CHANGING CONCEPTIONS, CHANGING PRACTICES

CHANGING CONCEPTIONS, CHANGING PRACTICES

Innovating Teaching across Disciplines

EDITED BY
ANGELA GLOTFELTER,
CAITLIN MARTIN,
MANDY OLEJNIK,
ANN UPDIKE, AND
ELIZABETH WARDLE

UTAH STATE UNIVERSITY PRESS
Logan

Published by Utah State University Press
An imprint of University Press of Colorado
245 Century Circle, Suite 202
Louisville, Colorado 80027

Printed in the United States of America

The University Press of Colorado is a proud member of the Association of University Presses.

The University Press of Colorado is a cooperative publishing enterprise supported, in part, by Adams State University, Colorado State University, Fort Lewis College, Metropolitan State University of Denver, University of Alaska Fairbanks, University of Colorado, University of Denver, University of Northern Colorado, University of Wyoming, Utah State University, and Western Colorado University.

∞ This paper meets the requirements of the ANSI/NISO Z39.48–1992 (Permanence of Paper).

ISBN: 978-1-64642-303-3 (paperback)
ISBN: 978-1-64642-304-0 (ebook)
https://doi.org/10.7330/9781646423040

Library of Congress Cataloging-in-Publication Data

Names: Glotfelter, Angela, editor. | Martin, Caitlin, editor. | Olejnik, Mandy, editor. | Updike, Ann, editor. | Wardle, Elizabeth (Elizabeth Ann), editor.
Title: Changing conceptions, changing practices : innovating teaching across disciplines / edited by Angela Glotfelter, Caitlin Martin, Mandy Olejnik, Ann Updike, and Elizabeth Wardle.
Description: Logan : Utah State University Press, [2022] | Includes bibliographical references and index
Identifiers: LCCN 2022040216 (print) | LCCN 2022040217 (ebook) | ISBN 9781646423033 (paperback) | ISBN 9781646423040 (epub)
Subjects: LCSH: English language—Rhetoric—Study and teaching (Higher) | Academic writing—Study and teaching (Higher) | Interdisciplinary approach in education. | Curriculum change. | College teaching—Vocational guidance. | Educational innovations.
Classification: LCC PE1404 .C4728 2022 (print) | LCC PE1404 (ebook) | DDC 808/.0420711—dc23/eng/20220920
LC record available at https://lccn.loc.gov/2022040216
LC ebook record available at https://lccn.loc.gov/2022040217

Support for this publication was generously provided through the Roger and Joyce Howe Distinguished Professor of Written Communication account at Miami University.

Cover photograph by Nkosi Shanga

To all the changemakers enacting progressive visions of education inside broken systems.

CONTENTS

FOREWORD

Elaine Maimon

Travel with me in the time machine to 1977, almost forty years to the day before the founding of the Howe Faculty Writing Fellows Program, which was established at Miami University in spring 2017.

In spring 1977, I was a junior faculty member at Beaver College (now Arcadia University), waiting for word from the National Endowment for the Humanities (NEH) about a proposal, "Writing in the Humanities," which I had submitted on January 2. Program officers at NEH had indicated NEH was willing to regard writing—rhetoric—as a humanity. Hurrah for the ancient Greeks, who knew it all along. But to the federal government before 1977, anything to do with writing was considered to be skills oriented and under the purview of the Office of Education (no US Department of Education until 1980). In US higher education, writing was then generally defined as a matter of talent for those who might eventually write fiction—or literary criticism. For all other students, sentenced to a year of first-year composition, writing was for the most part a matter of correct punctuation and spelling—control of what we now call *surface features.* A tsunami-like sea change was about to occur.

In July 1977, NEH funded the expansion of the Berkeley/Bay Area Writing Project into the National Project. And, more to the point of my personal story, Beaver College, a small liberal arts college in suburban Philadelphia, received the largest federal grant in its history to implement writing across the curriculum. We would channel the sea change into the sensemaking described in this book. We didn't have the term then. We did not think in terms of threshold concepts. What we were doing felt more like keeping our heads above water. We were teaching underserved students—today's New Majority—in ways outlined in Mina Shaughnessy's 1975 MLA keynote, "Diving In" (sea metaphors abound!), and in her 1977 book *Errors and Expectations* (Oxford

https://doi.org/10.7330/9781646423040.c000

University Press). We would transform the idea of student deficiencies into opportunities for nonlinear, messy education. We would stay true to a democratic agenda of educating citizens to be independent writers and thinkers.

As I reflect on those long-ago days, I see my colleagues and I were committed to what we now call *inclusive excellence*. We were enthusiastic innocents acting instinctively. We intuited important concepts, but we did not always name what we knew. We lacked the vocabulary to fully understand the enormity of the project. Now we do. Forty years later we have a history of practice and a viable theoretical framework. *Changing Conceptions, Changing Practices: Innovating Teaching across Disciplines* is the book I wish I had had in 1977.

Readers committed to transformational change in teaching and learning have a better chance today of bringing about deep change. The authors of this book achieve the overall goal of presenting "a conceptual framework based on a set of research-based principles."

Even without this book, writing across the curriculum has made a huge difference, which will now be enhanced by the work at Miami, described in this book. When I first gave presentations on WAC, some audience members treated it as a fad. That fad has outlasted the century in which it was named. Deep change has occurred in definitions of writing, not only in higher education but also in K–12. Much more must be done, and this book will help. Human beings crave simplicity and resist what is complex and messy. It's difficult to measure the nonlinear, and yet scholars seek means of assessment, and the public demands it. We waste money and time in measuring the wrong things. And because what we measure defines what we do, we then do things that are wasteful and teach what is beside the point. *Changing Conceptions, Changing Practices* puts us on a path toward counting the things that count, if we are going to count at all.

A great strength of this book is the discussion by scholars of the threshold concepts in their fields. From the beginning, WAC leaders aspired to help students to think like a philosopher, psychologist, economist, art historian, and so forth. The idea of threshold concepts clarifies what we mean by these varying conceptual frameworks. The book provides excellent examples. In chapter 5, for instance, philosophers ask, "What is a universal human right?" They then refer to Hannah Arendt and the contrast between Eichmann following orders and following orders because one does not know how to question the orders.

In chapters 7 and 12, psychologists write about the undue emphasis placed on APA style as a threshold concept as opposed to being merely formatting and mechanics. They confess they could not write their own articles if they were forced to do so in the way they were imposing on students. In 1981, when my colleagues and I published *Writing in the Arts and Sciences* (Winthrop), the first WAC first-year composition text, it was a big deal that we included APA style as well as MLA. We did so to encourage English-composition instructors to teach students to differentiate situations and contexts rather than see literary criticism as the only topic for writing. Our point was that MLA documentation puts an appropriate emphasis on page numbers because the text is important. APA style for good reason highlights the dates of previous research. I am pleased to read Miami psychologists understand that missteps in the details of APA style may make it easy to count student mistakes but do not teach the synthesizing of information central to writing in psychology.

Art historians in chapter 8 articulate a threshold concept in their field, "It is not easy to write what you see." That simple statement brought back memories of my own first-year art history course at the University of Pennsylvania. After weeks of showing us slides and lecturing, the professor told us the midterm would involve looking at slides and writing what we saw. I was terrified and mystified. What was I supposed to see? What was I supposed to write? Students at Miami will no longer be in that situation.

A professor of global art history in chapter 9 writes "telling is not teaching" and identifies that statement as a threshold concept. I've said since the late 1970s that I want a t-shirt that says, "I know I taught it because I heard myself say it."

In the early 1980s, I consulted at the University of Pennsylvania on the establishment of the Writing Across the University (WATU) program. Professor Robert Lucid, the chair of the English department at the time, intuited the idea of threshold concepts. We decided to pay stipends to English PhD candidates to sit in on disciplinary courses and to interview professors on writing and thinking in their fields. Professor Lucid called these graduate students "moles" because they were infiltrating courses outside English. We never published the findings. We should have.

Changing Conceptions, Changing Practices: Innovating Teaching across Disciplines will accelerate reform at a time when it is most needed. The trifecta of disease, racial reckoning, and economic challenge makes deep change in higher education essential. Deep change is disruptive and requires creativity and courage. This book provides a research-based conceptual framework and practical strategies for transforming colleges and universities. The underserved minorities of the late 1970s are now the New Majority in higher education. We must stop expecting the student population to change its identity and instead work on deep change at our educational institutions. Writing across the curriculum is the first and most generative of the high-impact practices. Shore up your courage and use this book as a starting point for transformation.

ACKNOWLEDGMENTS

We would like to gratefully acknowledge the following people:

Rachael Levay, who has been supportive and enthusiastic about this project from its initial conception through to final publication.

Roger and Joyce Howe, whose vision and financial support enabled the creation of the program described in this book.

All the Miami faculty members who have participated in the Howe Faculty Writing Fellows Program, many of whose projects do not appear in this book. Their tireless efforts to enact innovative and collaborative pedagogy inspire us.

The Fellows who contributed to this book, which was written during the biggest disruption to higher education in memory. Their goodwill and dedication have made this book possible.

Adrianna Kezar, whose scholarship on leading change has inspired us and helped develop our thinking about the role of faculty development leaders.

Elaine Maimon, who has not only supported our efforts in this book but has also supported many of us personally and professionally. Her feminist mentoring of other women is the standard to which we aspire.

CHANGING CONCEPTIONS, CHANGING PRACTICES

PART I

Developing and Researching Models for Deep Change through Educational Development Programs

1
WRITING-RELATED FACULTY DEVELOPMENT FOR DEEP CHANGE

An Introduction and Overview

Angela Glotfelter, Caitlin Martin, Mandy Olejnik,
Ann Updike, and Elizabeth Wardle

Misconceptions of writing (and writers) have dominated higher education for over a century—despite the best efforts of writing studies scholars. More broadly, the culture around learning in US higher education over the last fifty years has embraced what Randy Bass (2016) calls the "disintegrative" view of learning, which "emphasizes dimensions of education that can be commodified" (295). This disintegrative view has moved conceptions of learning away from the complex and messy to simpler, more linear measures of success. Combating these harmful conceptions and approaches to teaching and learning requires methods for helping faculty members work together to surface misconceptions and then, in turn, intentionally design courses, curricula, programs, and policies that enact more accurate and meaningful conceptions of writing, learning, and teaching, that is, to help faculty engage in collective *sensemaking* leading to deep change around learning. Sensemaking, or collectively looking at old ideas in new ways in order to change underlying conceptions, attitudes, and even identity, is a prerequisite for enacting "deep change," a process through which a person or institution transforms both its underlying beliefs and values and its actual day-to-day practices (Kezar 2018).

We argue in this collection that deep change through sensemaking is necessary if writing-related faculty development programs (Martin 2021) want to accomplish long-standing goals such as changing the culture of writing and learning on campus, helping all faculty take responsibility for teaching writing, or supporting faculty in recognizing the role of writing in learning. Changing the culture of writing and learning on campuses is difficult work, however. Through the research and narratives in this collection, we suggest writing-related faculty development

https://doi.org/10.7330/9781646423040.c001

programs might be most successful at facilitating deep change if they engage intra- and interdisciplinary teams of faculty in meaningful sense-making about writing and learning. As this collection illustrates, helping faculty to first change their conceptions about how writing and learning work empowers them to then reimagine not only their individual assignments and courses but also their programmatic curricula and, in some cases, departmental culture.

In this chapter, we briefly discuss the misconceptions of writing and learning that govern current notions of higher education and explain why deep change is necessary to overcome these harmful views. We then provide an overview of the principles and curriculum of the program we designed for faculty teams through the Howe Center for Writing Excellence (HCWE) at Miami University (Ohio) to combat these misconceptions. We conclude with an overview of the remainder of this book. Our aim is to provide not *the* answer to combating misconceptions of writing and learning but, rather, to present a conceptual framework based on a set of research-based principles we have found useful in working to innovate teaching and learning with faculty from across disciplines and contexts.

A NOTE ABOUT AUDIENCE

Before we begin, we want to directly address our audience for this collection. Careful readers will note that in introducing our project above, we use the term *writing-related faculty development.* This is a term we borrowed from one of our editors, Caitlin Martin (2021), who points out in her dissertation that "the activity of helping faculty across the curriculum learn to teach writing . . . is often a part of writing across the curriculum programs, but it might also happen in teaching and learning centers, in writing centers, and even through English departments" (3). It is our hope in this collection to speak to the varied audiences Martin has pulled together through her definition: those involved in writing across the curriculum efforts, writing centers, teaching and learning centers, and any other sites where the goal is to support faculty members from all disciplines in innovating their pedagogical practices, particularly with writing.

Historically, educational developers[1] (a term we use following Cheryl Amundsen and Mary Wilson [2012], Catherine King and Peter Felten [2012], and the POD Network [2021], among others) and writing across the curriculum leaders have not participated in the same scholarly conversations. Our conferences and other professional conversations tend to be quite separate. The POD Network annual conference, for example, attracts some writing scholars but not as many as one might expect—in 2020, only 2 presentations out of 141 explicitly contained content about writing (POD 2020)—and movement in the other direction seems even less common, with few educational development scholars attending writing studies conferences. (A notable exception is the work at Elon University, where writing studies scholars lead educational development work and encourage extensive cross-pollination in their seminars, conferences, and special journal issues).

Despite the infrequently articulated connections between the groups, we see the fields as integrally connected in both purposes and methods. Support for improved teaching—overall and of writing in particular—developed as a result of changes in the nature, focus, and students of higher education: the more higher education was opened up to the non-elite, the more concerns were raised about student "deficiencies" in general and as related to writing in particular. Calls to address perceived student deficiencies led in part to the creation of WAC in the 1970s and 1980s. Centers for teaching and learning and other related educational development efforts followed, as there came a growing recognition that "scholarship" could include teaching (Boyer 1990) and that such scholarship needed support (Matthias 2019; Ouellett 2010; Russell 2002; Sorcinelli et al. 2006).

All pedagogically focused faculty development (educational development) efforts share a commitment to student learning and a recognition that effective teaching requires development and support and is, in fact, a scholarly activity. These efforts benefit from being aligned so as to bring the most resources to bear in efforts to invite students into the work of the academy, scaffold rigorous learning opportunities, and recognize writing as one means of learning. In the Howe Center for Writing Excellence, we have increasingly collaborated with our university's Center for Teaching Excellence (especially when COVID required marshalling all available resources) to provide support and training for faculty on matters such as curriculum development, assessment, peer review, assignment design, and so forth. Both centers have benefitted, as has the larger university community.

This collection is designed to address concerns of educational developers, broadly conceived, about how to support faculty in the teaching of writing and in creating broader change around teaching and learning. Moreover, our collection aims to provide support and examples to disciplinary faculty from varied institutions who have committed themselves to improving their teaching by participating in such programs and who are looking for examples of how to innovate their teaching with their colleagues. The accounts in part 2 of this collection, written by faculty from a variety of disciplines, provide such examples and demonstrate how faculty can enact long-term change across courses and programs with the support of educational development efforts.

Most important for our purposes in this collection is that all educational developers, whether focused on writing and learning specifically or teaching and learning more broadly, share a primary concern about the larger context(s) in which the faculty they support are working. This larger context has been informed for over a century by misconceptions about the nature of writing and learning to write and since the 1980s by an increasingly disintegrative characterization of learning. We turn now to these concerns about how higher education conceives of learning as the exigence for the work described in this collection.

THE EXIGENCE FOR THIS COLLECTION: THE NATURE OF LEARNING VERSUS THE CURRENT DOMINANT PARADIGMS OF HIGHER EDUCATION

What we know about how learning works (including learning to write and using writing for learning) conflicts with popular conceptions and enactments of learning. What we know from the scholarship is that deep learning—the kind of learning that changes thinking and practice and that the learner is able to transfer to new contexts—is messy, time consuming, recursive, and often troublesome (Ambrose et al. 2010; Meyer and Land 2003). In order for students to learn concepts and apply them (rather than simply memorize them), they need opportunities to reflect, practice, and apply them across time and with feedback (see Ambrose et al. 2010 and the National Research Council 2000). This sort of learning is neither quick nor easy. It typically does not happen in one class or one "unit" of one class. Rather, it happens across time, across classes, and across disciplines. We know there are high-impact practices that encourage this kind of learning, such as integrative general education programs, learning communities that integrate learning experiences, writing-intensive courses across the curriculum, collaborative projects that require students to work and solve problems with others, opportunities for students to engage in meaningful research projects, experiential or community-based learning, and creating reflective ePortfolios, among others (see Kuh 2008).

We know that learning to write, like all kinds of learning, takes time and practice and that applying skills and ideas about writing in new contexts and when writing new genres is difficult (see Linda Adler-Kassner and Elizabeth Wardle [2015] *Naming What We Know* for a brief overview of these principles). We know there is no simple, one-time inoculation for learning to write, learning with writing, or learning in general. For students to learn in deep and meaningful ways, rather than to simply memorize or regurgitate, requires faculty members to work together to design integrative, coherent, scaffolded learning experiences across time. Student learning must take place in varied sites, as well: thus, faculty from *across* disciplines must work together to design meaningful and coherent general education programs, and faculty *within* disciplines must work together to design coherent, engaging learning experiences for their undergraduate and graduate students.

All of this work is difficult. Most faculty members want to teach well, want to encourage student learning, and want their students to write well. Still, common narratives about education, learning, and writing have created systems that get in the way of their ability to do this. Most faculty members have little exposure to scholarship and theories of teaching and learning and are instead only asked to gain expertise in their content areas. The daily work of institutions of higher education typically leaves little room for faculty members to engage together in scholarly conversations about student learning and how to facilitate it. This point about working *together* to facilitate student learning is an important one. Faculty members are generally rewarded as individuals via the traditional promotion and tenure process and tend to be treated more as independent contractors than like-minded communities of practice working toward shared goals (especially when it comes to teaching). In addition, institutions of higher education are more and more rewarded (via state funding and national rankings) for high scores on "proxy metrics" (O'Neil 2016) for learning rather than for learning itself (for example, they are rewarded for retention and graduation rates, time to degree, and employment after graduation, not for whether and how well students actually learn and can apply their learning to solving meaningful problems in the world).

Such proxy metrics do not reward institutions of higher learning for devoting resources to developing challenging curricula that ask students to engage in supported but messy deep learning. Thus, faculty members who do want to devote their time and energy to understanding how learning works and to designing innovative curricula often find their efforts unrecognized or, even worse, penalized. Administrators tend to reward curricula that are "efficient" and that develop easily measurable outcomes that can be achieved in short periods of time. Their systems for counting programmatic value tend to focus on metrics such as credit-hour production, lower cost per credit hour, low DFW rates, and high retention and graduation rates rather than innovative curriculum designed to facilitate deep learning that cannot be easily quantified. Efficiency and accountability, not teaching and learning, are the watchwords of the day.

This tendency to prioritize efficiency and quantification over deep learning is one of the symptoms of what Bass (2016) calls the "disintegrative paradigm" for learning. This view of education "emphasizes dimensions of education that can be commodified: targeted online learning, granular or modular, driven by algorithms that deliver micro-data on student understanding, often with a diminishing role for faculty" (295). The disintegrative view of education stands in sharp contrast to a "fundamentally *integrative paradigm* for learning" that "assumes the interdependence of knowledge, skills, and the broader dispositions that constitute a way of being in the world, such as openness to learning, empathy, and resilience" (295). Bass argues that "the central tension of our time in education" is between these two visions for what education is and should be (295). Bass believes—and much of our daily experience as teachers likely confirms—that the disintegrative view is dominating our work in education. Tyler Branson (2022), in his book *Policy Regimes*, uses a slightly different lens to describe the same phenomenon, arguing that what we are experiencing is the result of the dominant policy regime, which he calls the "accountability regime" (22). All paradigms and policy regimes are changeable, however. Higher education has not always enacted a disintegrative or accountability approach. Branson (following Patrick McGuinn) describes the "equity" regime that dominated education until the 1980s. That regime left school governance to local administrators and saw the role of the federal government only as providing resources to promote "equity and access for poor students" (18). In the equity regime, faculty and institutions were rewarded for recruiting, retaining, and supporting the success of low-income students.

The point is that we are not doomed to a lifetime of conforming to the current accountability regime or disintegrative paradigm. If dominant paradigms around teaching and learning in higher education are changeable, we want to support educational developers of all kinds (and writing-related faculty developers in particular) in devoting attention to designing programs that help faculty members engage in curricular changemaking that resists the dominant narratives. Faculty members need and want opportunities to engage in meaningful scholarly conversations that enable them to rethink student learning in their programs and institutions. This book provides an example of one such program that considers one method faculty members might draw on to engage in meaningful work to enact deep change that runs counter to current narratives about teaching, learning, writing, and the role of higher education. There are, of course, other models that can address these same tension points and resist these narratives. We offer here one model from a writing-focused faculty development context in which we explicitly invite faculty to work together in disciplinary teams to examine principles of writing and learning theory in order to innovate curricular designs and pedagogical strategies that combat misconceptions of writing and the disintegrative narrative of higher education.

COMPONENTS NEEDED TO FACILITATE DEEP CHANGE

If dominant paradigms—of higher education in general and as filtered down to and embodied in particular institutions—are to be resisted and changed, we benefit from an understanding of how change happens. Theories of changemaking explain that paradigm shifts are in the category of "deep change" or "second-order change," as opposed to "first-order change" or surface-level changes to practices and behaviors without the underlying conceptual shift (Kezar 2018).

Deep change describes an ongoing change process through which "underlying values, assumptions, structures, processes, and culture" transform (Kezar 2018, 71) as individuals within a system/context "[make] new sense of things" (87). Deep change involves the "transformation" of an entire system; in the case of higher education, this system could be a full institution or one of its academic departments or programs. This change process stands in contrast to "first-order" change, which occurs in a linear process and focuses on processes and behaviors rather than underlying belief systems. One reason deep change is so difficult, however, is that deep changes "are likely to encounter resistance from within and outside the institution," and "when change is too radical or is vastly different from the existing system, the change threatens the environment, thus causing it to encounter stronger resistance" (71). Because of this difficulty, deep change is fundamentally a learning process that occurs at both the individual and collective levels.

In other words, *individuals* may undergo a process of considering and reimagining their assumptions and ideas—about writing and learning, for example (and they must do so as part of deep change efforts)—but deep change *across programs and institutions* does not happen unless groups of people ("communities of practice," to use Etienne Wenger's

[2000] term) engage in this work together. One way this collective work can be facilitated is through *sensemaking*, a process through which "individuals attach new meaning to familiar concepts and ideas" or "develop new language and new concepts that describe a changed institution" (Kezar 2018, 87). When groups of people engage in sensemaking together, they shift their conceptions (for example, about the role of higher education, the nature of learning, the role of writing in learning) and then change their practices from the ground up. In other words, sensemaking leads to changed ideas and changed culture, and those changes manifest in attitudinal or cultural shifts (how groups and individuals interact with each other, the kinds of conversations that occur between individuals, and moving away from old arguments and beliefs) and structural changes (pedagogy, curriculum, assessment, policies, budgets, and other institutional decision-making structures) (Eckel 2002; Eckel and Kezar 2003; Kezar 2018). (We discuss sensemaking and change theory more in chapter 3.)

Proceeding from this work in change theory, we suggest educational developers can play a central role in paradigm shifts if they intentionally design programs that provide opportunities for groups of faculty to engage in sensemaking around teaching, learning, and writing. If program- or institution-wide culture shifts and deep change are the goal, change theory suggests educational development programs might consider the following principles for that design:

- Programs consist of *teams of people from the same program or department* so there are enough people undergoing conceptual change at the same time to shift the culture of their programs and departments. Simply working with *individuals* from programs may result in meaningful individual change but will not result in deep change across a program. (Chris Anson and Deanna Dannels's [2009] and Pamela Flash's [2016] writing-enriched curriculum practices are two of the few WAC initiatives that proceed from this central tenet.)
- These teams *have the opportunity to also engage with teams from other programs and departments.* These cross-disciplinary interactions provide a helpful means for those with shared conceptions and values to compare their ideas with others who understand teaching, learning, and writing differently. They also provide a greater likelihood that sensemaking will impact ideas and thus practices across the institution rather than simply in one department or program. Those cross-departmental interactions during sensemaking also provide opportunities for faculty from very different disciplines to become allies who share conceptions and vocabulary in future efforts to enact change on institution-wide committees and planning groups. (While nearly all educational development programs are cross-disciplinary, we do

not know of any that engage *teams* of faculty from disciplines in this cross-disciplinary engagement in intentional ways. Other programs typically consist of individuals from various disciplines attending workshops, seminars, or learning communities together.)

- The program *takes place across time, with plenty of opportunity for participants to read, think, talk, and apply ideas.* One-time workshops are unlikely to provide the necessary time for participants to reflect deeply, imagine new ways of thinking, and change their conceptions. (This practice of longer-term seminars is becoming more and more common in both WAC and educational development; Stephen Wilhoit [2013] makes this an explicit recommendation in the description of his WID seminar at the University of Dayton, noting that "changing faculty behavior, values, and commitments take time" [126]).
- The program provides participants with *theoretical frameworks for thinking about their ideas and practices and with the opportunity to engage with scholarship around teaching and learning.* The roots of the very first WAC seminars with Elaine Maimon and Harriet Sheridan were guided by this approach; faculty learning communities also function from a similar principle. Maimon (2018) argues quite persuasively that "curricular change depends on scholarly exchange among faculty members" (45). While the initial impulse might be to focus on practice, change theory suggests engaging scholarship and theoretical frameworks first is most likely to result in innovative changes to practice that have real staying power. Educational developers have been arguing for this as well. Sarah Bunnell and Daniel Bernstein (2012) describe this as "scholarly teaching, the act of systematically examining the links between one's teaching and student learning," necessitating an understanding of "teaching as an inquiry-based process"—and note that it "remains a challenging idea" (14).

As we note above, many of these principles for sensemaking projects are or have been enacted in various educational development programs (again, notably, at Elon University's Center for Engaged Learning [n.d.] through their multi-institution and multidisciplinary research seminars and publications, as well as through national projects such as the American Council on Education's [2021] ACE Transformation Labs). Our goal here is to articulate the need for *all these aspects of program design* to be facilitated *together* and *intentionally* from within an institution in order to create deep cultural shifts within that institution that resist dominant paradigms of teaching and learning and instead imagine and embody paradigms that enact what we know about how learning and writing really work.

The leadership team at the HCWE designed one such program with these principles in mind. In the following section, we provide a brief overview of the program, which is one example of how educational development programs with the goal of deep change can be designed, implemented, and facilitated. We assume, of course, as we say above, that there are many other ways to enact the preceding principles. Our goal here is to demonstrate what *one* enactment looks like and then to illustrate throughout the collection what the results of that enactment have been.

THE HOWE FACULTY WRITING FELLOWS PROGRAM

The Howe Faculty Writing Fellows Program (hereafter referred to as "the Fellows Program") was established at Miami University in spring 2017. It is carried out by Elizabeth Wardle (the director of the Howe Center for Writing Excellence), Ann Updike (the associate director from 2013 to 2021), and doctoral students from the composition and rhetoric program who serve as graduate assistant directors (coauthors and editors of this collection Angela Glotfelter, Caitlin Martin, and Mandy Olejnik have all served in this capacity). In designing the system, we were guided by a passionate belief about what education systems should be designed to do: they should teach for deep learning and critical thinking that is transferable across contexts and that will enable learners to be productive and innovative citizens in a democracy. In our role as an educational development support center serving the entire university, we want to advocate for what Tone Solbrekke and Ciaran Sugrue (2020) describe as *higher education as and for public good.* To model those principles for faculty, we sought to design a space for reflection, dialogue, and deep learning where faculty could grapple with ideas about the role of education, how learning works, the nature of learning and knowledge in their disciplines, and the role of writing in that system. In these efforts, we were guided by learning theory, the threshold concepts framework, and decades of scholarship about writing.

The Fellows Program proceeds from the deep change principles we outline in the previous section, which are enacted in the following specific ways.

Deep changes in curriculum and institutional writing culture require stakeholders to change—or at least bring to conscious awareness—their conceptions of writing. Participants can best engage in this critical reflection when they engage as *departmental teams* (of at least three members). Together, as departmental teams, they are better able to name and draw on their shared assumptions, values, and expertise. Moreover, after the program, the team has a greater likelihood of making changes in their larger departmental cultures than a lone faculty member would.

Departmental teams' ways of thinking and acting are colored by their community goals and purposes and by the history of their work together. This is true of their methods for working, as well as for their conventions for writing and communicating. However, faculty experts who have long been enculturated into their disciplinary and professional communities of practice are often unaware of how specialized their ways of thinking, practicing, and writing are—and thus how strange those practices can be for outsiders, newcomers, and learners (McCarthy 1987). They also, as chapter 12 illustrates, may be unaware of the built-in biases of their conventions and practices. Thus, expert faculty have implicit knowledge[2] (Ambrose et al. 2010) and can often see their genres and conventions as "genres in general" (Wardle 2004) rather than specific embodiments of disciplinary practice and values that mediate activity. We have found faculty can more easily bring their conceptions, values, and beliefs to conscious awareness against the *backdrop of disciplinary difference.* Thus, every Fellows cohort consists of teams from at least two and as many as five different programs or departments. This enables participants to see similarities and differences across their communities of practice.

Participants need to be engaged as scholars in thinking about teaching and learning. Most faculty want their students to engage in deep learning, but typical faculty members in US universities have little or no background in pedagogy or learning theories, having focused primarily on disciplinary knowledge during graduate training. Thus, we believe providing opportunities for faculty to engage with research about how learning works enables them to rethink their practices *for themselves* in light of and coupled with their own disciplinary expertise. The program therefore begins by providing a *framework for thinking about learning and expertise* (the threshold concepts framework, discussed more below), and then introduces participants to research and theory about how learning works, the role of writing in learning, and the nature of writing itself. Participants spend the first two-thirds of the seminar thinking about theory and naming their expert practices. Seminar activities help faculty explore their ideas and uses of writing, unpack their disciplinary knowledge, and see themselves as experts in writing by making *explicit* what they already know implicitly about writing and learning in their disciplines. This framework therefore positions faculty as the experts in disciplinary writing who are best able to make decisions about and to teach disciplinary writing conventions, values, and beliefs to their students.

Participants need time to engage ideas and reflect on what they are learning. Thus, the cohorts *meet regularly and intensively* for one and a half hours weekly for a full semester (about fifteen weeks), or for three hours daily for two or three weeks in the summer, in order to discuss and explore ideas and practices of writing in their own lives, disciplines, and teaching.

For deep change to occur, those who have engaged in sensemaking need *opportunities to put their new ideas and shared conception into practices that will have an influence beyond individual classrooms.* Thus, teams spend the final third of the semester engaged in a changemaking project of their choosing, which they present to the other teams and invited stakeholders on the last day.

The HCWE Faculty Writing Fellows Program relies heavily on the threshold concepts (TC) framework, though it is clearly possible to design sensemaking projects that rely on other conceptual frameworks, and we hope readers will imagine what those might be. We have had success with the threshold concepts framework, as the accounts in part 2 of this book illustrate. For that reason, we want to spend a short time here explaining what it is and how it works well with learning theory and conversations around teaching. However, we want to emphasize we are not arguing for a threshold concepts approach to all educational development. Rather, we are arguing that *some* robust conceptual framework around teaching and learning should serve as the backbone for team and cross-disciplinary sensemaking, and the work of this book illustrates how the threshold concepts framework serves that role in our program.

The Threshold Concepts Framework as One Conceptual Foundation for Sensemaking

The threshold concept (TC) framework is well aligned with a concern for integrative education as a public good that "[enables] students to make connections and integrate their knowledge, skills, and habits of mind into an adaptable and critical stance toward the world" (Bass 2017, 145). In fact, Ray Land (2016) calls the framework "a counter-discourse to the commodification of learning" because of "its emphasis on transformation through troublesome knowledge and shifts in subjectivity" (18–19). In other words, it asks disciplinary experts to name and interrogate their ways of thinking and practicing for the explicit purpose of creating more effective teaching and learning environments. The TC framework is influenced by research on learning transfer (Perkins and Salomon 1988, 1989, 1992; Tuomi-Gröhn and Engeström 2003) and also has led to a great deal of scholarship examining the role of learners' prior knowledge and experience in their learning and the nature of liminality and recursivity in learning these most difficult disciplinary ways of thinking and practicing (see, for instance, the massive bibliography maintained by Michael Flanagan on pedagogical research that uses threshold concepts theory as a foundation: www.ee.ucl.ac.uk/~mflanaga/thresholds.html).

While disintegration has become "common sense" in the way we talk about and enact education today, threshold concepts theory presents a way to name and challenge problematic "common sense" beliefs (Cousin 2006). The theoretical framework is well suited to tackling the task of naming and showing a better alternative to disintegrative visions of education. Further, because of its theoretical lineage, the TC framework aligns with the field of writing studies' deep commitments to seeing learning and transfer of knowledge through writing as complex and context bound (Driscoll 2011; Gorzelsky et al. 2017; Moore 2017; Wardle 2009).

The threshold concepts framework emerged from a United Kingdom national research project centering on characteristics for strong teaching and learning within disciplines (Cousin 2006). Ray Land, Glynis Cousin, Jan Meyer, and Peter Davies (2005) define threshold concepts as "concepts that bind a subject together, being fundamental to ways of thinking and practising in that discipline" (54). They are "akin to a portal" and "[open] a new and previously inaccessible way of thinking about something" (53). Threshold concepts, then, fundamentally change the way a learner views and approaches a subject, and learners internalize threshold concepts as they come to fully participate in a discipline. The resulting threshold concepts framework recognizes each discipline entails some learning thresholds through which newcomers to the discipline must struggle to pass in order to do the work of that discipline. Threshold concepts thus represent transformational ways of understanding, interpreting, or viewing something (Meyer and Land 2003). They are ways of thinking *and* ways of practicing. They entail and embody disciplinary values and epistemologies. Most important for our purposes in this collection, TC theorists recognize that learning threshold concepts is time intensive, recursive, messy, and troublesome. There is no linear path to learning threshold concepts, and learners can struggle in a liminal space for some time as they engage threshold concepts not just by reading but by doing. When students are in uncomfortable liminal spaces, they need support from a variety of teachers and mentors who all recognize learning is hard and are willing to together create safe and scaffolded environments for that learning. TC theorists devote extensive time to the nature of learning in liminal spaces and how to design learning environments that support students through this work. If we want students to learn ideas that transform their understanding of particular subject matter and the world around them, the TC framework reminds us there is no shortcut, there are no proxies for measuring learning, and learning must be integrated. The disintegrative view of education is deeply at odds with what TC theory and other learning theories tell us about the nature of transformative learning.

The implications of this framework for teaching and for learning are profound. In a higher education paradigm that values efficiency and accountability, commodifies learning, and encourages teachers to disaggregate the learning process, teachers and program directors need a conceptual framework that supports them in designing courses and course sequences, learning activities, and assessments that encourage and support messy, troublesome, recursive learning across time. Teachers need support for designing learning environments that plunge students into uncertainty and for helping students embrace that uncertainty when they have been trained more often to follow directions (Wardle 2012). The threshold concepts framework directly embraces the messiness of deep and transformative learning and simply accepts that such learning cannot easily be commodified and is difficult to measure; evidence of threshold concepts having been learned lies in how people view and conceptualize what they see and what they then do in response to those conceptions. In nearly every way, an educational experience designed around threshold concepts is antithetical to the disintegrative view of learning and to the accountability paradigm. It recognizes learning is messy, cannot easily be quantified, and is not particularly efficient. Learning must happen in context and over time with members of a community who share ways of thinking and practicing.

We are not the first to argue for the relevance of the threshold concept framework to educational development in general or even to writing across the curriculum faculty development efforts. As Meyer (2012) notes in an article for a special 2012 issue of *Journal of Faculty Development* specifically devoted to threshold concepts, "From the outset the TCF [threshold concepts framework] has attracted the attention of the faculty development community" (9) (the "outset" he refers to being the foundation of the framework developed by Meyer and Land in two seminal papers in 2003 and 2005). And Chris Anson (2015), in *Naming What We Know,* outlines threshold concepts that might inform WAC work. The concepts Anson names have been taken up in scholarship by Bradley Hughes and Elisabeth Miller (2018) and Christopher Basgier and Amber Simpson (2019, 2020), among others. The way we use the threshold concepts framework in Fellows, however, is somewhat different, as we explain below.

The Fellows Curriculum

The HCWE Fellows seminar begins with an introduction to threshold concept theory with short readings, minilectures, discussion, and activities for teams to identify their own disciplinary threshold concepts (Cousin 2006; Meyer and Land 2003). Next, participants are introduced to threshold concepts of writing from *Naming What We Know* (Adler-Kassner and Wardle 2015), followed by discussion and activities to examine how they use writing in their professional and daily lives. By interrogating their own practices, uses, and forms of writing, faculty come to understand the myriad ways that writing is used to achieve multiple purposes and that those forms follow their purpose or function. A final activity in this segment asks faculty to consider how this new understanding could inform their use of writing in the classroom beyond the often limited purposes and forms frequently assigned.

Participants then explore how disciplinary values and epistemologies are enacted in disciplinary writing conventions. The participants read Ken Hyland (2000) and John Swales (1990) to acquire language and a process for examining disciplinary texts, and then they perform a cross-disciplinary genre-analysis activity. Participants exchange research articles with participants from another discipline and look for what they find similar, surprising, or strange in regards to how citations work, what counts as evidence, how evidence is presented, and so forth. This activity, seemingly more than any other, helps participants conceptualize how difference plays out in writing across disciplines and how much variety there is. Participants gain a new appreciation for students who move between multiple disciplines daily and begin to realize that, as teachers, they must explicitly name for both themselves and their students what they mean by writing and "good writing." With this new understanding, each team defines "good writing" in their disciplines and explains it to the other teams to check its clarity for outsiders.

In the next stage, participants read and discuss theories of learning (Ambrose et al. 2010), specifically the role of prior knowledge, stages for moving from novice to mastery, experts' implicit knowledge, and knowledge transfer. We follow up with activities to identify all the ways they use writing when researching, learning something new, and writing a research article. After unpacking all this implicit knowledge, participants read and discuss ideas for scaffolding, teaching with writing, and responding to writing (Bean 2011). They practice scaffolding a course concept or assignment previously packed with implicit knowledge and skipped steps (their invisible assumptions) in an effort to make the implicit explicit for students.

In the final third of the semester, teams discuss among themselves what changes they would like to see surrounding teaching and learning in their programs or departments and then identify a project on which to work. These projects range from designing brand-new courses to designing and aligning course sequences to researching where and how writing is assigned across their majors to designing workshops they will facilitate for their departmental colleagues who did not participate in the Fellows Program, redesigning departmental assessments around ePortfolios, and more. (A full list of projects is included in appendix A.) Teams present their projects to the full cohort on the last day as part of a final showcase; the audience also includes invited guests such as department chairs, deans, associate provosts, and departmental colleagues. (A complete semester schedule is included in appendix B.)

Once the program ends, the teams return to their departments and implement their changes. We have continued to support their change efforts through a variety of changing initiatives, which have included:

- follow-up workshops to give Fellows time and space to continue redesigning their courses and assignments;
- alumni lunches to create space for discussing their ongoing work with Fellows from other cohorts;
- Chairs Leadership and Change Reading Group, for Fellows who are department chairs, to discuss books on change theory;
- grants to support their continued work, conference attendance, and publications;
- peer writing associates for their courses;
- training for their graduate teaching associates;
- departmental workshops.

Our program, then, includes a constellation of ongoing support for Fellows alumni, which they've cited as important and helpful to their continuing understanding of how learning and writing work in their disciplines and classrooms.

Readers interested in how to design a similar program within their own institutional contexts will find some suggestions in the concluding chapter of this collection (chapter 14). Here we want to emphasize that the costs of such an approach are important considerations but need not be prohibitive, and the semester-long design could be adapted to a shorter series or set of workshops distributed across time. What matters most are the *transferable organizing principles*:

- engaging faculty members in programmatic teams, enabling them to think beyond their own individual courses;
- providing opportunities for faculty from various disciplines to compare and contrast their practices and values in order to bring them to conscious attention;
- working from a theoretical framework that centers the difficulties of learning and invites faculty to consider how to collectively design coursework across time that invites students into the ways of thinking and practicing of a discipline.

The goal is to engage groups of faculty in group sensemaking that can result in deep change around teaching and learning—first within departments and programs and then across so many departments and programs that the changes take hold at the institutional level. As we describe in the next two chapters, we have worked with numerous departments and teams since 2017 and have achieved promising results, which the accounts in part 2 of this collection, written by Fellows alumni, serve to illustrate.

OVERVIEW OF THE REMAINDER OF BOOK

This book is organized into three parts. The remainder of this part, "Developing and Researching Models for Deep Change through Educational Development Programs," continues with a chapter that overviews research collected from Fellows Program alumni regarding their conceptual and practical changes after participating in the program. In that chapter, we describe how moving from change in one classroom to change in a full program (and later, change across a full institution) is difficult. This is the challenge we take up in chapter 3, outlining the difficulties of engaging in deep change efforts, including limited support and reward for faculty leadership.

Having established in part 1 the framework for deep change focused educational development, provided data about the impact of one such project, and described the challenges to deep change, we then provide in part 2 a series of accounts written by Fellows alumni, "Accounts of Faculty-Led Change Efforts." First, teams of economists and philosophers outline in chapters 4 and 5 how they underwent conceptual shifts in their thinking about writing, teaching, and learning that, in turn, helped them enact deep and fundamental changes across their departmental curricula. Chapters 6, 7, 8, 9, and 10 look more deeply at how the threshold concepts framework helped faculty members design effective (albeit messy and liminal) learning environments for students. In chapter 6, two gerontologists describe their efforts to name their field's threshold concepts and work to enact them across their graduate curriculum in order to invite students into the work of their fairly new and deeply interdisciplinary field. In chapter 7, three psychologists describe how they came to recognize that their expectations of student writers and their practices for assigning research writing to students were deeply misaligned with how professionals in their field write—and how they worked to reimagine learning environments that provide the same supports, time, and scaffolding professional psychologists have. In chapter 8, three art historians describe several threshold concepts they identified together and how they worked to engage students in the messy challenge of giving words to what they see. In chapter 9, one of those art historians discusses yet another threshold concept, Otherness, and how he invites students to grapple with it despite their own discomfort. In chapter 10, a historian describes the challenges inherent in historical thinking and why these challenges can make coherent curricular design difficult.

The next set of accounts shifts focus to the macro level, asking readers to take a critical and reflective stance in thinking about both threshold concepts and large-scale change. In chapter 11, three scholars of American, Latino/a, and Caribbean studies outline how they embraced the difficulties of inviting students into an interdisciplinary field that is, through its own history, contentious and disunified. Their discussion of using writing to teach students to engage the threshold concepts of their field illustrates the ways institutional positioning can influence a program or department's work. In chapter 12, a psychologist and woman of color describes her own painful journey to engage the threshold concepts of her field, only to realize what this process cost her. She urges readers to critically engage their fields' foundational ideas and gatekeeping practices, asking whose values they embody and who they silence or exclude. In chapter 13, three teacher education scholars describe their department's painful journey in addressing systemic racism, not only in their field and its efforts to make pedagogy appear value free but also in their own department, where a faculty member was recently outed in a quite public way for long-standing racist beliefs he enacted across decades of training future teachers. These accounts illustrate some of the many difficulties changemakers can expect to encounter when they try to enact change beyond their own individual classrooms.

We conclude the collection with Part 3, "Taking Stock and Moving Forward." In chapter 14, we glean lessons from the case studies and provide some suggestions for educational developers who may want to engage in similar efforts. We offer an afterword that considers the origins of the disintegrative paradigm and how its terms and framing impede efforts to make meaningful, grassroots change within higher education.

CONCLUSION

We offer this book as one optimistic example of how educational development programs can be explicitly designed to enable groups of faculty to lead from research-based principles of teaching and learning, reflect about their positionality and disciplinary practices, and work to enact an integrative view of learning via sensemaking and distributed leadership. Changing cultures (and conceptions) is hard work and takes a long time. It is also work that cannot be done by one person, instead requiring teamwork and collaboration across programs and units. But we are confident that challenging the disintegrative view of higher education and learning *is* possible and that meaningful changes *can* be made. We also believe there has never been a better time for this work than now, as the future of higher education seems to hang in the balance.

NOTES

1. Peter Felten, Alan Kalish, Allison Pingree, and Kathryn M. Plank (2007) define educational development as "helping colleges and universities function effectively as teaching and learning communities" (93). The Professional and Organizational Development (POD) Network prefers the use of the term "educational development" over "faculty development" for the ways it encompasses the wide breadth of the work POD Network communities engage in, which spans across levels, audiences, and subfields.
2. Ambrose et al. (2010) use the term "expert blind spots" to refer to the invisible assumptions held by experts who are no longer aware of all they know and therefore do not always teach this tacit knowledge to students.

REFERENCES

Adler-Kassner, Linda, and Elizabeth Wardle, eds. 2015. *Naming What We Know: Threshold Concepts of Writing Studies.* Logan: Utah State University Press.

Ambrose, Susan. A., Michael W. Bridges, Michele DiPietro, Marsha C. Lovett, and Marie K. Norman. 2010. *How Learning Works: Seven Research-Based Principles for Smart Teaching.* San Francisco: Jossey-Bass.

American Council on Education. 2021. "Ace Transformation Labs." https://www.acenet.edu/Programs-Services/Pages/Professional-Learning/Transformation-Labs.aspx.

Amundsen, Cheryl, and Mary Wilson. 2012. "Are We Asking the Right Questions?: A Conceptual Review of the Educational Development Literature in Higher Education." *Review of Educational Research* 82 (1): 90–126. https://doi.org/10.3102/0034654312438409.

Anson, Chris M. 2015. "Crossing Thresholds: What's to Know about Writing across the Curriculum." In *Naming What We Know: Threshold Concepts of Writing Studies,* edited by Linda Adler-Kassner and Elizabeth A. Wardle, 203–19. Logan: Utah State University Press.

Anson, Chris M., and Deanna P. Dannels. 2009. "Profiling Programs: Formative Uses of Departmental Consultations in the Assessment of Communication Across the Curriculum." In "Writing Across Disciplines and Assessment: Activities, Programs, and Insights at the Intersection." Special issue, *Across the Disciplines* 6. https://wac.colostate.edu/atd/assessment/anson_dannels.cfm.

Basgier, Christopher, and Amber Simpson. 2019. Trouble and Transformation in Higher Education: Identifying Threshold Concepts through Faculty Narratives about Teaching Writing. *Studies in Higher Education* 45 (9): 1–13.

Basgier, Christopher, and Amber Simpson. 2020. Reflecting on the Past, Reconstructing the Future: Faculty Members' Threshold Concepts for Teaching Writing in the Disciplines. *Across the Disciplines* 17 (1/2): 6–25.

Bass, Randall. 2016. "Well-Being, Disintegration and the Rebundling of Higher Education." In *Well-Being and Higher Education: A Strategy for Change and the Realization of Education's Greater Purposes*, edited by Donald W. Harward, 295–99. Washington, DC: Bringing Theory to Practice. https://bttop.org/wp-content/uploads/2020/08/Well-Being-and-Higher-Ed-FINAL-PDF.pdf.

Bass, Randall. 2017. "Coda: Writing Transfer and the Future of the Integrated University." In *Understanding Writing Transfer: Implications for Transformative Student Learning in Higher Education*, edited by Jessie L. Moore and Randall Bass, 144–54. Sterling, VA: Stylus.

Bean, John. 2011. *Engaging Ideas: The Professor's Guide to Integrating Writing, Critical Thinking, and Active Learning in the Classroom*. 2nd ed. San Francisco: Jossey-Bass.

Boyer, Ernest L. 1990. *Scholarship Reconsidered: Priorities of the Professoriate*. Lawrenceville, NJ: Princeton University Press.

Branson, Tyler. 2022. *Policy Regimes: College Writing and Public Education Policy in the United States*. Carbondale: Southern Illinois University Press.

Bunnell, Sarah L., and Daniel J. Bernstein. 2012. "Overcoming Some Threshold Concepts in Scholarly Teaching." *Journal of Faculty Development* 26 (3): 14–18.

Cousin, Glynis. 2006. "An Introduction to Threshold Concepts." *Planet* 17 (1): 4–5. https://www.tandfonline.com/doi/full/10.11120/plan.2006.00170004.

Driscoll, Dana Lynn. 2011. "Connected, Disconnected, or Uncertain: Student Attitudes about Future Writing Contexts and Perceptions of Transfer from First Year Writing to The Disciplines." *Across the Disciplines* 8 (2): 1–29.

Eckel, Peter D. 2002. "Assessing Change and Transformation in Higher Education: An Essential Task for Leaders." *Metropolitan Universities* 13 (2): 80–93.

Eckel, Peter D., and Adrianna Kezar. 2003. *Taking the Reins: Institutional Transformation in High Education*. Westport, CT: American Council of Higher Education/Praeger.

Elon University Center for Engaged Learning. n.d. https://www.centerforengagedlearning.org/.

Felten, Peter, Alan Kalish, Allison Pingree, and Kathryn M. Plank. 2007. "Toward a Scholarship of Teaching and Learning in Educational Development." In *To Improve the Academy: Resources for Faculty, Instructional and Organizational Development*, edited by Douglas Reimondo Robertson and Linda B. Nilson, 93–108. San Francisco: Jossey-Bass.

Flanagan, Michael. 2020. *Threshold Concepts: Undergraduate Teaching, Postgraduate Training, Professional Development and School Education: A Short Introduction and a Bibliography from 2003 to 2018*. www.ee.ucl.ac.uk/~mflanaga/thresholds.html.

Flash, Pamela. 2016. "From Apprised to Revised: Faculty in the Disciplines Change What They Never Knew They Knew." In *A Rhetoric of Reflection*, edited by Kathleen Blake Yancey, 227–49. Logan: Utah State University Press. https://doi.org/10.7330/9781607325161.c011.

Gorzelsky, Gwen, Carol Hayes, Ed Jones, and Dana Lynn Driscoll. 2017. "Cueing and Adapting First-year Writing Knowledge: Support for Transfer into Disciplinary Writing." In *Understanding Writing Transfer: Implications for Transformative Student Learning in Higher Education*, edited by Randall Bass and Jessie L. Moore, 113–21. Sterling, VA: Stylus.

Hughes, Bradley, and Elisabeth L. Miller. 2018. "WAC Seminar Participants as Surrogate WAC Consultants: Disciplinary Faculty Developing and Deploying WAC Expertise." *WAC Journal* 29: 7–41.

Hyland, Ken. 2000. *Disciplinary Discourses: Social Interactions in Academic Writing.* New York: Longman.

Kezar, Adrianna. 2018. *How Colleges Change: Understanding, Leading, and Enacting Change.* New York: Routledge.

King, Catherine, and Peter Felten. 2012. "Threshold Concepts in Educational Development: An Introduction." *Journal of Faculty Development* 26 (3): 5–7.

Kuh, George D. 2008. *High-Impact Educational Practices: What They Are, Who Has Access to Them, and Why They Matter.* Washington, DC: Association of American Colleges and Universities.

Land, Ray. 2016. "Toil and Trouble: Threshold Concepts as a Pedagogy of Uncertainty." In *Threshold Concepts in Practice*, edited by Ray Land, Jan H. F. Meyer, and Michael T. Flanagan, 11–24. Rotterdam: Sense.

Land, Ray, Glynis Cousin, Jan H. F. Meyer, and Peter Davies. 2005. "Threshold Concepts and Troublesome Knowledge (3): Implications for Course Design and Evaluation." In *Improving Student Learning, Diversity and Inclusivity*, edited by Chris Rust, 53–64. Oxford: Oxford Center for Staff and Learning Development.

Maimon, Elaine P. 2018. *Leading Academic Change: Vision, Strategy, Transformation.* Sterling, VA: Stylus.

Martin, Caitlin. 2021. "Facilitating Institutional Change through Writing-Related Faculty Development." PhD diss., Miami University.

Matthias, Laurie R. 2019. "Faculty Development: A Review of the (Relatively Recent) Literature and Implications for Christian Higher Education." *Christian Higher Education* 18 (4): 260–75.

McCarthy, Lucille P. 1987. "A Stranger in Strange Lands: A College Student Writing Across the Curriculum." *Research in the Teaching of English* 21 (3): 233–65.

Meyer, Jan H. F. 2012. "'Variation in Student Learning' as a Threshold Concept." *Journal of Faculty Development* 26 (3): 9–13.

Meyer, Jan, and Ray Land. 2003. "Threshold Concepts and Troublesome Knowledge: Linkages to Ways of Thinking and Practising within the Disciplines." *ETL Occasional Report 4.* Edinburgh: University of Edinburgh. http://www.etl.tla.ed.ac.uk/docs/ETLreport4.pdf.

Meyer, Jan H. F., and Ray Land. 2005. "Threshold Concepts and Troublesome Knowledge (2): Epistemological Considerations and a Conceptual Framework for Teaching and Learning." *Higher Education* 49 (3): 373–88. https://doi.org/10.1007/s10734-004-6779-5.

Moore, Jessie L. 2017. "Five Essential Principles about Writing Transfer." In *Understanding Writing Transfer: Implications for Transformative Student Learning in Higher Education*, edited by Jessie L. Moore and Randall Bass, 1–12. Sterling, VA: Stylus.

National Research Council. 2000. *How People Learn: Brain, Mind, Experience, and School.* Washington, DC: National Academies Press.

O'Neil, Cathy. 2016. *Weapons of Math Destruction: How Big Data Increases Inequality and Threatens Democracy.* New York: Crown.

Ouellett, Mathew L. 2010. "Overview of Faculty Development: History and Choices." In *A Guide to Faculty Development*, 2nd ed., edited by Kay J. Gillespie and Douglass L. Robertson, 3–20. San Francisco: Jossey-Bass.

Perkins, David N., and Gavriel Salomon. 1988. "Teaching for Transfer." *Educational Leadership* 46 (1): 22–32.

Perkins, David N., and Gavriel Salomon. 1989. "Are Cognitive Skills Context Bound?" *Educational Researcher* 18 (1): 16–25.

Perkins, David N., and Gavriel Salomon. 1992. "Transfer of Learning." In *International Encyclopedia of Education.* 2nd ed. Oxford: Pergamon.

POD Network: Professional and Organizational Development Network in Higher Education. 2020. "Schedule." https://drive.google.com/file/d/109aRDF5E4WI6qL4TCqO-Q93cqWXd2hFNo/view.

POD Network: Professional and Organizational Development Network in Higher Education. 2021. https://conference.podnetwork.org/schedule-2021/.

Russell, David. 2002. *Writing in the Academic Disciplines, 1870–1990: A Curricular History.* Carbondale: Southern Illinois University Press.

Solbrekke, Tone Dyrdal, and Ciaran Sugure. 2020. *Leading Higher Education As and For Public Good: Rekindling Education as Praxis.* New York: Routledge.

Sorcinelli, Mary Deane, Ann E. Austin, Pamela L. Eddy, and Andrea L. Beach. 2006. *Creating the Future of Faculty Development: Learning from the Past, Understanding the Present.* Bolton, MA: Anker.

Swales, John M. 1990. "Research Articles in English." In *Genre Analysis: English in Academic and Research Settings,* 110–76. Cambridge: Cambridge University Press.

Tuomi-Gröhn, Terttu, and Yrjö Engeström. 2003. *Between School and Work : New Perspectives on Transfer and Boundary-Crossing.* Advances in Learning and Instruction Series. Amsterdam: Pergamon.

Wardle, Elizabeth. 2004. "Can Cross-Disciplinary Links Help Us Teach 'Academic Discourse' in FYC?" *Across the Disciplines* 1. https://wac.colostate.edu/docs/atd/articles/wardle2004.pdf.

Wardle, Elizabeth. 2009. "'Mutt Genres' and the Goal of FYC: Can We Help Students Write the Genres of the University?" *College Composition and Communication* 60 (4): 765–89.

Wardle, Elizabeth. 2012. "Creative Repurposing for Expansive Learning: Considering 'Problem-Exploring' and 'Answer-Getting' Dispositions in Individuals and Fields." *Composition Forum* 26 (Fall). https://compositionforum.com/issue/26/creative-repurposing.php.

Wenger, Etienne. 2000. *Communities of Practice: Learning, Meaning, and Identity.* Cambridge: Cambridge University Press.

Wilhoit, Stephen. 2013. "Achieving a Lasting Impact on Faculty Teaching: Using the WPA Outcomes Statement to Develop an Extended WID Seminar." *The WPA Outcomes Statement: A Decade Later,* edited by Nicholas N. Behm, Gregory R. Glau, Deborah H. Holdstein, Duane Roen, and Edward M. White, 124–35. Anderson, SC: Parlor.

2

CHANGING CONCEPTIONS, CHANGING PRACTICES

Effects of the Howe Faculty Writing Fellows Program

Angela Glotfelter, Caitlin Martin, Mandy Olejnik,
Ann Updike, and Elizabeth Wardle

In the previous chapter, we argue for a set of design principles that could inform educational development programs whose goal is effecting deep change in curriculum. There we suggest that providing faculty with opportunities to rethink common misconceptions of writing and learning through the lens of learning theory and threshold concepts would empower them to intentionally design courses, programs, and practices for their own contexts that align with their new, more accurate conceptions. We then outline one approach for guiding faculty through that process—the Howe Faculty Writing Fellows Program at Miami University. In this chapter, we present some change-related outcomes of the Fellows Program by sharing IRB-approved survey and interview data collected from Fellows alumni, which illustrates evidence of individual changes in conceptions and practices, as well as more limited but promising evidence of wider changes across programs. One of our guiding assumptions has been that helping faculty surface their tacit assumptions about their disciplines, writing, and student learning can empower them to innovate teaching and learning in ways that fit the goals and values of their disciplines, programs, and departments. Our research—and the additional chapters throughout this collection—illustrates this is often the case. Before presenting that research, however, we begin with a brief history of the ways *change* has been discussed in writing-related faculty development scholarship in order to illustrate the historical trajectory of how faculty-related change has been understood in writing across the curriculum (WAC) efforts.

https://doi.org/10.7330/9781646423040.c002

CHANGE AS A GOAL OF WAC

At the start of the writing across the curriculum (WAC) movement in the 1970s, the faculty workshop model (now commonplace) was a new innovation: "The workshops were not committee meetings, graduate seminars, or parties, but somehow they combined the best features of all three" to become "settings for communal scholarship applied to pedagogic problems" (Maimon 2018, 45). Today, workshops for faculty remain a core feature of writing across the curriculum programs, although WAC programs have established other methods of working with faculty who teach writing, including brown-bag lunches to discuss teaching writing, support for creating department-level writing plans, individual consultations and departmental workshops, sponsoring travel to conferences, and offering in-house publications (Thaiss and Porter 2010). These methods support a host of local program goals: ensuring students have opportunities to write across their academic careers, increasing engagement in learning, increasing student writing proficiency, creating a campus culture that supports writing, and creating a community of faculty around teaching and writing (Cox et al. 2014). And these program goals suggest the variety of changes possible as a result of WAC's broad writing-related faculty development work.

One of WAC's strengths as a site of educational development is its focus on grassroots change and community building around student learning. Early WAC programs aimed to bring faculty members together to talk about student writing, and that approach continues today. These sites of "communal scholarship" applied to "pedagogic problems" are sites of *sensemaking*, which, as we discuss in chapter 1, is a process in which participants attach new ideas to familiar concepts and practices and is a prerequisite for deep change (Kezar 2018). WAC scholarship has tended to focus on the *structural* outcomes of participating in writing-related faculty development programs, such as changes to pedagogies, curriculum, and student-learning assessment, with much of the WAC research focused on individual participants. More recently, there has been a shift to understanding how WAC educational development might lead to *conceptual* changes in how faculty participants understand writing in their courses and disciplines, as we outline below.

FACULTY CHANGE AS A SITE OF WAC RESEARCH

From its beginnings, WAC scholarship has documented a variety of changes that can result from faculty participation in writing-related faculty development programs, including changed pedagogy and curricula and improved student learning (Fulwiler 1988). Some WAC leaders have asked workshop participants to describe changed pedagogical practices, such as the example syllabi and assignments included in the program profiles in *Programs That Work: Models and Methods for Writing across the Curriculum* (Fulwiler and Young 1990). In that collection, for example, James Slevin, Keith Fort, and Patricia O'Connor (1990), contributors from Georgetown University, include sample courses from environmental zoology, sociology, and theology. Faculty discussions of "sample courses illustrate some of the basic strengths of our program," they write, including "our commitment to the integrity and independence of individual faculty and our confidence that, by increasing their concern with student writing, making student writing a central concern of the course, individual teachers can only improve what they already do best" (26). Similar descriptions of classroom practices are presented in Mary Segall and Robert Smart's (2005) *Direct from the Disciplines: Writing Across the Curriculum.* Student papers that are easier to read and grade become evidence of the value of writing-to-learn activities (Duffy 2005), while end-of-course evaluations capture student perceptions of change (Hudd 2005).

WAC program leaders have often used follow-up surveys to document faculty change after participation in specific programming (Hughes and Miller 2018; Smithson and Sorrentino 1987; Wilhoit 2013), a strategy that has also become common in broader educational development (Saroyan, Amundsen, and Li 1997). In these approaches to understanding change, researchers or WAC program leaders identify specific pedagogical practices (such as including peer response in courses from across the disciplines) and gather data that illustrate the number of WAC program participants who have adopted these strategies in their classes. Research on Virginia Tech's 1980 faculty writing workshop provides one example. Isaiah Smithson and Paul Sorrentino (1987) distributed surveys immediately after the Virginia Tech workshop and again five years later. They found that, five years after participating in the 1980 workshop, all but one faculty member reported they still used writing to teach their subjects (328–29). More recently, Stephen Wilhoit (2013) found that twenty-one faculty participants from the University of Dayton's writing in the disciplines (WID) seminar felt "the seminar effected lasting changes in their teaching," including changes in how they design assignments and respond to students, how much writing they assign in their courses, and how they use writing to "promote learning" (134).

Such existing research has identified promising changes in faculty pedagogical practices and curriculum development. Additionally, some scholars have noted that changes in faculty conceptions and attitudes are more long lasting than their initial pedagogical changes. Barbara Walvoord, Linda Hunt, H. Fil Dowling Jr., and Joan McMahon (1997) were among the first to reach this conclusion. Based on data collected from three WAC programs over multiple years, they illustrate how faculty members at these institutions changed "their teaching philosophies and attitudes" (78). WAC had influenced faculty members' "*theories* about the nature of teaching and learning," "*habits of mind* during the planning and teaching process," "*sense of confidence* in teaching," "*enthusiasm* for teaching," and "*roles in relation to students*" (79). These areas represented conceptual shifts that enabled faculty to reimagine their role as teachers and to adapt their pedagogical behaviors. One faculty member explained how WAC helped "disabuse" them of "the myths" that "students wrote poorly in their biology courses because they didn't spend enough time doing it and/or they had not been adequately trained in English 101" (Walvoord et al. 1997, 127). Such changes had not previously been highlighted in research on the impact of WAC educational development efforts.

Recently, more scholars have begun to identify attitudinal or conceptual changes as a result of their WAC educational development work. Bradley Hughes and Elisabeth Miller (2018) illustrate how faculty and graduate students involved in their WAC seminar took up foundational beliefs about writing, turning to threshold concepts to analyze how participants talk about writing. When analyzing videotapes of participant conversations about writing assignments, they found a variety of examples of participants recognizing writing's disciplinary nature. Paired with survey data, these findings illustrate that their seminar activities helped prompt conceptual changes about writing. In a similar vein, Pamela Flash (2016) identifies how a process of "choreographed reflection" helped faculty come to new ideas about writing and its teaching as they worked with the writing-enriched curriculum program at University of Minnesota. In this program, departments are engaged in reflective conversation about student writing and writing in their disciplines in order to create a departmental writing plan, which identifies when and where students are taught to write in disciplinary classes. Flash and other members of the WEC team have helped departments surface their unstated assumptions about writing and student writing ability. Through this process, faculty assumptions about writing have shifted. "When faculty members deliberate accurate ways of describing desired writing abilities," Flash explains, "an assumption that writing can be generally described and that students can be expected to understand what is meant by such commonly used grading criteria as logical, substantive, or clear . . . begins to shift" (237). This more recent research provides compelling examples of conceptual change in programs designed to help faculty develop courses and assignments (Hughes and Miller 2018) and departmental writing plans (Flash 2016).

While this turn to documenting changed conceptions in WAC research is relatively new, these results are perhaps not surprising given WAC's historical focus on helping disciplinary faculty see the role writing could play in their courses. WAC founder Elaine Maimon (2006) has described how faculty who participated in her first NEH workshop at Beaver College (now Arcadia University) often came in with assumptions that "a writing workshop would be about commas and semicolons, or, at best, about gerunds and gerundives" but "found out that writing was an ancient art, a challenging craft, and, in many ways, thinking made visible" by reading and discussing scholarship in rhetoric and the emerging field of writing studies (25). Maimon collaborated with Harriet Sheridan to build on "the first *official* WAC program" Sheridan launched at Carleton College (Palmquist et al. 2020, 10). At Beaver College, Maimon (2018) invited multiple guest speakers over four days to share research and ideas about writing and how students learned, "leaving the fifth day for our own reflection, synthesis, and application of concepts" (45). These early workshops emphasized, then, conceptual understanding of writing, although they did not specifically use that term at the time. The curricular changes that resulted from these workshops were less the result of advocacy of specific pedagogical practices (Palmquist et al. 2020) and more about the driving principle that "curriculum change depends on scholarly exchange among faculty members" whose "creativity and ownership" led them to envision "applications that made sense in our own context and for our own students" (Maimon 2018, 45).

WAC scholarship, then, has illustrated the ways practices and conceptions can change as a result of participating in writing-related faculty development programs. Conceptual change has long been a driver of this work, even if it is not always an explicit goal of programming (Martin 2021). Like Maimon, Sheridan, and Flash, however, our work in the Fellows Program puts surfacing and discussing tacit assumptions about writing and learning—that is, *sensemaking*—at its center.[1] As we outline in chapter 1, our goal for the Fellows Program was to provide a reflective and scholarly space where faculty members could engage together with ideas about writing and learning. We wanted to ensure participants were empowered as experts and teachers to use what they were learning and what they already knew to revise or create learning environments, curricula, assignments, and practices most effective for their own contexts. In other words, we thought that by providing them an opportunity to do what academics do—read, reflect, think, and engage in dialogue using frameworks and scholarship—they would then engage in meaningful changes *they* initiated. Below, we present our research findings from the first three and a half years of facilitating faculty through our Fellows Program. The results illustrate the kinds of change—both conceptual and practical, individual and programmatic—that can result when sensemaking around teaching, learning, and writing is a central component of a writing-related faculty development program. They also illustrate the challenges of this work.

SITES OF CHANGE RESULTING FROM HOWE FACULTY WRITING FELLOWS PARTICIPATION

As we discuss in chapter 1, change theory tells us collective sensemaking on a topic leads to conceptual changes about that topic and subsequently to altered behavior and language. Conceptual change requires an internal transformation, a deep change that occurs when individuals alter their belief systems or existing schema related to the change effort. Signs that deep change have occurred include attitudinal and cultural evidence (i.e., the ways groups interact with each other or the way concepts are discussed), as well as the presence of structural elements (redesigned curricula, new departments, funds allocated to support initiatives). Conceptual change in WAC work therefore might be seen when individuals take up new language to discuss writing and its teaching or give up on prior arguments, such as who is responsible for teaching writing or simplifications about student writing ability.

In order to determine what changes might have occurred as a result of participating in the Fellows Program, we have collected a variety of data via an IRB study: we conducted a survey of all Fellows alumni in spring 2020 (eighty-eight at that time, from which we received twenty-five responses); we distribute surveys at the end of each program; we have conducted focus groups with alumni; and we conduct follow-up interviews with Fellows on their teaching practices that we highlight in our Miami Writing Spotlights. As part of our ongoing research, we conducted thematic analysis of this data for emerging trends related to conceptual, pedagogical, and institutional change. The findings suggest that (1) individual conceptions of writing *do* change (often quite dramatically) to align more with conceptions of writing from the field of writing studies research as a result of the program, (2) faculty subsequently demonstrate mindfully changed practices informed by their new conceptions, and (3) participants often also seek changes at the program/department level, but such efforts face numerous obstacles. In what follows, we first describe some of the individual changes around conceptions and practices and then turn our attention to broader change efforts. These data are encouraging in suggesting that the sorts of conceptual and pedagogical changes we hope for are happening: faculty are innovating their practices based on more informed, research-based principles of writing and learning, which they have applied to their unique contexts as experts (that is, second-order change), rather than simply implementing practices suggested or mandated by others (that is, first-order change).

Individual Change

Individual changes in both conceptions and practices were frequently reported in surveys and interviews with Fellows. An important goal in our study was to understand how participants' changed *conceptions* preceded and initiated subsequent changes in their *practice*. Below we discuss changed conceptions and changed practices in turn. These findings suggest expanded conceptions of writing lead to changed teaching and assessment practices.

Underlying Changes in Conceptions about Writing

The spring 2020 survey of all Fellows alumni found that, since completing the program, 92 percent noticed changes in the way they think and talk about writing. Fellows participants noted having and using new and expanded language to identify and talk about specific writing phenomena, not only in terms of individual self-reflection but also in conversations with colleagues about writing. Often, this change in vocabulary for talking about writing was connected specifically to a disciplinary understanding of writing within their own field. For instance, one Fellow noted the program provided them with "the concepts and vocabulary necessary to begin to understand and articulate what it means to write in a specific discipline, and to engage others in that process of discovery." Other Fellows noted an increased awareness of discipline-specific writing characteristics and subsequent easing of tension around disciplinary conflict when writing with colleagues from other fields. For example, in a focus group, one Fellow mentioned that making disciplinary beliefs about writing explicit allowed her to work better with a long-time writing colleague from a different discipline, mentioning that it was helpful to "[make] apparent the implicit that guides us, especially when working across disciplines."

Fellows also noted a marked change in their own perceptions of and internal dialogue about writing and how it works. Across the data we collected, increased awareness of disciplinary characteristics, genres, broader conceptions about what counts as writing, and feelings of ownership over teaching disciplinary writing were all features of Fellows' expanded thinking about writing.

Many Fellows noted that attending the program alongside other disciplinary teams was a transformative experience for them in realizing just how different writing is across disciplines. Often, this awareness of disciplinary differences translated into increased empathy for students who might be experiencing a disorienting onslaught of disciplinary writing expectations as they simultaneously take courses across the disciplines, especially general education courses. One Fellow was "struck by . . . how different our norms of good writing are from our colleagues. . . . It was a very, very vivid wakeup call. That's the prior knowledge that students are bringing to the course, so I'm . . . trying to just break it down more." Another Fellow framed his understanding of the disorientation students experience in terms of genre and what counts as "good writing," saying that he

> [gained] a greater awareness of the multiple genres which students have to write. [Students] always come in with this operating assumption about . . . a good way to write—there's one type of good writing, and we can all recognize it. We can all appreciate it. [The interdisciplinary nature of the program] made me realize that there are multiple genres and that the students in my class—when I say, "I want this to be a well-written essay," "well-written" has a completely different meaning depending on the disciplinary background of the student, and *that* has been really helpful.

In addition to the insights gained from the cross-disciplinary nature of the program, several Fellows cited the importance of attending as a disciplinary team with colleagues who share their values and practices. Having dedicated time to talk with department colleagues about teaching and the nature of their disciplines was a luxury they don't have in their daily lives and was important to extending their thinking. As a philosophy Fellow said in a team interview, the Fellows Program "wasn't just about teaching . . . it was about teaching philosophy in particular;" her colleague responded, "Right . . . not just teaching writ large with a diverse group of people where it's hard to have conversations that are discipline specific . . . but having them [colleagues from philosophy] and having everybody there from different disciplines was extraordinarily helpful to get some reflection on what we actually do as a discipline and what makes us unique." Another philosophy Fellow agreed, comparing her experience in Fellows to being in another seminar where she was the lone faculty member from philosophy: "I [didn't] have that kind of moral support of my colleagues [in the other seminar]. . . . It's like the balance of having people who do understand me and people who don't understand me at the same time [in Fellows] was . . . immensely helpful." (The results of her team's changed ideas are discussed in chapter 5.)

Faculty also developed a broader conception of what counts as writing. For instance, one Fellow from economics described how his understanding of disciplinary practices was expanded during the program because he adopted a more capacious view of what counts as writing:

> If you'd asked me before we started, "Do your Intro to Econ students write?" I would have said, "No. They don't write; they just solve this equation; they graph it. And they might explain the implications of that a little bit." But having our discussions here showed me that when I asked them to do that on the exam, they're actually writing. It's not a formal paragraph but that still constitutes writing. And I thought that was really interesting to learn and kind of see how we actually do a lot of writing, just not in a traditional format. (See chapter 4 for more on changed conceptions of writing among economics faculty.)

With this new understanding of what writing like an economist entails, the economics Fellows also developed a new sense of ownership of writing instruction within the discipline, stating, "It is incumbent upon us to teach students the particular things valued in economics, as they will not have learned them in a course from other departments."

We noticed several faculty talking about citation practices differently after being exposed to the Hyland and Swales readings and analyzing academic articles across disciplines. Rather than telling students to follow rules and put commas in the right place, faculty talked about citation practices as socially constructed and reflecting disciplinary values and goals. A faculty member from social work explained:

> It wasn't until after the workshop that I had language to talk about, "What does it mean to say, 'So-and-so and so-and-so, paren., date,' as opposed to a little footnote and what that conveys?" . . . That has been . . . a great way to not only talk about citations, but the whys behind and the importance of it, and that's . . . changed the plagiarism conversation. . . . I'm talking about honoring the ancients, if you will. And *that*, students get.

Changes in Teaching Practices

Our assumption and hope had been that if Faculty Fellows changed their conceptions of writing and learning, they would apply their own disciplinary expertise to change their practices around teaching writing, even though the program does not explicitly focus on what practices to change or how to go about making those changes. (We do provide faculty a copy of *Engaging Ideas* by John Bean [2011] and *How Learning Works* by Susan Ambrose et al. [2010], and they share their own teaching practices quite frequently.) Rather, we hope to learn what they have innovated as a result of their changes in thinking about writing and learning itself within their own disciplinary contexts, something we cannot do for them as disciplinary outsiders. The data we have collected have borne out our prediction. In the spring 2020 survey, 96 percent of respondents said they had changed their courses in ways they thought were related to their work as Fellows, with only one person saying they had not. The kinds of changes they shared in the survey included redesigning assignments to more closely align with learning outcomes, introducing lower-stakes writing-to-learn assignments, rewriting assignment prompts to be more explicit about expectations, modeling threshold concepts, incorporating more and earlier feedback on student writing, and breaking up large projects into smaller parts.

As one Fellow from history put it, the threshold concept framework in particular enabled deeper reflection on why he was assigning writing. He said, "[I began to] just continually [ask] myself and [prompt] myself to think about and to articulate why am I assigning this piece of writing," asking "What is this going to accomplish? What is the goal of this piece of writing?" This meta-awareness of purpose when assigning writing was echoed by a philosophy Fellow who emphasized reflection on his pedagogy. He described Fellows as prompting him to ask questions like "How do you want to change your pedagogy?" and "How do you want to change your teaching in light of [Fellows]?," describing the process as "a whole other level of reflection." (See chapter 5 for more about the philosophy team's pedagogical changes.) Although the program is a writing-related faculty development program, its focus on learning theory, as tied to writing and underlying any purposes for using writing in a classroom, led Fellows to often report rethinking their approaches not only to teaching writing but also to teaching overall.

Multiple Fellows also reported placing more emphasis on the writing process in their teaching. In a focus group, a Fellow from gerontology, for example, described redesigning a graduate-level professional seminar so it emphasized introducing students to writing in the field.

> This fall, the first two weekly meetings, we had faculty come in and talk about the process of writing and how they approach writing. That worked really well . . . [students] get to learn what the faculty do, but

> then faculty—we had groups of four come in—were really honest about how they approached writing and what resources they use and what the challenges are, and I think that helped humanize [the writing process] a lot. I think it set a really nice tone for "this is a process; we all work on this together; we do it differently and you have to find your way but here are the commonalities." (See chapter 6 for more about the changes the gerontologists made in their curriculum.)

Enacting the writing threshold concept that reflection and metacognition are important for improving as a writer, a Fellow from political science described more purposefully helping students reflect on their writing and peer-review processes: "One of the things I have them do . . . between that rough draft and the peer review and when they turn the final thing in is to do a cover letter . . . to address 'what aspects of the peer review did I take on and were helpful' and 'here's how I worked to address those items.' And that's helpful for them, I think, to think through that process and to think through if they did and how they did address those issues; it's helpful as a grader to also see that as well."

To a lesser extent, Fellows also experienced changes in how they assessed and responded to writing: 68 percent of Fellows reported they had changed their assessment of and response to writing while 32 percent reported they had not. Echoing the threshold concept that writers benefit from practice and feedback, one respondent described providing students with more feedback and revision opportunities as a result of Fellows, reflecting, "Previously I would spend much time at the end of the semester making comments on final drafts of papers, which students would not read (unless they got a bad grade!). This past year, I restructured my assignments and invested more time on the rough draft of the paper. As a result, the final drafts were much more polished and I was impressed with the final product by most of my students."

Also recognizing the importance of providing feedback throughout the semester and not just on the final paper, a historian reported that during Fellows he recognized not only "the importance of feedback" but also the importance of the *timing* of feedback. He pointed out that previously, when he assigned an end-of-term essay, it "goes into this void; they will never see or request or ask for any kind of feedback on this final assignment." As a result, he moved larger essays "into the middle of the course so that we're working with it and I'm giving them feedback all along the way on the steps that I built into it." He also now gives students "feedback in class and require[s] them to come and talk to [him] about it."

As noted in the previous section, by uncovering their invisible assumptions, as well as witnessing disciplinary differences through the program's readings and activities, faculty gained an appreciation for the difficulty students experience as they switch from discipline to discipline throughout the day. Consequently, many Fellows reported being more explicit in their communications with students. A respondent in an end-of-program survey described how they "retooled their expectations" and used "far more examples so students can first 'mimic' what they read and write and move on from there." A philosophy professor said, "I guess we have never really tried to make explicit what the threshold concepts are. And having done that . . . now I feel like . . . something invisible has been made visible for me and now I can make it visible for my students as well."

Additionally, after learning about and identifying threshold concepts in their fields, faculty have learned to model and *show* disciplinary threshold concepts as a way to guide students through them rather than simply lecture about the ideas. A Fellow from history explains:

> I try to model the kinds of practices—disciplinary practices—that are very much associated with the threshold concepts. For instance, contextualization—that's, for me, is very fundamental—that is to say that, when you read a text . . . you don't think about the merits or value of the arguments that are being presented on their own terms, but that you try to situate those arguments within the historical context. For that reason, I'm constantly . . . prodding them to read for clues that can be connected to the contextual knowledge that they have or that they can acquire, so that's one of those ways in which I try to *show* rather than *explain* threshold concepts at work.

For another example of teaching threshold concepts though modeling, see chapter 9's extended description of how an art historian changed the way he taught the threshold concept of Otherness to his students, moving from lecturing *at* them to providing activities and assignments that helped students come to a deeper understanding of the concept themselves.

Overall, we see changes in both conceptions and practices in the Fellows' responses and experiences, with changed conceptions preceding and being integral to eventual changed practices. Faculty not only changed certain writing practices (e.g., redesigning a peer-response worksheet) but first evolved in their understanding of and beliefs about writing (e.g., realizing the social nature of writing and how important feedback is in learning how to write). These results, as a whole, seem to support our hypothesis that changing *conceptions* of writing helps faculty change *their own practices* in ways that make sense given their own context and expertise.

BROADER CHANGE

Our assessment indicates individual Fellows change their conceptions of writing and thus their practices surrounding the teaching of writing as a result of attending the seminar. Faculty experienced changed conceptions of writing that have been leading to many (and varied) changed practices in their classrooms—practices initiated and designed *by them* to work within their disciplinary contexts. However, our research suggests that making larger, programmatic changes proves more difficult, though such changes are possible under certain conditions. In the spring 2020 survey of all Fellows alumni, Fellows reported fairly frequently that they continued to engage in discussions around teaching, writing, and curriculum design (see figure 2.1). They less frequently reported curricular, assessment, or policy changes at the department/program level, as seen in figure 2.2.

These survey results suggest faculty have been less successful in instituting wider departmental change. Yet we think these survey results require some additional investigation. The obstacles Fellows encountered on the way to change may have led them to respond on the survey that they had not definitively "made changes"; our interactions with them (as some of the chapters in this book illustrate) suggest they more likely saw what they were doing as *trying* to make changes at the program level and not always succeeding. The survey here does not tell the full story (as is frequently the case with quantitative measures). After completing the program, many of the Fellows teams have invested in numerous, time-intensive efforts to try to implement changes that go beyond a single person's classroom. Many of the chapters in this collection describe their larger efforts for change.

- A number of teams have continued to revise their general education courses (philosophy, chapter 5; social work and family science; art history, chapters 8 and 9; biology; international studies) or particular aspects of pedagogy that extend across their undergraduate courses (for example, writing across the major, economics, chapter 4; team writing, psychology, chapter 7).
- Some have made significant and ongoing revisions to their major's capstone courses (geography, political science) or other aspects of their undergraduate major (history), including implementing a portfolio for their undergraduate majors (philosophy, chapter 5, and geography).

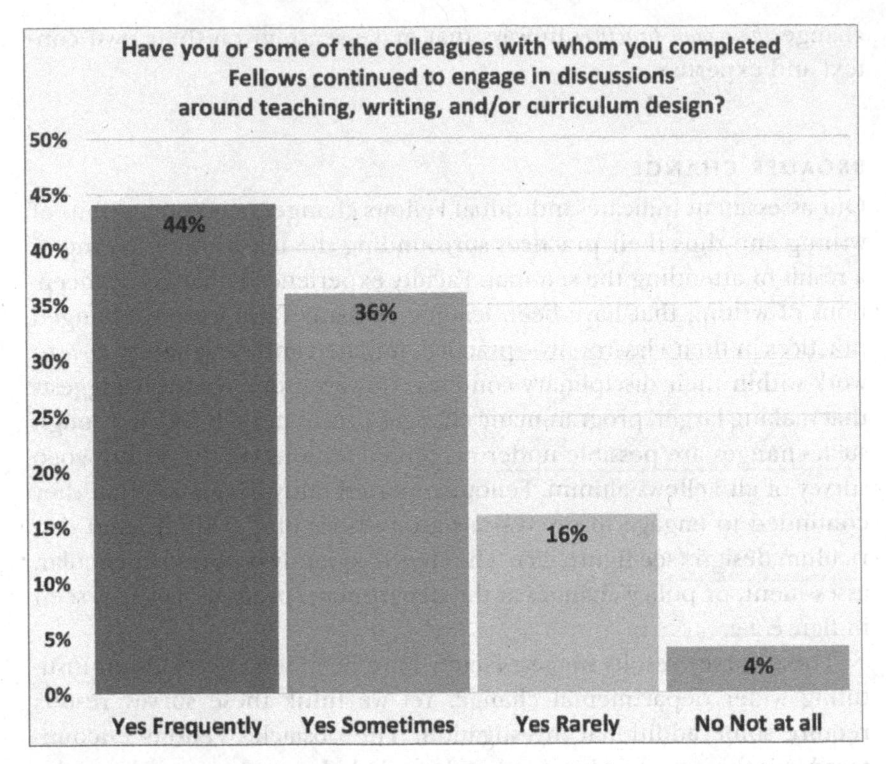

Figure 2.1. Fellows alumni survey results regarding continued discussion around teaching, writing, and/or curriculum design.

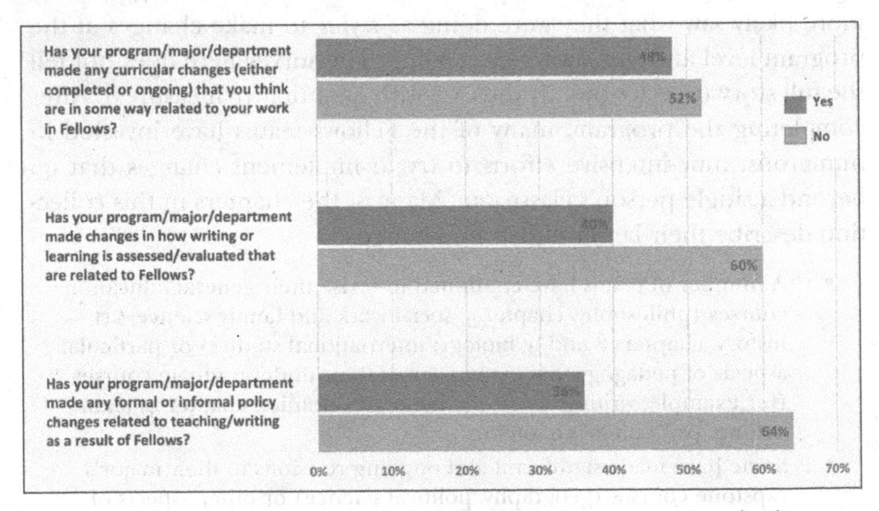

Figure 2.2. Fellows alumni survey results regarding curricular, assessment, and policy change at the department, major, or program level.

- Other groups have worked to make changes across their graduate programs (gerontology, chapter 6; music; mechanical and manufacturing engineering).
- One group (who sent four different teams to Fellows) revised their department mission and strategic plan following the program (teacher education, chapter 13).

We have noticed in our follow-up work with these teams that they face a variety of constraints and obstacles to fully implementing the changes they want to initiate. One such constraint is conceptual: while the Fellows team members spend an entire semester reflecting collaboratively and across disciplines on conceptions of writing and learning, colleagues in their departments do not. Thus, Fellows face on a smaller, departmental scale the problem we outline earlier: without collaborative sensemaking, their colleagues do not understand the rationale for the changes the Fellows want to make, their conceptions of writing and learning have not changed, and there is limited time (or precedent) in the life of a typical academic department to engage the full faculty in such reflection and thinking. Some teams made concerted efforts to set aside time for exploring the conceptual shifts the Fellows themselves had experienced during their departmental activities. Philosophy, history, and teacher education, for example, all set up extended workshops for their full departments to invite everyone to engage with threshold concepts and considerations of the role of writing in their curriculum. In those three cases, the department chairs were part of the Fellows teams, an important affordance we take up further in chapter 3. When full departments are not engaged in this thinking and reflection, Fellows find their ideas for change can stall due to prevalent misconceptions about writing and teaching. For example, one team advocated for a particular set of writing practices and assignments to be taught within their program. The response from their colleagues was supportive—but only if the Fellows themselves taught the course(s) and did not ask others to participate in the work. This response demonstrates a lack of understanding of the need for students to write for and receive feedback in multiple courses and contexts rather than receiving a writing "inoculation" in one course or from one faculty member.

Another significant barrier to change is inflexible institutional structure, including external pressures for expediency, cost reduction, and evidence of return on investment (as we discuss in chapter 1 and investigate in detail in the afterword). Even in programs where everyone participated in thinking and reflecting about writing and everyone was engaged in imagining subsequent changes, the reality of disintegrative bureaucratic systems often served as an impediment. The university has been trying to scale back its curricular offerings and reduce what some administrators call "curricular bloat." As a result, new course and requirement proposals sent forward by Fellows and their departments were sometimes blocked by deans and curriculum committees. In at least one case, the requirements the team proposed were approved and implemented for one year with resounding success (as measured by student learning), only to be terminated the following year as a result of budget cuts and other administrative mandates around course enrollments and credit-hour requirements.

Another team designed an ambitious disciplinary writing course that introduced students to writing in the two major fields in their department; they implemented it for one year, only to determine that the writing of their two fields was so incompatible as to not be teachable in a single course. In addition, they recognized what many in writing studies have long recognized: teaching students about genres and conventions outside of (and prior to) the context in which they are used has limited value. They determined they needed to refocus their efforts and do something even more challenging: create a sequence of courses that teach ways of writing in their professional fields across time. The work of getting just one course approved and scheduled had been excessive; doing this all over again with a series of courses, and involving the full department to ensure all faculty members are teaching it, is an even more daunting task. Their efforts seem to currently be stalled. Is this an example of success or failure? In our view, what is successful here is that the group understood underlying principles of teaching, learning, and writing and designed an innovative course based on those principles. When that effort did not work as planned, they understood why, and they knew what changes to make. But the nature of a bureaucracy made the new efforts slow going. In some ways, we see this as a great success because the Fellows did not abandon their efforts to teach writing when their first attempt failed. They continued to believe that teaching writing was their own responsibility and that they knew how to undertake it themselves rather than trying to outsource it to English faculty. Whether their deep understanding can eventually lead to a new set of revised practices even in the face of institutional inflexibility and pressure remains to be seen.

Other teams faced issues of rank and power when attempting change, and some faced the consequences of a system that relies heavily on contingent (and thus constantly changing) labor. One department sent two different teams through Fellows, but both consisted of untenured faculty members or visiting faculty members. Several members of those teams have since left the university, and the remaining (and still untenured) faculty have found themselves unable to navigate the terrain of their department to introduce changes senior faculty are uninterested in considering. Multiple teams have lost faculty members (untenured, visiting, and non-tenure-track) to other jobs and universities, which makes coherent curricular design and implementation difficult. Other teams, though consisting almost entirely of tenured faculty, were simply unsure how to proceed in introducing new ideas to their colleagues and engaging them in reflective conversations. Other teams found their departments (and sometimes their entire disciplines) were so splintered, fragmented, or siloed that any department-wide conversation about creating coherent curricula for their students was nearly impossible.

As this section discusses, our data reveal the promising potential of a program to promote changed conceptions leading to changed practices but also points to the very real barriers to wider implementation. The nature of academic programs and departments results in many individuals with their own conceptions and practices, even if grouped together by way of academic discipline. The challenge, then, seems to be encouraging broader departmental and programmatic change, which necessarily takes longer and includes embracing distributed leadership.

CONCLUSION: TEACHING FACULTY TO LEAD CHANGE

What we have learned from implementing a deep change–focused, writing-related educational development program has encouraged us but also demonstrated there is much more we must do if we are to meaningfully support faculty members not only in changing their conceptions of teaching and learning and changing their own practices as a result, but also in supporting them as they work to change cultures and structures around teaching, learning, and writing in their own departments. In essence, we have learned educational development programs benefit from including direct discussion of why faculty members can and should lead change efforts, what that kind of leadership entails, and how change efforts can be meaningfully enacted. We take up these issues in chapter 3, where we consider more deeply why efforts to lead broader change are so hard, why the current US system of higher education generally leaves academics ill prepared for this work, and how change and leadership theories can help explain these difficulties and assist faculty in leading broader change efforts.

NOTE

1. We discuss the rationale, principles, and underlying theories of the Fellows Program in chapter 1 and include a sample program schedule in appendix B. For a more detailed discussion of the Faculty HCWE Writing Fellows Program, see Glotfelter, Updike, and Wardle's chapter in Lesley Bartlett, Sandra Tarabochia, Andrea Olinger, and Margaret Marshall's (2019), *Diverse Approaches to Teaching, Learning, and Writing Across the Curriculum: IWAC at 25*.

REFERENCES

Ambrose, Susan. A., Michael W. Bridges, Michele DiPietro, Marsha C. Lovett, and Marie K. Norman. 2010. *How Learning Works: Seven Research-Based Principles for Smart Teaching.* San Francisco: Jossey-Bass.

Bartlett, Lesley Erin, Sandra L. Tarabochia, Andrea R. Olinger, and Margaret J. Marshall, eds. 2019. *Diverse Approaches to Teaching, Learning, and Writing Across the Curriculum: IWAC at 25.* Perspectives on Writing series. Fort Collins, CO: WAC Clearinghouse. https://doi.org/10.37514/PER-B.2020.0360.2.10.

Bean, John. 2011. *Engaging Ideas: The Professor's Guide to Integrating Writing, Critical Thinking, and Active Learning in the Classroom.* 2nd ed. San Francisco: Jossey-Bass.

Cox, Michelle, Susan Chaudoir, Michael Cripps, Jeffrey R. Galin, Jonathan Hall, O. Brian Kaufman, Suzanne Lane, Mary McMullen-Light, Mya Poe, Teresa Redd, et al. 2014. "Statement of WAC Principles and Practices." https://wac.colostate.edu/docs/principles/statement.pdf.

Duffy, Sean P. 2005. "Writing in Political Science." In *Direct from the Disciplines: Writing Across the Disciplines,* edited by Mary Segall and Robert Smart, 115–24. Portsmouth, NH: Heinemann.

Flash, Pamela. 2016. "From Apprised to Revised: Faculty in the Disciplines Change What They Never Knew They Knew." In *A Rhetoric of Reflection,* edited by Kathleen Blake Yancey, 227–49. Logan: Utah State University Press. https://doi.org/10.7330/9781607325161.c011.

Fulwiler, Toby. 1988. "Evaluating Writing Across the Curriculum Programs." *New Directions for Teaching and Learning* 36: 61–75.

Fulwiler, Toby and Art Young. 1990. *Programs That Work: Models and Methods for Writing across the Curriculum.* Portsmouth, NH: Boynton/Cook Heinemann.

Glotfelter, Angela, Ann Updike, and Elizabeth Wardle. 2019. "'Something Invisible . . . Has Been Made Visible for Me': An Expertise-Based WAC Seminar Model Grounded in Theory and (Cross) Disciplinary Dialogue." In Diverse Approaches to Teaching, Learning, and Writing Across the Curriculum: IWAC at 25, edited by Lesley Erin Bartlett, Sandra L. Tarabochia, Andrea R. Olinger, and Margaret J. Marshall. Perspectives on Writing series. Fort Collins, CO: WAC Clearinghouse. https://doi.org/10.37514/PER-B.2020.0360.2.10.

Hudd, Suzanne S. 2005. "Evaluating Writing Across the Curriculum Programs." In *Direct from the Disciplines: Writing Across the Disciplines,* ed. Mary Segall and Robert Smart, 125–36. Portsmouth, NH: Heinemann.

Hughes, Bradley, and Elisabeth L. Miller. 2018. "WAC Seminar Participants as Surrogate WAC Consultants: Disciplinary Faculty Developing and Deploying WAC Expertise." *WAC Journal* 29: 7–41.

Kezar, Adrianna. 2018. *How Colleges Change: Understanding, Leading, and Enacting Change.* New York: Routledge.

Maimon, Elaine P. 2006. "It Takes a Campus to Teach a Writer." In *Composing a Community: A History of Writing Across the Curriculum*, edited by Susan H. McLeod and Margot Iris Soven. West Lafayette, IN: Parlor.

Maimon, Elaine P. 2018. *Leading Academic Change: Vision, Strategy, Transformation.* Sterling, VA: Stylus.

Martin, Caitlin. 2021. "Facilitating Institutional Change through Writing-Related Faculty Development." PhD diss., Miami University.

Palmquist, Mike, Pam Childers, Elaine Maimon, Joan Mullin, Alisa Russell, and David R. Russell. 2020. "Fifty Years of WAC: Where Have We Been? Where Are We Going?" *Across the Disciplines* 17 (3/4): 5–25.

Saroyan, Alenoush, Cheryl Amundsen, and Cao Li. 1997. "Incorporating Theories of Teacher Growth and Adult Education in a Faculty Development Program." *To Improve the Academic* 16 (1): 93–115.

Segall, Mary, and Robert Smart. 2005. *Direct from the Disciplines: Writing Across the Disciplines.* Portsmouth, NH: Heinemann.

Slevin, James, Keith Fort, and Patricia E. O'Connor. 1990. "Georgetown University." In *Programs That Work: Models and Methods for Writing across the Curriculum*, edited by Toby Fulwiler and Art Young, 9–28. Portsmouth, NH: Heinemann.

Smithson, Isaiah, and Paul Sorrentino. 1987. "Writing Across the Curriculum: An Assessment." *Journal of Teaching Writing* 6 (2): 325–42.

Thaiss, Chris, and Tara Porter. 2010. "The State of WAC/WID in 2010: Methods and Results of the U.S. Survey on International WAC/WID Mapping Project." *College Composition and Communication* 61 (3): 543–70.

Walvoord, Barbara E., Linda L. Hunt, H. Fil Dowling Jr., and Joan D. McMahon. 1997. *In the Long Run: A Study of Faculty in Three Writing-Across-the-Curriculum Programs.* Urbana, IL: NCTE.

Wilhoit, Stephen. 2013. "Achieving a Lasting Impact on Faculty Teaching: Using the WPA Outcomes Statement to Develop an Extended WID Seminar." In *The WPA Outcomes Statement—a Decade Later*, edited by Nicholas N. Behm, Gregory R. Glau, Deborah H. Holdstein, Duane Roen, and Edward M. White, 124–35. Anderson, SC: Parlor.

3

DEEP CHANGE THEORY

Implications for Educational Development Leaders

Caitlin Martin and Elizabeth Wardle

INTRODUCTION

While chapters 1 and 2 explore the promise of theoretical frameworks for making conceptual change that leads to innovative action around teaching and learning in higher education, they also point out the challenges to this kind of work as teams of faculty strive to lead change in their programs and departments after completing the program. To summarize our claims thus far: one of the goals for the HCWE Faculty Writing Fellows Program is to empower faculty who participate to return to their departments to make programmatic changes—changes they identify as central to their work and values and program culture. The kinds of changes we advocate for in the Fellows Program are initially conceptual—that is, we support faculty in learning new ideas about writing and assume they will then use their new conceptions to initiate change in curriculum, pedagogy, assessment, and so forth. We don't tell them how to assign or teach writing in their courses but instead support them as they think through their own ideas for innovation. As many chapters in this collection illustrate, and as chapter 2 already illustrates, such change is possible, but it is not without challenge.

Since 2017, as we have followed and supported Fellows alumni as they have tried to promote larger changes in their departments and programs, we have been repeatedly struck by the challenges they face. We have come to recognize their challenges are representative of a set of systematic challenges to leading change in higher education: many individuals who want to act as change agents have no formal training in leadership or how to lead change. In addition, cultural norms, including those of departments and institutions, as well as individual disciplines and fields, serve to powerfully regulate behavior and constrain change efforts while also remaining largely unrecognized or invisible to those seeking to make change (Kezar 2018).

https://doi.org/10.7330/9781646423040.c003

Ultimately, our argument in this chapter is that if educational developers seek to support faculty in making deep, meaningful change around not only how they teach but also how students learn and how curricula are designed across programs and universities, then educational development programs can't stop at providing seminars on research-based practices and theories of writing and teaching. Rather, they benefit from including direct discussion of what leadership entails, why faculty members can and should lead change efforts, and how change efforts can be meaningfully enacted. We have never seen a writing-related faculty development program that does this work—and our program at Miami has not historically done it, either. We came to the conclusion that we *should* be doing it only after watching our colleagues return to their departments and programs and face constraints and obstacles to enacting and leading change.

In this chapter we discuss the challenges of institutional and departmental culture change and the challenges of supporting faculty in seeing themselves as change agents who seek to make deep change in higher education. First, we outline two types of change that educational development leaders might find useful in meeting their own change goals and supporting others in changemaking efforts. We then discuss the challenges for faculty who attempt to lead deep, meaningful change around teaching and learning in higher education systems. We end with some methodologies that faculty leaders can employ to make change in their programs and departments.

A BRIEF OVERVIEW OF TYPES OF INSTITUTIONAL CHANGE

In order to act as change agents, individuals benefit from understanding different types of change and the ways those change efforts are led. As we briefly discuss in chapters 1 and 2, change theorists distinguish between two general types of change: *first-order changes* include changes to behavior and practices, while *second-order change, or deep change,* involves changing underlying belief systems that in turn change behavior and practice (Kezar 2018). First-order and deep changes involve different change processes, with first-order changes being more linear and rational while deep change is ongoing and recursive (Kezar 2018). The types of changes educational development leaders often seek can fall into both categories. Curricular change, for example, can be a first-order change that occurs in a linear and straightforward way, such as when it is mandated by a campus leader or committee. Curricular change can also be evidence of an accompanying deep change, such as if changed conceptions lead teachers and faculty to make changes in their curriculum so it better aligns with their understanding of teaching and learning. Those seeking to make change around teaching and learning benefit from understanding both types of change in order to determine what change process best aligns with their desired outcomes.

If faculty members think about change, they typically think about first-order change, which often occurs in a planned, linear fashion. First-order changes often lead to new processes for doing work without necessarily changing the underlying mindsets or beliefs around that process. For example, the registrar's office may create a new process for overenrolling students in courses. This new process is communicated to faculty and students, who will take up the new process without changing their ideas about acceptable class size or why they might enroll students beyond the designated course cap. In this example, there is likely a designated leader or group of leaders who can help faculty and students understand the change and act in new ways. First-order approaches to change are already common in higher education contexts, such as organizational development, strategic planning, and total quality management, and, according to Adrianna Kezar (2018), there is a wealth of research available on leading first-order change.

In fact, first-order change actually dominates scholarship in change theory and also dominates the daily lives of most faculty members (often to their frustration). First-order changes can easily be pointed to and assessed, which likely accounts for the attention paid to these efforts in a culture where efficiency and accountability are the watchwords of the day. Programs and universities can easily point to new requirements as evidence of change. However, as we discuss in chapter 2, such first-order changes, while potentially important and useful, do not necessarily ensure something meaningful is happening in daily practice. If the problem is as we outline in chapters 1 and 2—that the current focus on efficiency and accountability does not in fact lead to deep learning—then deep change in the values and culture of the system itself must be pursued.

In contrast to first-order change, deep change is a change "that is so substantial that it alters the operating systems, underlying values, and culture of an organization or system" (Kezar 2018, 85). Deep change is, as might be expected, extremely difficult; as Kezar puts it, "Research is not encouraging" for individuals who want to lead deep change. Deep change is often likely to be resisted, especially if "change is too radical or is vastly different from the existing system" (71). Deep change *does* lead to structural changes of the same sort that might be led through first-order change strategies, including "substantial changes to the curriculum, new pedagogies, changes in student learning and assessment practices, new policies, the reallocation of funds, the creation of new departments" (86). These changes represent deep change when they are accompanied by implicit evidence of deep change, which does not lend itself to traditional assessment and reporting approaches, such as change in attitude and culture shifts, the "way groups or individuals interact with one another, the language used by the campus . . . or the types of conversations that occur, as well as the abandonment of old arguments or the emergence of new relationships" (86). The difficulty, of course, is knowing when a first-order change has meaningfully resulted from deep change or whether it is the result of surface-level mandates.

One of the fundamental challenges to leading the kinds of deep change we advocate is that it cannot be mandated. It requires more than changing practices that can be easily tracked or assessed. Instead, deep change "involve[s] constantly helping others to understand the nature of the change and reinforcing why it is important for learning" (Kezar 2018, 71). Deep change requires, then, an ongoing learning process using methods like sensemaking and organizational learning, through which higher education stakeholders are introduced to new ideas and given the time and space to integrate these new concepts with their existing beliefs before developing new approaches to curriculum or pedagogy. Because of its underlying emphasis on change as a learning process, deep change benefits from distributed leadership that involves a variety of institutional stakeholders. As educational development leaders, we are most interested in how faculty members can, from the bottom up, lead deep change in their programs and departments, not just in their individual classrooms. Yet supporting faculty to lead these meso- and macrolevel changes requires a deeper understanding of institutional culture and appropriate methods for leading change. These system changes also face a variety of challenges, to which we now turn.

CHALLENGES TO MAKING DEEP CHANGE

If educational development leaders want to lead deep change or empower others to do so, they benefit from considering the wide variety of challenges change agents might face. Institutional and departmental cultures can afford or constrain change efforts, and many change agents will need support in navigating multiple layers of institutional culture in order to lead change. In addition, faculty may not see themselves as change agents, and the nature of the promotion and tenure system typically does not reward curricular leadership.

Institutional and Departmental Culture

Any effort by individuals or groups within a university setting to effect deep change around teaching and learning is bound by larger rules of the game. Institutional and departmental cultures are important considerations for all change initiatives but particularly so when leaders want to facilitate deep change. Culture is a "powerful norm" that can regulate behaviors (Kotter 2012), but "the cultural system is implicit," so "change agents often overlook it" (57). Faculty members pursuing change, then, must understand the existing culture (of their department, of the university, of the system of education overall and its current embodiment of a disintegrative view of learning), a task that requires them to bring to consciousness tacit assumptions and conventions. The work of uncovering existing cultural norms and assumptions can help potential changemakers understand the relationship between existing culture and the change they seek. In higher education in particular, there may be multiple cultures to navigate within a single institutional context, including departments and institutions themselves, as well as the norms and practices of individual academic disciplines. While not all changes require cultural change to be successful, the culture always bears on what any potential change agent can do.

One way of understanding how cultures bear on local change efforts is to think about Pierre Bourdieu's conceptions of field and *habitus*. Programs, departments, divisions, and universities are all part of what Bourdieu describes as a "field"—in this instance, the field of higher education. Thus, no person or program, no matter how powerful, operates with complete agency. Rather, "our modus operandi are bound in various ways by 'the rules which define the ordinary functioning of the field' " (Bourdieu 1991; Bourdieu and Wacquant 1992, 101). Everyone working in universities is a "social agent" (Bourdieu and Wacquant 1992, 115) in the "social game." For the most part, we as individuals feel the pull of the larger field and its rules on all we do, even if only with a vague sense of frustration. For example, our program budgets may be cut while we are also required to provide more formal assessment reports; we are frustrated, but we may not recognize the way the rules of the game have changed, resulting in this frustration: what states view as valuable and worth funding has changed over time, and thus education budgets are cut while accountability initiatives are increased (Newfield 2018), a point we return to in the afterword. Individual faculty feel the results of this change even if they are never explicitly told what the larger "rules of the game" are. This frustration matters for our purposes in this collection because it is important to recognize that no individual or team who completes an educational development program is simply free to make any change they desire. They are constrained by the "rules which define" the "ordinary functioning" of the field of higher education. And they are additionally constrained by the rules that define the functioning of their local institution, their division, and their department.

Each institution has what Tone Dyrdal Solbrekke and Ciaran Sugrue (2020) call a "dominant institutional orientation" (19), and the leaders of those institutions have "implicit leadership theories" that influence what those dominant institutional orientations are. These are rarely if ever explicitly named or discussed, but together, these orientations "create a force field in which . . . employees and students are obliged to play the game" (19). We all, of course, have some agency, but this agency has limits. Sometimes the resistance individuals feel around change efforts is linked to implicit attitudes, values, orientations, and dispositions that are never named but clearly influence how easily particular changes can be effected. In chapter 2 we suggest conceptual change around writing, teaching, and learning that leads to changed practices should be a goal of writing-related faculty development (and other educational development) programs. This goal, much more than smaller goals around specific curricular practices, is likely to butt up against the *habitus*[1] of the field—the local university and larger education system—in ways that can make change very difficult. If, for example, faculty recognize that deep learning of threshold concepts or disciplinary ways of thinking and practicing require students to fail and struggle for extended periods of time within liminal spaces, the types of assessments typically mandated in higher education as imperative evidence of accountability must be dismantled. Such a change would require taking on currently accepted rules of the game, leading change in the system or field itself. This work is extremely difficult and requires faculty members to understand how leadership works within bureaucratized systems and how change can be effected within such systems.

Leadership in an Academic Environment

So far in this chapter, we have established that the deep changes we want to support faculty in making are difficult. While faculty teams who have changed their own conceptions of writing return to their departments with plans for changed coursework, curriculum, and assessment, they often encounter roadblocks identified in chapter 2. Others in their department do not share the same ideas of writing, teaching, and learning that the departmental teams have developed and as a result might be apathetic or even antagonistic toward the changes individuals want to make. In addition, larger cultural assumptions and values of their universities and the educational system in general are always influencing what changes can be made. At this stage of changemaking efforts, then, leadership is crucial (as is an understanding of the nature of and constraints to change). Yet faculty members (and department chairs and program directors) rarely have training in either leadership or leading change efforts (Collins 2014; Solbrekke and Sugrue 2020). James Collins (2014) has outlined a number of problematic assumptions about academic leaders that have resulted in "many institutions of higher education" simply not offering "leadership-training programs for the average faculty member, even after someone commits to administration" (561). This overall lack of leadership preparation, paired with the difficulty of making some types of change, is a key challenge for change agents to act on their changed conceptions as they hope to.

When educational development leaders lead programs like the Faculty Writing Fellows Program at Miami, they assume and hope faculty will return to their departments and programs and lead, formally or informally, meaningful change in curricular design and implementation of research-based pedagogical practices. Neither of these is a given. More often, faculty tend *not* to see themselves as leaders, not to know *how* to work to effect change beyond their own classrooms, and not to be prepared when the larger changes they seek encounter resistance from a field that enacts quite different values and assumptions.

Let's consider the first obstacle. Faculty may not see themselves as leaders for many reasons; one is that in the US promotion and tenure system, faculty members are typically *not rewarded* for leading pedagogical efforts. "The reward for committing seriously to education [and] education leadership is perceived to be very much less than that gained through commitment to and success in research" (Beckman 2017, 156). As Jose Coll (2007) puts it, the only advice new faculty members tend to get is "publish as early as possible and develop a research agenda that could garnish [*sic*] external funding." Faculty are rewarded for publishing and, at some schools or in some roles, for teaching effectively. They are not rewarded most of the time in any tangible way for rocking the boat and trying to effect large-scale curricular changes; quite often, they are actually punished for this behavior instead. Institutional culture, in terms of the lack of value it places on innovating pedagogy and curriculum, can limit whether individuals who *want* to make change see themselves as change agents who can lead change efforts. This reality may be even more complicated for faculty in some kinds of teaching-track positions, where they may not be rewarded for doing *any* institutional service (although at some schools, non-tenure-track teaching innovations are rewarded, as chapter 4 discusses). Faculty without long-term contracts or job security may feel the frustrations of institutional culture and want to make change but realistically be constrained by their own positions within the university hierarchy and lack of job security.

Implicit assumptions about who is able to lead in higher education may also present challenges for individuals, especially faculty members who want to lead change but may not already see themselves as change agents. Many individuals view leadership as inherent in "persons" or "positions" (Grint 2013); that is, a person either has inherent qualities that make them a leader, or they hold a formal institutional position that grants them leadership authority. In higher education hierarchies, faculty members may not see themselves as holding the authority to lead changes they want to make. And there are "few programs designed to cultivate a broader number of individuals or the structures to support shared leadership" (Kezar and Holcombe 2017, v)

When faculty members *do* see themselves as change agents or decide to lead changes despite the limited rewards for doing so, there is another obstacle: many individuals, even those in formal leadership positions, lack "systematic training" in leadership (Solbrekke and Sugrue 2020, xx). In most academic disciplines, training in pedagogy and curriculum are scarce, and scarcer still is training in how to work across a full program or department to lead innovative change in pedagogy and curriculum. When faculty try to lead, there are no scripts for them in leadership roles. As a result, the burden to define and find such leadership scripts falls "largely on the individual" (21; see also Henkel 2002). Formal academic leaders such as provosts, deans, and chairs without formal leadership training tend to fall back on their personal ideas about leadership. According to research conducted by Solbrekke and Sugrue (2020), this leads to implicit leadership styles that tend to focus on "influence directed toward the achievement of goals" and overlook questions such as, "What is the source of the goals to be pursued?" and "By what process is influence to be exerted?" (22). This focus on achieving specific goals may lead to a focus on first-order changes because the cultures, conceptions, or attitudes that underlie those goals are invisible to leaders. Because they work from implicit approaches to leadership, individuals may actually be hindered in their attempts to lead change as they draw on strategies that are not beneficial to their goals (Kezar 2018).

We don't identify these challenges to faculty leadership as criticisms of the alumni of the Fellows Program. As this collection illustrates, many

Fellows do see themselves as change agents and are working toward deep change in their programs and departments. As we have worked to support faculty in these efforts, however, we have identified ideas and strategies in the leadership and change scholarship that we can explicitly include in our educational development in order to support faculty as agents of deep change around teaching and learning in their programs and departments.

Educational development leaders who want to support faculty as change agents might begin by reframing leadership, challenging the personal and positional views in favor of process-oriented leadership (Grint 2013). Solbrekke and Sugrue (2020) suggest helping faculty reconceive of leadership by asking them to explore the idea that "leading implies teaching, and teaching implies leading" (72). In our view, helping faculty think of leadership as teaching and teaching as leadership is a promising avenue for helping them embrace their role as leaders. Those who come to educational development programs tend, for the most part, to see themselves as teachers if not as leaders. Helping them see teaching as leading might be a first step toward reimagining their role as potential leaders. This shift is particularly important for individuals who desire to lead deep change, as effecting such change requires an ongoing learning process on the part of participants.

In addition to seeing "leadership" as "teaching," faculty also benefit from understanding a "distributed" perspective of leadership (see Solbrekke and Sugrue 2020, 72; Spillane 2006), or what Kezar (2018) describes as "collective" or "shared" leadership (134; see also Pearce and Conger 2003), with both formal and informal leaders (Solbrekke and Sugrue 2020, 20). This view sees leadership as not "vested exclusively in the most senior personnel in higher education organisation" but rather as "both formally and informally enacted across the whole organisation, in vertical as well as horizontal relational dynamics" (24). This is a grassroots method of leadership, rather than a traditional top-down method that relies on "positions of power" (Kezar 2018, 135). Distributed leadership seeks to understand the goal of change as a "shared responsibility." Faculty who return to departments after educational development seminars to try to enact meaningful, research-based changes cannot act alone. However, enacting a distributed model of leadership is not simple. It requires creating "cultures and structures" that empower and motivate individuals to work with others to be responsible for change and "build collaborative and trusting relationships" (Carbone et al. 2017 quoted in Solbrekke and Sugrue 2020, 29). A distributed leadership model is likely quite a different model of leadership than faculty typically imagine when they hear the word *leader*. There is often a sense that upper administrators (not faculty) are the ones who lead, and at many institutions faculty distrust these leaders, feeling high-level decisions are made without regard for deep learning or faculty expertise. This concern seems to be increasing for reasons we allude to in chapter 1 and take up further in the afterword, as institutions of higher education embody "apparent instrumentalist entrepreneurialism that privileges competitiveness, internationalisation, and rankings" (Solbrekke and Sugrue 2020, 18). In other words, the disintegrative paradigm in which we are currently operating may mean faculty members (typically focused on learning and research) and administrators (typically focused on operations) may struggle to find common frames for approaching problems and enacting change.

A challenge for those leading educational development programs "is [how] to encourage colleagues to take ownership of" their shared leadership responsibility for pushing for meaningful change around learning in their programs but also in the larger educational system. Achieving this aim requires engaging faculty in "an ongoing, deliberative process" and suggests an opportunity for educational development leaders to act as brokers as they work to help faculty engage in this way with the work of the university[2] (Solbrekke and Sugrue 2020, 31).

METHODS FOR LEADING CHANGE

Once educational development leaders are aware of the challenges faculty members face in leading change and determine they want to directly support these change efforts, developers need methods for leading change that are available to different kinds of institutional stakeholders.

Change theorists note that not all individuals who desire to lead change have the same methods available to them. Leaders who are invested with institutional power and authority have methods for leading change that most faculty do not. They have at their disposal strategic plans, mission and vision statements, budget and resource allocation, rewards and incentives, and the ability to hire and restructure. These leadership strategies are, as Kezar (2018) puts it, only available to "organizational elites" (136) and thus are not our focus here. Rather, we want to consider how faculty teacher-leaders can act from a distributed-leadership model to effect deep change. Those leading from the bottom up have other strategies available to them. Kezar describes nine strategies they can leverage, some of which are hard or even impossible for top-level leaders to leverage. These include creating intellectual forums, providing meaningful faculty development opportunities, recruiting like-minded applicants for pivotal positions, finding seed money to test out innovative ideas, creating coalitions with students, generating awareness and consciousness through classroom practice, gathering and using data, joining networks with common interests and goals, and partnering with key external stakeholders (139–42; see also Kezar and Lester 2011).

In order for shared or distributed leadership to be successful, change agents must learn to work in leadership groups, something faculty members (and leaders in general) are sometimes not adept at. Kezar (2018) notes that successfully working in such leadership groups requires cultivating a number of skills:

- "interpersonal skills such as conflict resolution, empathy, communication, and emotional competence" (145);
- an understanding of how groups work and how to create functional processes and bring newcomers on board (145–46);
- how to create a "shared sense of purpose, values, and goals" (146);
- how to facilitate "shared cognition" or "similar mental maps regarding their internal work, as well as the nature of the external environment" (146) while also recognizing that shared cognition "does not mean groupthink" and instead supporting diverse perspectives and establishing trust over time (147);
- facilitating regular and ongoing communication; and
- addressing differing levels of power and status among the members of the leadership group (148).

While this advice regarding strategies to leverage and skills to cultivate is useful, it can feel somewhat abstract. What, specifically, can groups of faculty do when they return to their departments and programs and seek to effect deep change that extends across the program's courses and faculty? Solbrekke and Sugrue (2020), along with Molly Sutphen, Tomas Englund, and Kristin Ewins (2020), argue for the role of *deliberative communication* "wherein participants agree to have or try out a set of dispositions, including a willingness to reflect on one's biases . . . ; to engage in collective will-formation; to be open to the views of others" (81). This form of communication, developed by Englund (2006) and based on the work of John Dewey and Jurgen Habermas, is intended to help "create conditions for participants to reflect on a problem or situation and be used for a public good" (Sutphen, Englund, and Ewins 2020, 81). Deliberative communication asks participants to reflect both individually and collectively, allows all voices to be heard, hears and respects different perspectives, but also asks participants to reach "legitimate compromises in a web of possible contesting commitments" (Bergh, Solbrekke, and Wickstrom 2020, 92). It also stimulates collective learning (Bergh, Solbrekke, and Wickstrom 2020), without which meaningful change within a community of practice is unlikely to occur.

Deliberative communication is similar to what Kezar (2018) calls "sensemaking," which "is about changing mindsets, which in turn alters behaviors, priorities, values, and commitments" (87). One way "people undergo sensemaking is that they develop new language and new concepts that describe a changed institution" (87). One example of sensemaking is the first four weeks of the Fellows Program, which we describe in chapters 1 and 2. As Fellows participants examine their disciplinary written practices and discuss them with people from other disciplines, their mindsets and ideas change—they are making new sense of writing and its teaching. A forum/space must be carefully designed to facilitate this kind of sensemaking. For an example of deliberative communication or sensemaking in action at the level of a full department, see chapter 13 of this collection, in which teacher education revised its mission statement, guiding principles, and curriculum around social justice.

Faculty members who return to their departments hoping to enact change could invite their colleagues into deliberative communication around conceptions of writing and the implications for teaching. While they might initiate the conversation, the goal of deliberative conversation is to ensure that all voices are heard and that people with expertise can bring their ideas to the table and reflect. Thus, distributed leadership is enacted. We have seen some Fellows alumni return to their departments to do something very much along these lines. Teacher education, history, and philosophy all facilitated some version of deliberative communication. Their chosen structures for these follow-ups were very much democratic and dialogic, without one expert or authority leading them. Philosophy and teacher education asked the two of us to assist with at least the first conversation, while history facilitated its own discussion. In all three cases, the department chair had participated in the Fellows Program, making it easier for the conversations to be scheduled with ensured participation. Even the most deliberative and democratic model of leadership and shared learning across departments requires someone to suggest and schedule times for conversation. And, given the nature of academic institutions, participants need to feel their time will be valued in some demonstrable way—which is easier for a chair to ensure than a rank-and-file faculty member. However, in all three of these cases, the chair did not assert authority over the discussions themselves; the chair simply ensured the discussions happened. To build on our argument in chapter 2, then, we note that it is helpful for chairs to be part of the Fellows teams, but we want to clarify that this participation is not so they can force others to adhere to their changed ideas about teaching and writing but rather so they can set the table where meaningful discussion about teaching and writing can happen among the full faculty.

CONCLUSION

In this chapter we argue that leading deep change that supports creating meaningful learning environments for students requires challenging and changing systems and their culture or *habitus*. Faculty need support if they are to return to their departments and take on such change efforts. They benefit from understanding the nature of distributed leadership and the resources they can leverage in their efforts, and from having access to programs that will support them in building the skill sets around teamwork that academia has historically rarely provided.

In the process of making this argument, we greatly complicate and extend the nature of the work that educational development leaders do: in addition to facilitating training in teaching and learning, we might also provide support for leadership and change. While we can't lead change *for* programs and departments, we can support them in these efforts, acting as boundary brokers (Wenger 2000) and modeling the same learning and sensemaking processes faculty might use to lead change themselves.

We note at the beginning of this chapter that our own program has not historically done the work we are currently calling for. It is through our efforts to support Faculty Fellows in their leadership and change efforts that we have come to articulate the challenges they face and have begun to develop programming around supporting change initiatives. After working with department chairs in philosophy, teacher education, and history, for example, we invited four Fellows who served as program or department chairs to engage in a leadership and change reading group focused on higher education change theories we discuss here. Now, we are developing programming specifically aimed at empowering Fellows as leaders in their change efforts, regardless of their academic positions. In the 2020–21 school year, we piloted a year-long initiative called the Leading Change Institute. Even though we had not initially articulated the need to support faculty in their change efforts, we have nonetheless seen powerful examples of Fellows leading change in their programs and departments. The next two chapters illustrate how the Fellows Program served as a sensemaking opportunity in which faculty engaged in deliberation about writing, teaching, and learning in their disciplines in ways that led to changes in their programs and departments. These chapters from economics and philosophy faculty teams illustrate what happens when faculty are successful at leading change from within.

NOTES

1. Bourdieu (1990) defines *habitus* as "a system (i.e., a set of interacting elements) of durable, transposable dispositions" (53). John Thompson, his editor, summarizes Bourdieu's view of *habitus* as "a set of dispositions which incline agents to act and react in certain ways. The dispositions generate practices, perceptions, and attitudes which are 'regular' without being consciously co-ordinated or governed by any 'rule.' The dispositions which constitute the habitus are inculcated, structured, durable, generative, and transposable" (Bourdieu 1990, 12).
2. While it is not the focus of this chapter, we believe educational development leaders are working as what Etienne Wenger calls "boundary brokers" who participate in multiple communities of practice and introduce practices from one into the other and vice versa. For more on this role see Wenger's *Communities of Practice* (2000).

REFERENCES

Beckman, Elizabeth A. 2017. "Leadership through Fellowship: Distributed Leadership in a Professional Recognition Scheme for University Educators." *Journal of Higher Education Policy and Management* 39 (2): 155–68.

Bergh, Andreas, Tone Dyrdal Solbrekke, and Johan Wickstrom. 2020. "Deliberative Communication: Stimulating Collective Learning?" In *Leading Higher Education As and For Public Good: Rekindling Education as Praxis,* edited by Tone Dyrdal Solbrekke and Cianan Sugure, 92–106. New York: Routledge.

Bourdieu, Pierre. 1990. *The Logic of Practice.* Redwood City, CA: Stanford University Press.

Bourdieu, Pierre. 1991. *Language and Symbolic Power.* Edited by John Thompson. Translated by Gino Raymond and Matthew Adamson. Cambridge, MA: Harvard University Press.

Bourdieu, Pierre, and Loic Wacquant. 1992. *An Invitation to Reflexive Sociology.* Chicago: University of Chicago Press.

Carbone Angela, Julia Evans, Bella Ross, Steve Drew, Liam Phelan, Katherine Lindsay, Caroline Cottman, Susan Stoney, and Jing Ye. 2017. "Assessing Distributed Leadership for Learning and Teaching Quality: A Multi-Institutional Study." *Journal of Higher Education Policy and Management* 39 (2): 183–96. https://doi.org/10.1080/1360080X.2017.1276629.

Coll, Jose. 2007. "Rethinking Leadership Development in Higher Education." *The Evolllution.* https://evolllution.com/managing-institution/operations_efficiency/rethinking-leadership-development-in-higher-education/.

Collins, James P. 2014. "Leadership and Change in Twenty-First Century Higher Education." *BioScience* 64 (7): 561–62. https://doi.org/*10.1093/biosci/biu080.*

Englund, Tomas. 2006. "Deliberative Communication: A Pragmatist Proposal." *Curriculum Studies* 38 (5): 503–20.

Grint, Keith. 2013. *Leadership: A Very Short Introduction.* Oxford: Oxford University Press.

Henkel, M. 2002. "Emerging Concepts of Academic Leadership and Their Implications for Intra-Institutional Roles and Relationships in Higher Education." *European Journal of Education* 371 (2): 9–41.

Kezar, Adrianna. 2018. *How Colleges Change: Understanding, Leading, and Enacting Change*, 2nd ed. New York: Routledge.

Kezar, Adrianna, and Elizabeth Holcombe. 2017. *Shared Leadership in Higher Education: Important Lessons from Research and Practice.* Washington, DC: American Council on Education. https://www.acenet.edu/Documents/Shared-Leadership-in-Higher-Education.pdf.

Kezar, Adrianna J., and Jaime Lester. 2011. *Enhancing Campus Capacity for Leadership: An Examination of Grassroots Leaders in Higher Education.* Stanford, CA: Stanford University Press.

Kotter, John P. 2012. *Leading Change.* Boston: Harvard Business Review Press.

Newfield, Christopher. 2018. *The Great Mistake: How We Wrecked Public Universities and How We Can Fix Them.* Baltimore: Johns Hopkins University Press.

Pearce, Craig L., and Jay A. Conger. 2003. *Shared Leadership: Reframing the Hows and Whys of Leadership.* Thousand Oaks, CA: SAGE.

Solbrekke, Tone Dyrdal, and Ciaran Sugure. 2020. *Leading Higher Education As and For Public Good: Rekindling Education as Praxis.* New York: Routledge.

Spillane, James. 2006. *Distributed Leadership.* San Francisco: Jossey Bass.

Sutphen, Molly, Tomas Englund, and Kristin Ewins. 2020. "Intellectual Virtues for Leading Higher Education." In *Leading Higher Education As and For Public Good: Rekindling Education as Praxis*, edited by Tone Dyrdal Solbrekke and Cianan and Sugrue, 80–91. New York: Routledge.

Wenger, Etienne. 2000. *Communities of Practice: Learning, Meaning, and Identity.* Cambridge: Cambridge University Press.

PART 2

Accounts of Faculty-Led Change Efforts

Part 2 provides a number of accounts from faculty across the disciplines who completed the HCWE Faculty Writing Fellows Program and, as a result, carefully reconsidered their conceptions of writing and learning in their fields. This part is further split into three sections: section 1, "Changing Conceptions and Making Values Visible"; section 2, "Designing Meaningful Learning Opportunities"; and section 3, "The Challenges of Systemic Change in Fields and Departments." These sections each tackle different levels of changed conceptions and practices, with section 1 taking up broader faculty conceptions and programmatic changes, section 2 focusing more on changes and innovations faculty have made in specific courses and programs, and section 3 tackling the difficulty in making changes across departments and wider disciplines.

The first two chapters in section 1, chapters 4 and 5, from economics and philosophy, specifically focus on what we think of as macrolevel concerns: changed conceptions among groups of faculty members and changed programmatic practices as a result.

The next chapters in section 2, chapters 6–10, provide accounts of faculty members and teams who have used threshold concepts to design meaningful learning opportunities for students in specific courses and programs. Their accounts range from collaborative discussions of disciplinary identity and what that means for classroom pedagogy to reflections of individual teachers who are looking for strategies and methods for engaging their students in the messy, liminal work of their discipline. These authors offer examples of how readers can reflect on and redesign the ways they assign, teach, and assess student writing. Overall, these chapters put many of the larger themes of this collection to work and provide compelling examples of how faculty innovate meaningful learning environments.

The final three chapters in section 3, chapters 11, 12, and 13, provide accounts of how faculty members in the very different fields of psychology, Latin American, Latino/a, and Caribbean studies, and teacher education seek to make change in their programs, departments, and disciplines.

https://doi.org/10.7330/9781646423040.p002

SECTION 1

CHANGING CONCEPTIONS AND MAKING VALUES VISIBLE

4

REDEFINING OUR UNDERSTANDING OF WRITING

Janice Kinghorn and Ling Shao
Economics

INTRODUCTION

In 2017, three faculty members in the economics department (the authors and another colleague who has since left Miami) participated in the Howe Faculty Writing Fellows Program. We were motivated by a sense of frustration about the ability of the economics department to constructively fulfill college and university writing requirements. The existing department writing plan was meant to satisfy an earlier requirement from the College of Arts and Sciences and was seen as a distraction from the core mission of teaching economics. While the plan required a paper directed toward a general audience with a minimum word count, it was embedded in courses focused on the use of formal theory to model economic phenomena (300-level core theory courses). Some faculty felt the way the requirement was constructed was at odds with students' development of clear and focused communication using the tools of mathematics and theoretical frameworks. Frustration increased when in 2015 a new university-wide writing requirement was mandated.

Our group entered the Fellows Program with a practical goal. We were looking for simple, ready-to-use techniques to make this new mandate less burdensome. However, participating in the Fellows Program made us realize that in seeking quick fixes we were at risk of repeating the error in the design of our previous writing plan, which had been developed to fulfill a mandate rather than to complement teaching and learning. We were also deeply touched by the Fellows guiding belief that higher education should "teach for deep learning and critical thinking that is transferable across contexts and that will enable learners to be productive and innovative citizens in a democracy" (this volume, chapter 1). Rarely have we been involved in a professional development program with such a sense of urgency and responsibility.

https://doi.org/10.7330/9781646423040.c004

The rest of the chapter details our experience with the Fellows' Program. First, we explain how our conception of writing was broadened through the Fellows use of the threshold concepts framework. Then we present results from two surveys on existing writing activity and writing instruction among our departmental faculty. Based on the survey results, we discuss the distinct features of writing in economics and reflect on how our departmental writing requirements could become key components of how we teach our students to describe and explain economic phenomena. Last, we document our assessment effort that ensures the continuing integration of writing throughout the major. We conclude by discussing the possibility of extending the assessment model to other disciplines beyond economics.

HOW THE FELLOWS PROGRAM CHANGED OUR CONCEPTION OF WRITING

Going into the Fellows Program, we thought it would present us with tips and tricks we could easily adapt in order to meet the university-wide writing mandate. During the first meeting, however, we were told that would not be the case. Instead, we were encouraged to think deeply about the transformative power of writing and how writing could be used to enhance teaching and learning in our discipline. To these requests, our initial responses were along the lines of, "Well, we have large enrollment introductory classes where writing is not really practical" and "Students will have already learned and know how to write papers when they take their upper-level courses." In other words, our definition of writing when we started the Fellows Program was based on a typical paper published in an academic journal. However, this view of writing, possibly entrenched in our minds since graduate school, was too restrictive both from a pedagogical standpoint and from the standpoint of meeting a mandate. By limiting our understanding of writing to papers of a certain length, we might have undervalued writing as an important way of learning economics, especially in large class sections. We might also have been inclined to regard any writing mandate as an additional burden when equated to a paper with specific word count.

Our conception of writing began to change when we were introduced to the threshold concepts (TC) framework. None of us had heard of this idea before, so it was quite surprising to learn economics actually was one of the disciplines studied extensively within this framework. For instance, Jan Meyer and Ray Land (2006) explain why opportunity cost is a threshold concept in economics. They also specifically use economics as an example to argue that in some disciplines, "ways of thinking and practicing" qualify as a vital threshold that learners need to pass in order to transform from novice to expert (15).

This last point proved particularly enlightening. The three of us had been teaching introductory economics for many years and were familiar with the phrase *think like an economist*, found in almost every beginning economics textbook. Yet despite our familiarity with the phrase, our experience suggested that upon graduation, only a small fraction of our students would somehow "get it" while for many students it would remain a lofty goal. We did not really ponder why economics majors would have trouble thinking like an economist. We assumed that as we taught economic concepts and showed their applications, students would come to think like economists over time. It then became difficult to genuinely desire a change if we accepted as a fact that no matter what we did, some students just would not master thinking like economists. Consequently, a lot of blame was placed on students' lack of critical thinking and quantitative skills.

Through the lens of a TC framework, we learned to acknowledge the difficulty in crossing the threshold of thinking like an economist. As the editors of this collection put it, due to the nonlinear and messy nature of thresholds, learners may find themselves stuck in uncomfortable liminal spaces, needing "support from a variety of teachers and mentors who all recognize that learning is hard and are willing to together create safe and scaffolded environments for that learning" (this volume, chapter 1). The realization that students' failure to think like economists might have less to do with deficiencies in their skill sets than with inadequate instructional support necessitates a set of pedagogical questions: How do people already in the profession overcome the hurdles? How could teachers help learners pass through the portal? What is the role of writing in the process?

Deirdre McCloskey (2000) in her book *Economical Writing* argues that "writing is thinking" and "you do not learn the details of an argument until writing it in detail, and in writing the details you uncover flaws in the fundamentals" (7). Steven Greenlaw (2009) claims that "the best way to learn economics is not to hear about it, or to read about it, but to do it. Doing economics means performing economic research" (1). We, as economists in the teaching profession, can easily relate to these words, but the TC framework adds an interesting perspective. We now recognize that once we successfully pass the portal, that is, once performing and writing about economic research become part of a routine, we may forget how we used to struggle in a liminal state and hence may skip the necessary hand-holding support for our students in this journey. Another connection we made through the TC framework is that if *think like an economist* is a threshold concept and writing is thinking, then *write like an economist* should also be a threshold concept. Whenever thinking happens, we can always find a written format to support that thinking. This greatly expands our conception of writing in economics, from an academic paper to any form of writing that reflects economic thinking, whether it is in words or in math equations.

Through interactions with participants of the Fellows Program from other departments, we were reminded writing could look quite different across disciplines. Economics seeks to understand human behavior within the constraint of limited resources. Principles such as incentives, trade-offs, and maximizing one's own welfare are fundamental in economic analysis. The economic way of thinking and writing is more aligned with other disciplines in social science, including psychology and sociology, than it is with humanities such as history or literature. While economic research is divided into theoretical and empirical types, both share the same structure. It starts with identifying an economic issue from which one can develop a research question. Then the question is formulated into a model, typically in mathematical form. Depending on whether the analysis is empirical or theoretical, real data or simulations are used to test the validity of the model.

Discussions with other Fellows participants shed light on different values placed on disciplinary writing. It is incumbent upon us to teach students the particular things valued in economics, as they will not have learned them in a course from other departments. In other words, this was our responsibility. For example, the work of Murray Simpson and Shireen Carroll (1999) resonated with us, and we identified writing quantitative research papers as something only we could teach. The instructors of typical writing classes would not have the disciplinary expertise. Likewise, only we could provide practice for students learning to present quantitative results to people lacking expertise in economic analysis. We recognized that as economists we write in particular ways and have been expecting our students to do likewise without systematic attention to how we teach them to do so.

We had some room for improvement. For example, the use of evidence is valued in economic writing. Students may not be aware of the extensive requirements to document claims expected in an economic argument. Novice writers often make general claims, such as "the growth rate was extraordinary," without being specific about what they mean by *extraordinary*. While such a descriptive word may be appropriate in another discipline, we require students to instead tell us what the growth rate was and, if they want to convey it was extraordinary, give us some evidence why. For example, they may compare it to previous years or other countries to give it that context.

Another challenge in the use of evidence occurs in referencing existing literature. Providing citations is a way to help the reader position the argument within existing literature, a concept new to many students. We must encourage students' awareness of the audience and purpose of their writing and thus acculturate them into our disciplinary community.

Clarity is also valued in economics. This again is an outgrowth of an awareness of audience and purpose. Much of our writing is intended to provide useful analysis to others. Sometimes it is difficult for students to understand that more words, more details, and longer pieces of writing are not always better. As we worked through the Fellows Program, we recognized and became better able to teach the skill of providing enough but not too much information. It also helped us articulate why a writing requirement with a minimum word count felt out of place in our curriculum.

Economists write for many audiences, and our writing should be adapted accordingly. When writing for fellow professionals, economists can use technical terms and reference theories that would be inappropriate when writing for a general audience. Sometimes students, having worked so hard to master the technical terms and theories, want to use them even when their audience does not share their understanding. On the other hand, they sometimes want to use general terms when technical language and illustrations would be clearer to the audience. The Fellows Program helped us see the need to teach students how to explain technical concepts to professional and general audiences.

WHAT WE CAME TO SEE AS CHALLENGES AND HOW TO ENGAGE THEM

As we developed our understanding of the values economists place on writing, we wanted to know whether the values were being encouraged in our current classrooms and, if so, how. Instead of looking at writing requirements as something to be added on, we researched ways writing, as we now understood it, was being used in our existing classes, the ways our faculty believed writing was important to professional economists, and the challenges faculty were experiencing with writing in their classrooms.

In early March of 2017, we sent an email to department faculty soliciting their responses to the following questions: (1) What do you think graduates of our department should be able to do with their writing? (2) What types of writing do you teach and/or assign in your courses? There was a strong consensus among faculty regarding the first question. Economics majors should be able to clearly explain complex economic concepts, correctly apply these concepts to real-world issues, and effectively communicate technical results to different audiences. The types of writing assigned by economics faculty vary depending on course levels. At the introductory level, writing assignments include short-answer exam questions, news-article analysis, interview reports, and reflections. In 300-level courses, faculty reported that they assign essay questions, literature reviews, opinion pieces, referee reports, and term papers targeted for a general audience. Faculty teaching 400-level field courses typically require students to write a term paper targeted for a specialist audience, as well as extended-response exam questions.

We were surprised about the widespread use of writing already occurring in our department. We and our colleagues had been so enculturated into our professional practice that often we did not realize what we were doing was a discipline-specific way of writing, and thus when the university asked us to incorporate writing in our courses, we were not always aware of the extent to which we were already doing this.

Our team also asked about the purpose of writing. We identified a cluster of courses that ask students to communicate technical results to a general audience (our 300-level theory courses) and another cluster that require communication to a specialist audience with graphs, equations, and tables (our 400-level electives). We found that across 300- and 400-level courses there was wide agreement within the department that we use words, graphs, and equations to interact with ideas: to critique arguments, to synthesize ideas of others, to identify reasoning behind ideas, and to apply economic theory to issues. Finally, we have a cluster of courses that ask students to develop economic arguments and support them with quantitative evidence.

These results helped the department realize we had a shared interest in teaching students to effectively communicate technical and quantitative results. There was also wide agreement that writing can be used to clarify thinking about economic arguments.

Responses from the initial email inquiry still left some unanswered questions about the quality of student writing as seen by faculty and what writing-related instruction faculty provided to students. We posed these questions in a survey administered during a faculty meeting in late April of 2017. Based on survey responses from fifteen faculty members, faculty identified as most problematic in student writing grammatical or mechanical errors (eleven votes), poor organization (ten votes), ideas not clearly conveyed through writing and arguments not well supported with sources (nine votes each). Other less common issues included invalid or incorrect arguments, lacking a central thesis statement or main idea, and intentional or unintentional plagiarism.

Regarding faculty instruction on improving student writing, we learned faculty provided opportunities for feedback on drafts (eleven votes) and taught students how to locate and cite scholarly sources (eight votes). Faculty spent less time on explicitly teaching students how to write a thesis statement or a good introduction and conclusion. While one faculty member did mention he continually discusses what constitutes "good writing" in economics—logical organization of hypothesis, test, and conclusion; the use of multiple sources of evidence; and avoiding overgeneralization—we did not get the sense that this instruction was widely practiced in the department. It echoed what we learned from the Fellows Program: once someone has passed the portal of writing like an economist, they might unintentionally assume everyone else writes in the same way they do.

This gap between faculty perceptions of where students have difficulty and corresponding classroom instruction on writing indicated what the department could do better. For example, clarity in writing and adequate support for claims are two issues widely held to be problematic in student writing. We now realize we were spending classroom time teaching *how* to locate and cite sources but sometimes we did not devote much instruction to *when* sources were needed to support claims or *why* that support is important to economists. We should have been more explicit on conveying these values in the classroom through discussions and scaffolded assignments. Also, we noticed the opportunities we gave students for instructor feedback were inconsistent. For example, several term papers offered no opportunity for feedback and little guidance for completing the assignment even though clarity was an important value. Defining our values, examining where they were taught, and where students were asked to practice using them, helped us see ways we could improve student learning.

Combining what we learned from the Fellows Program with the research on current classroom practice showed student performance on the economics department's learning objectives could be improved by having students practice supporting their arguments with appropriate economic principles and data. Because the transformation from novice to expert does not happen overnight, faculty can achieve the desired levels of competency only if at all levels of economics courses they make concerted efforts to allow students to go through the "portal" repeatedly. The extent to which writing was already occurring presented a key opportunity. How could faculty come to recognize learning opportunities in the writing students already do?

WRITING AS MORE THAN WORDS

Early in our project to improve writing instruction, we noted that types of writing we knew were being used in the classroom were not identified as such by our faculty. For example, we make extensive use of problem sets, which ask students to solve economic problems and convey the results using a variety of types of writing, such as constructing and interpreting graphs. We also ask students to perform and interpret empirical analysis and explain the findings using writing. Neither of these activities were identified by faculty when asked about the writing in their classrooms. Some faculty thought of them as doing economics, not as writing.

The reason faculty did not at first identify writing as crucial to economic reasoning was because of a misconception about what writing is. Perhaps because most of us first learned to write in high school English classes, and traditionally at the college level writing instruction has occurred in first-year composition courses, economics faculty thought of traditional essays or papers as writing and did not consider other ways economists communicate via written symbols. For example, when discussing growth and business cycles, it is impactful to illustrate the change in GDP over time rather than just writing about it in a narrative form. Figure 4.1 illustrates how this change may be effectively communicated. The same image may also be used to discuss business cycles, as the reader can see the fluctuations over time rather than being told about them. This form of communication is an example of writing consistent with economists' values of clarity and evidence.

To explain the concept of an exogenous shock leading to a change in market price of a good, an economist would use a graphical model as in figure 4.2. Using the graphical model to illustrate the effects of a decrease in demand, for example, communicates not only the effect on the demand curve but also why the price and quantity fall and what is concurrently going on with the supply curve. Because this model is part of the shared language of economists, it is important to teach students to read and write in that language.

Economists report empirical results using particular conventions other economists can easily understand. In our econometrics courses we teach students to communicate using these conventions. For example,

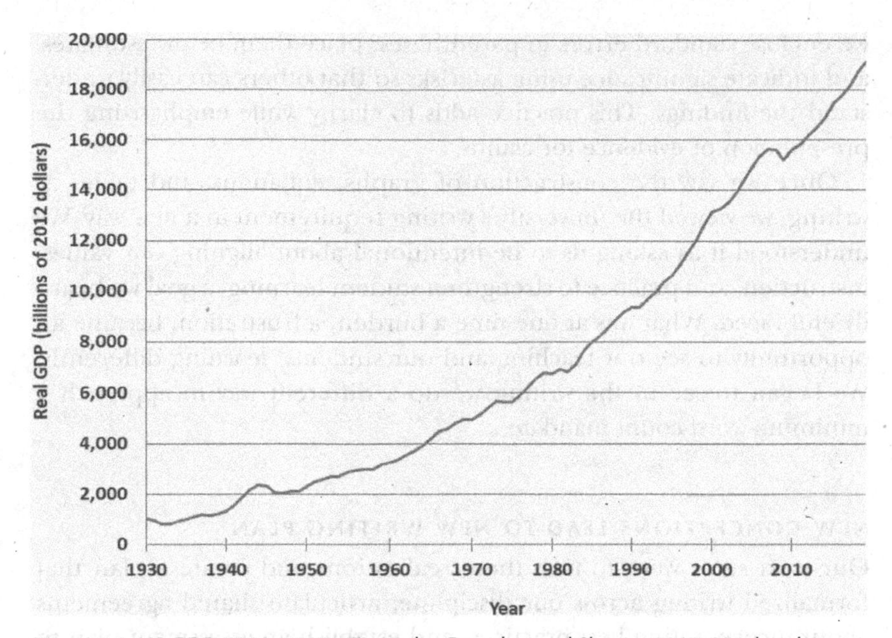

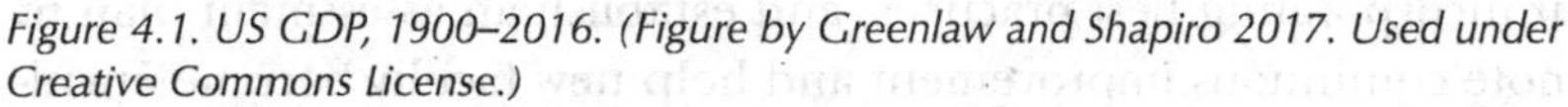

Figure 4.1. US GDP, 1900–2016. (Figure by Greenlaw and Shapiro 2017. Used under Creative Commons License.)

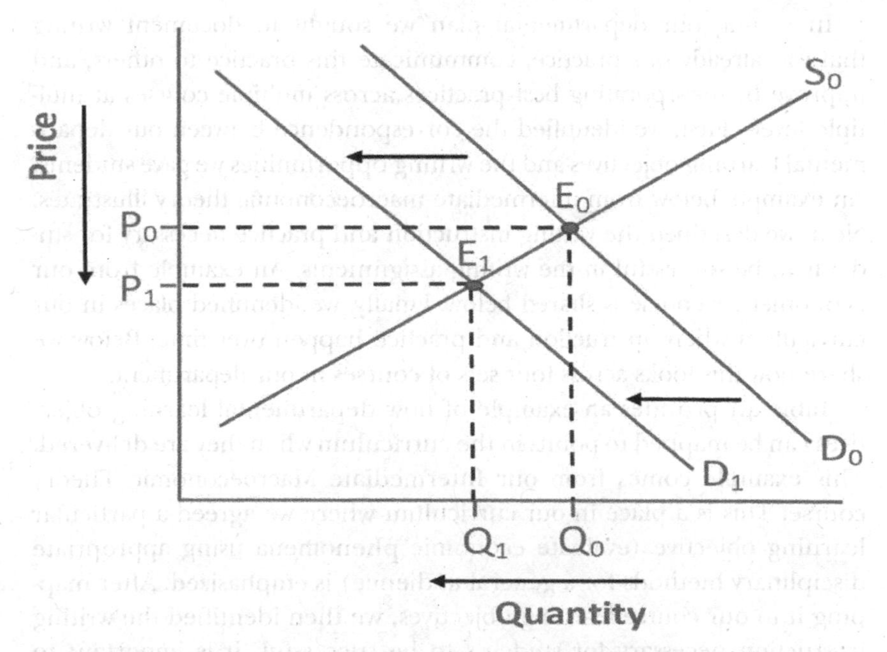

Figure 4.2. Modeling a market with a demand shift. (Figure by Greenlaw and Shapiro 2017. Used under Creative Commons License.)

we enclose standard errors in parentheses, place them below estimates, and indicate significance using asterisks so that others can easily understand the findings. This practice adds to clarity while emphasizing the presentation of evidence for claims.

Once we saw the construction of graphs, equations, and tables as writing, we viewed the university's writing requirement in a new way. We understood it as asking us to be intentional about aligning our values, instruction, and practice to strengthen student learning, a goal we heartily embraced. What was at one time a burden, a frustration, became an opportunity to see our teaching and our students' learning differently. We began to see in the writing we do a different way to approach a minimum-word-count mandate.

NEW CONCEPTIONS LEAD TO NEW WRITING PLAN

Our next steps were to take these realizations and create a plan that formalized writing across our discipline, articulate shared agreements about incorporating best practices, and establish an assessment plan to promote continuous improvement and help new faculty become enculturated to our practices.

In writing our departmental plan we sought to document writing that was already our practice, communicate this practice to others, and improve by incorporating best practices across multiple courses at multiple levels. First, we identified the correspondence between our departmental learning objectives and the writing opportunities we gave students. An example below from intermediate macroeconomic theory illustrates. Next, we described the writing instruction and practice necessary for students to be successful in the writing assignments. An example from our econometrics course is shared below. Finally, we identified places in our curriculum where instruction and practice happen over time. Below we share how this looks across four sets of courses in our department.

Table 4.1 provides an example of how departmental learning objectives can be mapped to points in the curriculum when they are delivered. This example comes from our Intermediate Macroeconomic Theory course. This is a place in our curriculum where we agreed a particular learning objective (evaluate economic phenomena using appropriate disciplinary methods for a general audience) is emphasized. After mapping it to our course learning objectives, we then identified the writing instruction necessary for students to be successful. It is important to note that this course was not one our faculty had in the past thought of as an appropriate place for writing instruction because we had a narrow

Table 4.1. Curricular mapping of departmental learning objectives

Course	*Departmental learning objective*	*Course learning objective*	*Writing instruction*
Intermediate Macroeconomic Theory	Evaluate economic phenomena using appropriate disciplinary methods for a general audience.	1. Apply models to analyze various economic events. 2. **Describe and interpret** the movement of important macroeconomic variables. 3. **Describe** the difference between long-run trends and short-run business cycles **for a general audience**.	Teach how to apply graphical and mathematical models to describe economic phenomena. Teach how to use appropriate disciplinary vocabulary to describe economic phenomena to general audiences.

Table 4.2. Description of writing instruction and practice within a course

Writing instruction in econometrics	*Writing practice*
Direct instruction in how to communicate a model and empirical results to a general and professional audience, including how to use economic terms, occurs most days through lecture and discussion.	1. Students use problem sets to practice for the exams that follow. 2. For the project, the instructor or trained consultant provides feedback and students revise. 3. Students demonstrate their ability to revise their work from the problem sets as they are given similar problems to complete on the exams.

view of what writing was, so this last step was an important change to the way we thought about teaching.

Describing the instruction and practice necessary for students to be successful is important because it encourages faculty to make explicit how students learn. Table 4.2 provides just one example from our Econometrics course below. Note that the course is quite technical, and in the past writing was not perceived by the faculty as an important component of the course because of our misunderstanding of what constituted writing.

After agreeing on the ways writing contributes to meeting our department learning objectives and the writing instruction and practice necessary for students to learn, we documented our expectation of how this pedagogy would work across different courses in our major, as we understood students need practice writing across time. Table 4.3 describes how this practice occurs throughout a student's time in the major.

In addition to the formal plan described above that ensures all our majors receive writing instruction and practice, many other courses in

Table 4.3. Writing practice across the curriculum

	Writing practice	*Feedback*	*Revised writing*
Econometrics (3rd year)	Homework problems Project	Instructor or trained consultant provides feedback on project.	Students revise project based on feedback. Two exams
Intermediate Microeconomic Theory (2nd/3rd year)	Problem set with explanatory analysis	Instructor provides feedback on three problem sets with explanatory analysis.	Revision occurs on exams (students are given similar problems to those on the problem sets). Three exams
Intermediate Macroeconomic Theory (2nd/3rd year)	Problem set with explanatory analysis	Instructor provides feedback on three problem sets with explanatory analysis.	Revision occurs on exams (students are given similar problems to those on the problem sets). Three exams
Upper-level electives (4th year)	Draft of final paper to professional audience Draft of paper to generalist audience	Peer and instructor or trained consultant provides feedback.	Final papers

the major contribute to these learning outcomes through the use of writing to teach economics. That is, our department has much more writing within our major than is reflected in our plan—our plan just documents the minimum instruction and practice for each student.

CREATING SUSTAINABLE CHANGE IN A DEPARTMENT

In the Fellows Program we learned meaningful and long-lasting learning takes a long time, is not linear, and is very messy—perhaps even emotionally or mentally difficult. It is thus not surprising that *organizational* learning also takes a long time, is not linear, and is very messy.

One of the obstacles to change identified in chapter 1, that faculty are rewarded for publishing and not for leading curricular change, may be ameliorated by the increasing importance of nontraditional positions and ranks within the university. The three department members who participated in the Fellows Program are teaching faculty and as such are rewarded for teaching excellence and strong service and are encouraged to develop areas of expertise that may include pedagogy.

Assessment of student writing is a critical part of ensuring our new learning about how to teach writing is firmly established in the major. The process of assessment allows faculty to revisit our learning and ask questions about how well we are teaching what we have come to understand is important.

The creation of a rubric with which to assess student work allowed us to discuss the different elements we wanted to see in student work. We realized different types of writing in economics display different qualities, so our rubrics were different depending on the purpose and audience. Agreeing on a common rubric allowed faculty to talk with each other about what they found important.

Our departmental assessment efforts promote deliberative communication, may make possible the conversation that leads to long-lasting learning among a broad range of faculty members, and thus may contribute to departmental change.

As of this writing we have completed a full assessment cycle with our intermediate economic theory instructors. They ask students to solve technical economic problems and convey the answers correctly to a professional (the instructor) and to a general audience. The process of assessment generated a conversation about students' ability to explain economic concepts clearly. Interestingly, the conversation did not center around student's writing, although the discussion was about how to write. The selection of artifacts to assess seemed to have been important to our discussions. Because we used authentic artifacts—assignments faculty already were asking students to do—our conversation centered around our students' ability to explain economic concepts rather than our students' ability to write, keeping the focus away from grammar and mechanics and onto student achievement of our learning objectives.

The robust discussion around assessment seemed to be an indication that the learnings were becoming integrated into what faculty members felt was important—they were integrated into economics. It is that discussion—what we hope will be the first of many discussions about our student's learning—that allows for the deliberative space and the creation of a shared understanding that may lead to sustained change.

CONCLUSION

Writing requirements approached from the standpoint of writing can lead to writing plans that are disconnected from disciplinary values and thus suffer from lack of support within departments. A writing plan that is instead the outcome of an examination of teaching and learning within a discipline may lead to a more appropriate curriculum and higher levels of faculty support. A key learning from our experience is that the focus of writing must be first and foremost discipline based.

Economics faculty are the experts on writing in economics. Writing across the curriculum programs can help support and guide us to think about how to best help students achieve our learning objectives. This case study details how the guidance provided through the Howe Faculty Writing Fellows Program helped us change the way we thought about writing. In essence it helped us embrace responsibility for our students' learning and thus caused us to authentically integrate instruction and practice in written communication within our major.

REFERENCES

Greenlaw, Steven A. 2009. *Doing Economics: A Guide to Understanding and Carrying Out Economic Research.* Mason, OH: South-Western Cengage Learning.

Greenlaw, Steven A., and David Shapiro. 2017. *Principles of Economics.* 2nd ed. Houston: OpenStax.

McCloskey, Deirdre N. 2000. *Economical Writing.* 2nd ed. Prospect Heights, IL: Waveland.

Meyer, Jan H. F., and Ray Land. 2006. "Threshold Concepts and Troublesome Knowledge: An Introduction." In *Overcoming Barriers to Student Understanding: Threshold Concepts and Troublesome Knowledge,* edited by Jan H. F. Meyer and Ray Land, 3–18. New York: Routledge.

Simpson, Murray S., and Shireen E. Carroll. 1999. "Assignments for a Writing-Intensive Economics Course." *Journal of Economic Education* 30 (4): 402–10. https://doi.org/10.2307/1182954.

5

TEACHING PHILOSOPHICAL READING AND WRITING BY MAKING INVISIBLE DISCIPLINARY PRACTICES VISIBLE

Keith Fennen, Elaine Miller, and Gaile Pohlhaus, Jr.
Philosophy

INTRODUCTION

As philosophy professors, we face the challenge of introducing an entirely new discipline to students, one that asks them to think in a way that has never been explicitly identified for them before. While disciplines like mathematics and physics are conceptual in nature, students have studied them in high school, so to a degree their requirements seem transparent. Philosophy, because it is expressed for the most part in ordinary language, appears to students to be a discipline analogous to the study of literature or history. Students reading a Platonic dialogue, for example, readily turn, in their initial analysis, to a discussion of the narrative plot or story of the dialogue, or to the historical context. Both of these elements may contribute to the meaning of the text, but what we ask them to do instead is to focus on the fundamental philosophical concepts upon which the arguments in the text depend. During the Howe Faculty Writing Fellows Program on threshold concepts (TCs), the three of us were asked to come up with a set of threshold concepts students in philosophy must grasp to fully enter into the discipline of philosophy. This task was more difficult than it first appeared. We soon came to realize the threshold concepts we were trying to articulate were simpler than we had initially thought but also, precisely for that reason, harder to articulate. The term *ontological shift* is a philosophically apt one to describe the process we were trying to put into words.

In this chapter, we explain our process of developing and utilizing threshold concepts as an effective way of introducing students to philosophical thinking and writing. We begin by describing our experience in the Fellows Program articulated in chapter 1. We then explain how we settled on the conceptual/empirical distinction as the threshold

https://doi.org/10.7330/9781646423040.c005

concept most essential for introductory students in learning how to think, read, and write in the discipline of philosophy. Next, we situate our own thinking in relation to work by other scholars on threshold concepts in the discipline of philosophy. We argue that the conceptual/empirical distinction is more fundamental to philosophy than TCs previously discussed by other philosophers, although there have so far been very few examples of this kind of analysis. We then articulate what we mean by the conceptual/empirical distinction and describe, by illustrating its role in a philosophical text, how conceptual thinking is a basic TC in philosophy that can be difficult to transfer to students given its double invisibility. Finally, we describe various exercises we employ in our classes to make conceptual thinking visible to our students, thereby helping them master the TC of conceptual thinking. We conclude by reporting on ways we integrated what we had learned into our departmental practices.

MAKING THINGS EXPLICIT TO OURSELVES

When we enrolled in the HCWE Faculty Writing Fellows Program, we were not quite sure what to expect. All three of us had participated in programs aimed at developing good pedagogy and specifically at developing good practices for teaching writing. However, these programs only took us so far. At best, we learned one or two new exercises we could implement in one of our courses. At worst, we felt we were being asked to stuff ourselves into a mold that really didn't fit our discipline or our experiences in the classroom. One of us had even been told by a facilitator at a workshop on improving student writing that philosophical writing was impenetrable and probably shouldn't be taught to students anyway. These sorts of experiences had left us at a loss, particularly because each of us genuinely cares about helping students become better thinkers and writers of philosophy. Our concern for teaching philosophical writing well was heightened by the fact that we had recently introduced a new Advanced Writing course within our department required of all majors to align with our university's updated liberal arts curriculum. Two of us had taught the Advanced Writing course already, and the third was about to teach it soon. Teaching an entire course on writing was new to all of us, and we were determined to do it well. So our initial thought was to enroll in the Fellows Program in order to think through our Advanced Writing course together.

Entering the program together as a cohort (which was a requirement for enrolling) made a world of difference in our professional development within the program. When we were introduced to new concepts, the three of us could really immerse ourselves in the liminal space of learning and working with those concepts from our disciplinary perspective, thinking through what each new concept might mean for us as *philosophy* professors. In other words, because we had each other, we did not have to explain what happens in the philosophy classroom before discussing how the concepts we were learning might play out in it. Moreover, discussing the concepts we were learning with each other as philosophers provided a way of making philosophy itself and the teaching of philosophy an object of knowledge for us in a manner no other pedagogy workshop really has. Thus we were able to think carefully and deeply about how the concepts we were learning might best inform the work we do in our classrooms, as opposed to trying to make our classrooms fit into a preordained mold. At the same time, because the group enrolled in the Fellows Program also contained two cohorts from other disciplines, once we had begun to fully articulate some of the concepts we were learning together and see how they might work for teaching our own discipline, we had an audience of nonphilosophers on which to try these new ideas out.

Overall, the learning we did together in the Fellows Program did far more than introduce us to best practices and individual exercises. Instead, it gave us a basis for developing best practices and new exercises of our own. What started out as an opportunity to work on a particular course together initiated a shift in how we approach the teaching of writing that we were able to bring back to our department and that has begun to inform the entirety of our curriculum. Specifically, the concepts we learned in the Fellows Program provided tools for making the practices we engage as philosophical thinkers and writers visible to us so we can in turn make them more visible to our students. In particular, the Fellows Program helped us see the challenges those outside philosophy face in trying to grasp philosophy's continual engagement with things that are by their nature invisible. This fact is so internal to philosophy that the need to thematically and repeatedly articulate it to our students was invisible to us. The workshop helped us to see our task is to guide students through this portal.

PHILOSOPHY AS THE ART OF ENGAGING INVISIBLES

Making the invisible implicit, and taken-for-granted practices of a discipline visible to practitioners and communicable to students is challenging. Philosophy operates first and foremost at a conceptual—not only at an empirical—level, pursuing conceptual clarity, evaluating the adequacy of concepts, modifying concepts, and creating concepts. Because philosophical inquiries and questions tend to be conceptual in nature, they cannot be answered simply by giving facts or information; we ask students to think about what Hannah Arendt calls "invisibles," or concepts that structure experience rather than things they can grasp with their senses. For virtually all new students to philosophy, the idea of investigating a topic without a clear link to the empirical can derail their progress from the start. Many practitioners of philosophy understand they work on the conceptual level, but they don't make it thematic or craft assignments to aid in mastering this TC. As a result of our work in the Fellows Program, however, we now explicitly return to this distinction throughout the semester, particularly when giving and explaining our writing assignments. Emphasizing this distinction helps students realize that when they are writing philosophy, they are engaged in conceptual work that calls for different methods (e.g., reasoning about ideas) than those with which they may be familiar in more empirically oriented disciplines (e.g., using data and facts gleaned from the library) or literary analysis.

To facilitate students' grasp of this distinction, it's helpful to show them that all disciplines, and many things important to them, such as justice and human rights, depend on concepts that defy empirical verification. One can ask an empirical question about how often a right was violated, but "What is a right?" isn't an empirical question. One cannot detect the nature of a right empirically. Other disciplines simply don't make conceptual inquiry their focus, although they employ concepts as an integral part of their study. Scientific theories that organize and link data are conceptual. Historical records or results of sociological or psychological surveys are empirical, but operationalizing definitions for use in surveys and making sense of records and results require the use of concepts. Moreover, conceptual structure explains why two economists can have the exact same data but predict two different trajectories, say, for the economy: they have two different ways of organizing the data based on two different conceptual frameworks. Where this example parts ways with philosophy is that when predictions are made, empirical verification is forthcoming.

We cannot lose sight of the fact that other disciplines use concepts all the time. Those at the forefront of their fields (notably, those who are doctors of philosophy of their discipline) sometimes argue about the concepts central to their fields. This has been true historically when disciplines undergo paradigm shifts, such as a Newtonian framework to an Einsteinian framework in physics, but is also true in the present day, such as debates around how to define a species in light of hybrids, asexual species, and DNA sequencing. Partaking in these debates, however, isn't essential to entering most disciplines. In fact, introducing students to conceptual debates too soon can be confusing to them within some fields, so for the most part they are not central to lower-level undergraduate education in these fields. However, for philosophy, concepts that resist empirical verification are always front and center. Philosophy seems particularly troublesome in this regard since it is one of the few fields that often questions the discipline's very nature. Rarely does a zoologist ask "What is zoology?" or a finance professor ask "What is finance?" Yet, the question "What is philosophy?" is a very real question for philosophers. Given that the nature of the discipline is contested, seeking a consensus on the discipline's TCs appears daunting. Indeed, in our own case, it took our participation in the Fellows Program, followed by much friendly debate and argument with our colleagues, to agree on a foundational set of TCs.

MAKING THINGS EXPLICIT TO OTHERS

Our departmental debates reflect the fact that contestation and argumentation are essential to the practice of philosophy, so much so that Shelagh Crooks (2020), one of a handful of educators from the discipline of philosophy who has written about threshold concepts in teaching, recently argued in her article "The Concept of Argument in Philosophy as a Threshold for Learners" that the "concept of 'argument' in the discipline of philosophy" is a TC (2). Crooks's focus appears to be on students who are committed to becoming specialists, that is, on philosophy majors. In her experience, she notes, it is only "late in their first year of study or in second year" that students in the discipline of philosophy start to tell her "that they find that they have a new way of interacting with materials they see in academic and popular culture" (7). We don't necessarily disagree with her emphasis on argument, but in thinking about writing, we want to focus as much on getting all non-majors in one semester to interact with the world and texts in a fundamentally new way as we do on majors. We agree with Crooks that argument is central to philosophy and could be considered a TC, but we argue that her account depends on the more fundamental TC of the conceptual/empirical distinction. To call this distinction a TC of philosophical thinking is to foreground the explicit way philosophy always presupposes the conceptual/empirical distinction. Thus, for conveying to a nonspecialist the nature of philosophical inquiry and expediting students through the liminal phase, argument is too complex as a starting point. This complexity partly results from the fact that philosophical argument very often, if not always, involves utilizing and arguing about invisibles. Without foregrounding and emphasizing the conceptual/empirical distinction, students can easily be misled into seeing philosophy as opinionated debate rather than philosophical argumentation about concepts/invisibles. Learning a TC involves an ontological shift, one that can be shaped and solidified through habitual practice; learning the conceptual/empirical distinction in philosophy renders one's view on every statement a critically discerning one, an irreversible shift in perspective.

Our formulation of TCs is guided by our goal of transitioning students into philosophy broadly speaking and not only into one topic. This focus sets us apart from Monica Cowart (2010), who, in her article "A Preliminary Framework for Isolating and Teaching Threshold Concepts in Philosophy," advances a protocol for selecting "core philosophical threshold concepts" (131–32) that results in selecting concepts too topical and narrow for the transformative shift required at the entry level.[1] We are interested in the threshold concepts that allow students to enter into the discipline of philosophy irrespective of the philosophic topic and question. Thus, Cowart's focus on the concept of personhood as an example of a "core philosophical threshold concept" is too narrow and specific for us. To be sure, by her criteria, personhood is a threshold concept, but her criteria also thereby make the full set of threshold concepts innumerably large. While her approach and case study on personhood reveal her method is effective for transitioning students into a philosophical debate about a specific question or concept, they don't really address the deeper question of foundational threshold concepts.

We agree with Jennifer Booth (2006) that the Socratic method is a useful tool for teaching students how philosophers think, but like Cowart, Booth's focus is too narrow. She identifies "representation," or "the idea that the contents of perception might be mental pictures which represent—truthfully or not—the objects of the world" (176) as a core TC in philosophy. While we find representation and personhood to be too specific, they do participate in the broader category conceptual/empirical distinction, which is the focus of our chapter. Specifically, representation and personhood are conceptual objects that are invisible (i.e., they cannot be observed as objects of perception) but nonetheless very real (i.e., they are objects of understanding concerning which we can reason). Philosophical thought engages with these sorts of objects.

So while Crooks and Booth are correct to identify personhood and representation as concepts that are part of our discipline, the type of thinking required to engage with them is a more fundamental TC for philosophy. In other words, they have identified particular conceptual content discussed in our discipline but haven't thematized the conceptual nature of the content itself, and thus students run the risk of not entering into the discipline itself.

During the 2018–2019 academic year, our department held pedagogy workshops in which we discussed and revised our initial formulation of the threshold concepts of our discipline. Through this process we achieved commitment from our colleagues to integrate the explicit use and identification of threshold concepts into our curriculum. It's worth mentioning them here with a brief description.

Threshold Concept 1: Conceptual/Empirical Distinction. Philosophy operates at a conceptual—not only at an empirical—level, pursuing conceptual clarity, evaluating the adequacy of concepts, modifying concepts, and creating concepts.

Threshold Concept 2: Transformative/Conceptual Reading. The goal of reading philosophical texts is to enter into different conceptual frameworks by following lines of reasoning and allowing them to speak to us.

Threshold Concept 3: Critical/Interpretive Reading. Philosophy practices hermeneutical reading skills, including reading a text for purpose, significance, structure, interconnection of ideas, presuppositions and implications, and nonargumentative as well as argumentative elements.

We think of these threshold concepts as complementary and mutually reinforcing but also placed in chronological developmental order in terms of student capabilities and complexity of learning. Threshold concept 1 is taught in all of our courses, beginning with introductory classes, and we hope the distinction between conceptual and empirical becomes a natural analytic capacity for all students. Threshold concept 2 is taught in introductory courses but especially developed in intermediate courses, as students begin to read more complex texts and build upon the philosophical knowledge and skills they have acquired. Threshold concept 3 and the writing ability it enables is fully developed at the advanced level, both in the Advanced Writing course and in upper-level seminars.[2]

These threshold concepts were always operational in our own writing and thinking, and, when mastered, allow students to enter into the practice of philosophy irrespective of the philosophical topic or question under consideration. Of these three, we wish to pay particular attention to the first TC (conceptual/empirical distinction,) as it is the most accessible to the nonspecialist student and is at the heart of virtually all philosophical inquiry. As a way into the first TC, it's helpful to notice that Cowart's example of personhood is a concept and that the question "What is personhood?" is a question that cannot be answered empirically. In fact, we argue that any concept that meets her definition of a "core philosophical threshold concept" resists an empirical answer, which is perhaps why these questions are troublesome for students.

THE CONCEPTUAL/EMPIRICAL DISTINCTION IN A PHILOSOPHICAL TEXT

Thematizing the distinction between empirical and conceptual questions and statements can confuse introductory philosophy students. Philosophy is not a subject to which most students have been introduced prior to the university; even though they utilize the distinction between conceptual and empirical statements naturally in speaking and writing, drawing attention to the difference between these kinds of statements or questions can seem confusing and counterintuitive. The bulk of secondary-education testing demands answers to empirical questions, such as "What is the chemical composition of water?" or "When did the French Revolution happen?" or "Which educational system results in the highest literacy rate?" Empirical questions can be answered by giving facts or information. Concepts, by contrast, might seem mysterious, but although they are abstract, students can come to recognize that they use them all the time to organize their thinking and that they literally could not think or communicate or even know without concepts. Some common examples of concepts students are introduced to in philosophy courses are justice, beauty, and truth, but concepts also include seven, blue, or big.

When we ask a philosophical conceptual question, we are usually inquiring into the nature of something or asking a question about how something is the way it is. Ancient philosophers such as Plato asked conceptual questions such as "What is goodness?" as the basis of philosophy. The statements, "That action is wrong," or "Knowledge is justified true belief," are conceptual. In order to illustrate this distinction, here we will consider a text sometimes taught in introductory philosophy courses, Arendt's (1971) "Thinking and Moral Considerations," in conjunction with Plato's early Socratic dialogues, which are more regularly taught in introductory philosophy courses.

Reading Arendt's article in conjunction with Plato's Socratic dialogues can be instructive for students in introductory philosophy courses when we teach the distinction between the empirical and the conceptual or ask students to make conceptual arguments. In this essay, Arendt considers the distinction between thinking and knowing and refers to concepts, especially the highest ideas referred to by Plato and Socrates, as "invisibles." The article is structured around an account of the trial of the Nazi war criminal Adolf Eichmann, convicted of responsibility for deporting, enslaving, sterilizing, torturing, and murdering millions of Jews during World War II, an event students already recognize as having significance for a reason that transcends an empirical account. At some, perhaps tacit, level, students are already attuned to the metaphysical weight of accounts of the Holocaust; they are used to thinking, in this context, of terms like *evil* as significant, going beyond explaining the motivation behind an action in purely descriptive terms. Consider the distinction between the following two explanations:

a. Eichmann directed the deportations to the concentration camps at Auschwitz because he was following orders from his superiors (in court, his own justification of his actions).
b. Eichmann followed the orders of his superiors because he didn't think to question them; this inability to think is the source of evil (Arendt's argument, simplified).

Students can understand the conceptual distinction between these two statements on some level, including the fact that the first one, by being couched in purely descriptive/empirical terms, remains unsatisfactory as an explanation, whether in a court of law or in a court of public opinion. They can also identify the distinction between the two sentences as involving the term *evil*. This step allows a mental shift from the empirical to the conceptual, as *evil* is a term that has no distinct material referent in the world.

Arendt (1971) writes, "To raise such questions as 'What is Thinking?', 'What is Evil?' has its difficulties. They belong to philosophy or metaphysics, terms that designate a field of inquiry which, as we all know, has fallen into disrepute" (419). Eventually, students can easily recognize questions such as "Is there a god?," "Do humans have freedom?," and "Is there life after death?" as metaphysical and conceptual. However, we do not necessarily want to lead students to think conceptual thinking is otherworldly. Arendt goes a step further, referring to these, and other, more mundane concepts such as "house" and "blue," as "invisibles." In other words, while we can point to particular houses and shades of blue, the concepts themselves (under which particular things are organized) are not tangible. She goes so far as to say that "the moment we start thinking on no matter what issue . . . it is as though we moved into another world" (423), the world of the conceptual or of thought. Starting to refer to concepts as "invisibles" in class helps reinforce the distinction between concepts and empirical reality and helps students understand it as a distinction that permeates the world of everyday reality, not something that exists in another, metaphysical realm.

From here, it is possible in class to begin to refer to rights, beauty, time, thinking, identity, and being as concepts and to show students how these invisibles permeate our everyday reality. In assignments, students can then be asked to consider concepts, to analyze and unpack the way philosophers use them, and perhaps to compare them across texts. For example, they might be asked, "Do animals have rights?" This question asks students to consider what a right is and whether it is the sort of thing an animal ought to or even could have. It does not ask whether or not there are laws on the books that actually give these rights. It also does not ask for their opinion on this question but for a reasoned position that draws on philosophical concepts and texts for support.

Showing students some further contrasting examples of empirical and conceptual questions allows them to broaden their understanding of the distinction. Although there will probably be an initial temptation on the part of students to answer some of these questions with empirical answers—for example, there are plenty of surveys that claim to show which country is the happiest and what a particular culture thinks beauty is—they come to understand that these answers, while interesting, don't ask and cannot answer the underlying philosophical questions, "What *is* happiness?" and "How *ought* we to define beauty?" At times, this correction on the part of the instructor might be met with resistance and be considered annoying or troublesome, another marker of a TC (Meyer and Land 2003, 7). Students might claim there are no answers to some of these questions other than empirical answers. Showing them that even if such a claim is true, it cannot be established empirically and would require an argument with concepts, may meet with further resistance. Mastery of this TC may be challenged by the overwhelming desire to revert to a common-sense understanding of the world; philosophical thinking can seem counterintuitive from this vantage point, and thus engagement in it may cause discomfort.

In fact, education in philosophy may actually be a radical challenge to common sense, as Itay Snir (2017) argues in "Making Sense in Education: Deleuze on Thinking against Common Sense" (299). The philosopher tries not to assume any concrete standpoint without critical examination. Whereas common sense extends a pregiven image of what thinking is to a new object, binding thought to a predetermined order, genuine thinking allows for something new or radical to appear. Not every experience "invites thinking," in Gilles Deleuze's words; when an experience involves a perplexing encounter in which the faculties of sensibility and understanding cannot recognize their object or react in an ordinary way, thinking can begin (306). Plato has Socrates call this kind of thinking a move toward transcendent ideas, where experience begins with an encounter with the world but goes beyond the limits of sensibility to the conceptual.

Arendt also conceives of philosophy as a radical dissolution of the prephilosophical common-sense world, drawing on Immanuel Kant's distinction between thinking and knowing. Where *knowing* builds up a world of informational content, *thinking* may break down some of the "facts" we thought we knew in the past. This activity of thinking fits well with the discussion of the liminality of TCs. As Jan Meyer and Ray Land (2003) note, fully grasping a new way of thinking requires students to let go of long-held habitual ways of thinking. Arendt (1971) calls the activity of thinking "the habit of examining and reflecting upon whatever happens to come to pass, regardless of specific content and quite independent of results" (418), a habit that, once cultivated, seemingly paradoxically undoes all other forms of nonphilosophical thinking. This activity of letting go and trying out new ways of thinking can forge a new identity, that of the critical analyzer of one's own assumptions, of texts, and of culture. Philosophy often breaks down previously held beliefs and assumptions, or at least demands they be replaced by views that can be supported by evidence and reason.

As Snir (2017) indicates, Deleuze refers to the pedagogy leading to this type of thinking as an "apprenticeship" in that it cannot be handed over ready-made to students as a set of instructions or definitive content; rather, students must practice philosophical thinking in the classroom side by side with the professor and other students, discern it in the readings they are assigned, and try it out in their writing, which will be revised in light of queries and objections raised by other interlocutors. Deleuze uses the example of swimming, which cannot be taught as an abstract, theoretical set of principles. When thrown into the water, one learns by apprenticing oneself to a situation, which breaks down any prior foundation (307).

Philosophy as a discipline strives to avoid the dual extremes of completely dismissive skepticism, on the one hand, and passive acceptance of reigning sociocultural views, on the other, both attitudes to which undergraduate students often are prone. Philosophical inquiry asks students to bracket what they have always believed and subject even their most confidently held presuppositions about themselves, their beliefs, and their culture to rigorous doubt. If all views were subject to this critical gaze, what would survive? This method of systematic testing and disintegration of established views can propel students into confusion in some cases and wild iconoclasm in others. The breakdown can lead to stumbling blocks on the way to mastering the threshold concepts in the classroom. We consider some of these obstacles and possible ways of navigating them in the classroom in the final part of this chapter.

TRANSFORMING THE CLASSROOM

To help students begin to engage careful conceptual thought, we have developed exercises used at the introductory level, within our Advanced Writing course, and even at the graduate level. In these exercises we seek not only to engage students in philosophical thinking but also to make visible the thing they are doing while they are doing it. For example, in our introductory courses, to make the distinction between the empirical and the conceptual explicit, we use an exercise in which students are given a list of different questions, some of which require empirical investigation ("How does the brain process knowledge?") and others that cannot be answered definitively through gathering data ("What is knowledge?"). Students are then asked to think about how a person could investigate answers to these questions, distinguishing those that require observation and data from those that require thinking about the meaning of a concept. Moreover, when working through this exercise in class, we discuss how the questions that require factual answers can be turned into questions that are conceptual. For example, "What time is it now?" can turn into "What is time?" or "What is the relation between now and time?" Changing questions that are empirical in nature into ones that are conceptual and asking students to do the same can give them a sense of how we are asking them to think when the object of knowledge is not something to which we can point. Discussing with students questions like "How would you begin to answer this type of question?" or "What would you need to know to answer this sort of question?" can help students to see that conceptual questions require a different sort of approach than empirical questions. While they may be confused about how to actually answer conceptual questions, they can often understand the importance of really thinking through these types of questions and not simply accepting answers to them without understanding the reasoning behind the answer. It might be fine, for example, to trust your roommate's yes or no answer to the question "Is a living wage listed among the United Nations' human rights?," particularly when you know they have recently read the UN document on this subject. But ought one to depend solely upon another's yes or no answer to the questions "*Ought* a living wage be considered a universal human right?" and "What *is* a 'universal human right'?"

In the Advanced Writing course we spend time simply devising questions about particular readings, reworking questions together so as to demonstrate how a really well-formulated question can help a reader enter and follow the line of reasoning present in a text. When students devise questions that require further research beyond the concepts in a particular text, we stop them and ask, "Can this question be reframed so it can be answered through direct engagement with the ideas as presented in the text alone?" Getting the questions right is often more important than the possible answers.

Important, conceptual thinking often requires students to follow a line of thought with the aim of seeing how it works but not necessarily agreeing with it. This approach can be confusing to students who are wedded to the idea that there is either a right answer or no point in thinking at all (where there is no right answer, suddenly all and any answer seems right). However, the student must let go of the assumption that right answers are the point. To help with this aspect of conceptual thinking, we often assign texts in which philosophers think through arguments for conceptual frameworks the philosopher rejects. For example, in the early Socratic dialogues, Socrates thinks through multiple lines of argument on a particular question without arriving at any particular answer, even while insisting there *is* an answer (not that we should give up on the enterprise of thinking things through). In the Advanced Writing course, one of us has regularly assigned "Two Concepts of Rules" by John Rawls in which Rawls, famous for rejecting utilitarianism, thinks carefully from a utilitarian perspective on how utilitarians might be able to address a classic charge used against the utilitarian perspective. Important, while engaging with this text, students must grapple with the fact that Rawls is providing a line of reasoning in defense of a conclusion he ultimately rejects, so the point must not be to arrive at a particular conclusion concerning utilitarianism but rather to understand how the ideas themselves *work*.

TRANSFORMING THE DEPARTMENT

To understand how our participation in the Fellows Program has affected our departmental practices requires a few preliminary remarks. Since 2012 our department has held an annual pedagogy workshop in which we discuss assessment and how to improve student outcomes and share assignments we find effective. Over the years, what emerged from these sessions was a skepticism about university assessment initiatives. Even though our department has been praised for the quality of our assessment, we've never seen it as very valuable. On the one hand, the viability of the statistics is questionable, and on the other hand, we've never found that assessment addresses our frustrations with student thinking and writing. Ostensibly, assessment should help with the latter insofar as it aims to push departments to change their practices and to measure the effectiveness of said changes. How, though, does one change? To be sure, everyone in our department engaged in workshops regarding assignment creation, and many participated in semester-long workshops that centered on the scholarship of teaching and learning (SOTL). Even so, there was a clear collective frustration that these workshops, assignment-creation exercises, and much of the SOTL literature either ignored or misunderstood the nature of philosophical thought and inquiry. Moreover, there always seemed to be a rush for quantifiable results with little or no regard for the liminal phase of learning. In other words, prior to the HCWE Fellows Program, we collectively felt invisible and misunderstood when engaging with other university entities and individuals regarding our pedagogical practices and assessment.

The HCWE Fellows Program helped us understand why we were often frustrated with student writing and how to overcome those frustrations via TC theory. Moreover, it introduced us to alternative forms of assessment. Thus, after our participation in the HCWE Fellows Program in 2018, we decided to schedule a series of three, rather than one, pedagogy workshops with our department in the fall of 2018. These workshops centered on sharing our work on TCs with our colleagues, refining our TCs and the writing guide we created for the HCWE website, reviewing our curriculum to map out where the threshold concepts would be introduced and cultivated, and discussing assignment design and changes to assessment. The most meaningful change, which is still in process, is the development of assessment within the major, and individual classes, through the use of writing portfolios.

For us, the biggest challenge to implementing substantial change at our departmental level is simple, namely sustained effort. To be sure, our vision of teaching is forever changed in fundamental ways, and yet there is a danger of stagnation, of not redesigning courses with TCs in mind, not implementing portfolio assessment. This potential stagnation results from everyone having entirely too many tasks and job responsibilities and surely not from laziness or a lack of desire for change. Our university is ranked as one of the most efficient in the country, and that efficiency partly reflects the ever-increasing number of responsibilities faculty have assumed since the 2008 recession and subsequent budget cuts. With that said, we've found having a Center for Writing Excellence that continually offers opportunities to foster our progress and continue our departmental transformation invaluable. Moreover, we are convinced that as long as the three of us commit to change, have regular meetings on how our courses are progressing, and regularly discuss relevant topics at our departmental meetings and pedagogy seminars, real tangible results will follow. What cannot be overlooked in this context is that we and our colleagues often disagree on nuanced points, but all of us are committed to improved student outcomes. We recognize the value of making visible and accessible to students what is natural and inherent to philosophy (and thus often invisible to us). This recognition has led to positive changes across our curriculum and program.

CONCLUSION

What began with a summer workshop involving three faculty members has so far expanded into a department-wide effort to foreground writing pedagogy. We began with a series of pedagogy workshops, which naturally resulted in an ongoing discussion in the department about teaching writing. In addition to thinking about strengthening our Advanced Writing course by approaching the question of writing in philosophy conceptually as a whole rather than piecemeal through particular assignments, we have developed a culture of thinking holistically about the connections among thinking, reading, and writing. We are also developing a writing-portfolio process of assessment of the major. This project would involve philosophy majors (and perhaps minors) collecting, from their first year on, samples of their best writing in philosophy, which would be collected in an electronic portfolio and assessed by the faculty before their graduation. Such a portfolio would allow us to readily see the progress made by students as they pass through the program, including their mastery of the threshold concepts. The Fellows Program helped us to really understand the value in this type of assessment.

The Fellows Program gave us the opportunity to think deeply and collectively about not only teaching writing but also the overall conception of philosophical thinking and writing we expect from students without, at least in the past, ever explicitly stating these expectations to them. The biggest insight we had from this experience was that because philosophy deals in invisibles, whether those are concepts or metaphysical ideas, making these concepts visible to students may be our biggest challenge. From our experience we gained an ability to formulate the distinctiveness of philosophical writing, its inextricability from philosophical thinking and reading, and the particularities of the ontological shift that takes place when one begins to read, think, and write philosophically. Being able to approach this task through a collective meditation on philosophical writing and thinking as a whole had a meaningful impact on our classes, on faculty discourse, and on our program as a whole. We would like to end by thanking the Fellows Program for providing a meaningful venue that allowed individual and departmental transformation to develop organically from within our discipline rather than trying to impose on faculty a nondisciplinary framework, teaching method, or mechanical assessment rubric, or attempting to teach us how to teach.

NOTES

1. Cowart (2010) defines these as "concepts that reside at the intersection of metaphysics, epistemology, and ethics" (134). These concepts reside in all three "since these concepts raise questions within each sub-discipline" (134). Thus, understanding the threshold concept requires understanding "the questions threshold concept x raises in metaphysics, ethics, and epistemology" (134).
2. In addition to these fundamental TCs, we identified four methods of getting at a problem that are not unique to philosophy but are used with more frequency than in other disciplines. These methods are notable in that they involve thinking about problems in what some might consider an artificial or abstract way in order to isolate the structure or "bones" of the argument. The four methods are (1) assuming something for the sake of argument, (2) assessing logical validity, (3) thought experiments, and (4) tracing the genealogy of ideas in terms of both their historical context and their conceptual interrelations.

REFERENCES

Arendt, Hannah. 1971. "Thinking and Moral Considerations." *Social Research* 38 (3): 417–46.

Booth, Jennifer. 2006. "On the Mastery of Philosophical Concepts: Socratic Discourse and the Unexpected 'Affect.'" In *Overcoming Barriers to Student Understanding: Threshold Concepts and Troublesome Knowledge*, edited by Jan H. F. Meyer and Ray Land, 173–82. London: Routledge.

Cowart, Monica. 2010. "A Preliminary Framework for Isolating and Teaching Threshold Concepts in Philosophy." In *Threshold Concepts and Transformational Learning*, edited by Jan H. F. Meyer, Ray Land, and Caroline Baillie, 131–45. Rotterdam: Sense.

Crooks, Shelagh. 2020. "The Concept of Argument in Philosophy as a Threshold for Learners." *Teaching Philosophy* 43 (1): 1–27.

Meyer, Jan H. F., and Ray Land. 2003. "Threshold Concepts and Troublesome Knowledge: Linkages to Ways of Thinking and Practising Within the Disciplines (1)." In *Improving Student Learning: Improving Student Learning Theory and Practice—Ten Years On*, edited by Chris Rust. Oxford: OCSLD.

Snir, Itay. 2017. "Making Sense in Education: Deleuze on Thinking against Common Sense." *Educational Philosophy and Theory* 50 (3): 299–311.

SECTION 2

DESIGNING MEANINGFUL LEARNING OPPORTUNITIES

6

DISCOVERING THE GERONTOLOGICAL VOICE AS AN EMERGING THRESHOLD CONCEPT IN SOCIAL GERONTOLOGY

Jennifer Kinney and Kate de Medeiros
Gerontology

INTRODUCTION

Three years ago, we were introduced to threshold concepts through the Howe Center for Writing Excellence's Faculty Writing Fellows Program at Miami University. The experience transformed our thinking about our discipline and led us to explore new ways to introduce graduate students to the discipline through writing. This chapter documents our process of working through the liminality to discover the gerontological voice as a threshold concept in social gerontology, presents the pedagogical strategies we created to help students develop their gerontological voice, and describes our ongoing efforts to further develop this threshold concept.

Social gerontology is a relatively new discipline that studies old age and later life, from the social structures that shape how people grow old to the personal experiences of being an older person. By virtue of its intellectual origins and focus of study, it is an inclusive discipline. For these reasons, at the graduate level, social gerontology attracts (and welcomes) students from diverse disciplines. But even entering an inclusive discipline can be challenging, as newcomers encounter unfamiliar vocabulary, concepts, conventions, and values. Challenges are further complicated by social gerontology's lack of a defined identity; many people who were trained in other disciplines identify as gerontologists. This motivated us to develop inclusive pedagogies that make writing in social gerontology explicit and that actively encourage students to engage in the development of their gerontological voice.

Although the context for our work is social gerontology, several aspects of our work can inform colleagues working on threshold

https://doi.org/10.7330/9781646423040.c006

concepts in other disciplines. Working with threshold concepts can be a messy process; this chapter highlights some of the challenges we confronted and strategies we used while traversing the liminal space. In addition, writing in each discipline has nuances that must be made explicit for novices in those disciplines. Disciplinary knowledge is necessary but not necessarily sufficient. We explain several strategies from other disciplines (e.g., cognitive academic language proficiency, conversational inquiry, rhetorical reading) that helped us articulate the nuances of writing in our discipline so they can be communicated to others. Finally, the threshold concept of the gerontological voice itself has the potential to inform approaches to writing in other disciplines.

THE CONTEXT FOR OUR WORK: GRADUATE EDUCATION IN SOCIAL GERONTOLOGY

In 2017, we participated in the Fellows Program with the intent of improving a specific course. However, as participants from several departments began to articulate the conventions of writing in their disciplines, we began thinking, "How can we revise our graduate gerontology curriculum to be more explicit in defining to students what values in gerontology are expressed in writing?" At first, we integrated what we had learned in the Fellows Program into the introductory and advanced graduate-level gerontological theory courses we each routinely taught. Our continued work led us to two outcomes described in this chapter: (1) the discovery of the gerontological voice as a threshold concept in social gerontology, and (2) assignments designed to promote development of the gerontological voice among graduate students from diverse undergraduate disciplinary backgrounds, both of which led to ongoing efforts to further develop the gerontological voice as a threshold concept in social gerontology.

Our decision to focus on the development of the gerontological voice in these courses was motivated by pragmatic, programmatic, and, most important, pedagogical considerations. Pragmatically, although we are both ultimately interested in second-order/deep change à la Adrianna Kezar and colleagues (Kezar 2018; Kezar and Lester 2011; see chapters 1, 2, and 3 of this volume), the exploratory nature of our work, including grappling with the complexities that underlie deep change, needed to progress on a small scale. The two theory courses provided a working laboratory in which we could engage students with our evolving ideas. Programmatically, the introductory theory course is required for all master's students during their first semester and recommended for the first-semester doctoral students who do not have a background in social gerontology. The advanced theory course is taken by all doctoral students, typically in their second year, and a subset of the master's students who wish to build their knowledge of gerontology. These courses guarantee early exposure to the threshold concept for almost all of our students and the opportunity for many of the students to formally revisit the threshold concept before completing their coursework. It also introduces the possibility of duplication and the need to work collaboratively on our content to enhance all students' learning.

OUR DISCOVERY OF THE GERONTOLOGICAL VOICE AS A THRESHOLD CONCEPT IN SOCIAL GERONTOLOGY

As the literature documents, identifying threshold concepts is not easy (e.g., Barradell 2013; Land 2011; Meyer and Land 2003); the prior socialization and culture a newcomer brings to a discipline can interfere with their ability to master the fundamentals of that discipline (Groundwater-Smith 2014). We initially attributed our struggle to identify threshold concepts in social gerontology to the multiple disciplines involved and gerontology's "newness." However, this refrain was common among colleagues from other new disciplines such as Latin American Studies and more established disciplines as well. Thus, we turned our attention to considering what prior knowledge, experience, and assumptions both novices and faculty trained outside gerontology typically bring to social gerontology. We believe our findings could be illustrative for colleagues working on threshold concepts in other disciplines as well.

At the student level, because formal education in social gerontology is not widespread, graduate programs accept students from a variety of backgrounds, the majority of which are not social gerontology. Given its subject matter and inclusive orientation, social gerontology welcomes students from diverse educational and experiential backgrounds, often with incomplete and/or inaccurate disciplinary assumptions about aging and older adults. For example, students with clinical backgrounds (e.g., nursing, social work, physical therapy) might erroneously assume all older persons are frail or in poor health since those are the characteristics of people who generally receive such services. Business students, accustomed to seeing ageist advertising campaigns directed toward consumers who are thirty years old or younger, likely have given little to no thought about the needs, interests, and buying power of older consumers. Even students with a more technical backgrounds such as statistics or demography may view an older person as a number without fully appreciating the many structures (e.g., income, gender, race, health status) that can affect how people and communities age. In addition, attitudes about and behaviors toward old people come from a variety of sources, including the media (e.g., advertising, television, film) and personal experiences (e.g., interactions with one's neighbors). Regardless of the source, students from nongerontology backgrounds might inappropriately apply their limited exposure to or experience with older adults to older adults as a group. Introducing students to the threshold concept of the gerontological voice in their first semester of graduate school is a tangible way to begin their socialization to the discipline.

With respect to faculty, as mentioned earlier, doctoral education in social gerontology is sufficiently new that the majority of faculty in social gerontology programs were trained in a traditional discipline (e.g., anthropology, psychology, sociology). As such, faculty bring their disciplinary rules, attitudes, theories, and assumptions to their teaching (and scholarship). This can contribute to a lack of shared understanding among faculty about the courses that should comprise a social gerontology curriculum and the content of those courses, let alone what might constitute a threshold concept. To further complicate matters, despite being an inclusive discipline with fluid boundaries, a distinct way of writing that is uniquely gerontology is only now emerging,[1] which is one reason the gerontological voice is so important to our work.

THREE STEPS TO A THRESHOLD CONCEPT

Step 1: *Ask yourself, "What does it mean to think (and write) like a social gerontologist?"*

We recognize the phrase *gerontological voice* needs some unpacking. Although one of us (Kinney) had used the phrase *gerontological voice* for more than twenty-five years, she had not clearly developed the concept. Focusing on the importance of being able to communicate knowledge and passion for the field, orally and in writing, to diverse audiences, her initial use of *gerontological voice* referred to an understanding of the then-unnamed characteristics that defined gerontology. Later, a graduate student used *gerontological voice* as a position of advocacy, referring to people who spoke on behalf of gerontology or to promote the evolving discipline. The most recent adopter of the concept (de Medeiros) provided a more developed definition in the syllabus for an advanced graduate theory course, and it is the definition we subsequently use throughout the chapter: "[The gerontological voice] means developing an understanding of how scholars in gerontology think about and apply theory in their written work to include tone, word choice, argument structure, and other aspects of writing in the discipline." Using this definition as the starting point, we thus began our quest to discover the threshold concept of the gerontological voice in social gerontology.

Step 2: *Identify Components of Cognitive/Academic Language Proficiency (CALP)*

We quickly realized the gerontological voice consists of more than concepts and frameworks. Because oral and written communication are key foci of the gerontological voice, the threshold concept needed to be sensitive to and incorporate the elements of rhetorical situations (i.e., audience, purpose, medium, and context), genre, and the conventions of writing in our discipline. We also conceptualized the gerontological voice as a developmental process, something that should be accessible to novices/students yet also informative for more experienced scholars/educators. Given these requirements, we looked to other disciplines and found the concept of cognitive/academic language proficiency (CALP) (Cummins 1979), which applies to any discipline, a useful framework to help us identify and articulate our emerging threshold concept.

Stephen Krashen and Clara Brown (2007) propose a three-component model of CALP. The two central yet interdependent components are (1) knowledge of academic language (i.e., vocabulary, lexicon, syntax, discourse style) and (2) knowledge of academic content (i.e., specialized knowledge about the subject matter). We use the example of successful aging from social gerontology to illustrate this interdependence. The notion of successful aging began in the 1950s whereby researchers noted a distinction between "normal" (i.e., gradual age-related changes over time such as memory loss) and "abnormal" (or "unsuccessful") aging (e.g., dementia) (Baker 1959). Later, "successful aging" referred to aspects of subjective life satisfaction (Havighurst 1961) and then was used to describe ways older persons use various strategies to successfully compensate for functional challenges (Baltes and Baltes 1990). More recently, John Rowe and Robert Kahn (1997) created their own definition of "successful aging" as the absence of physical, cognitive, and social decline. As illustrated, while successful aging may be part of gerontology's vocabulary, it has a particular history and series of meanings embedded in the field that might differ from other disciplines' understanding and/or use of the term (e.g., successful aging as synonymous with aging well). Therefore, acquiring proficiency was consistent with our conceptualization of the gerontological voice as a developmental process, and the integration of language and content was especially appealing since social gerontology is not a vocabulary-driven discipline.

Krashen and Brown's (1997) third component is academic proficiency strategies, or the tools that help students acquire both types of knowledge. Krashen and Brown propose a series of strategies that target either reading comprehension or problem solving. We return to these strategies below in the context of how we used the concept of the gerontological voice to structure assignments in our graduate-level social gerontology theory courses. Overall, the richness achieved by using CALP's multidimensional framework is in stark contrast to Kalia's cautionary characterization of psychology as having "ossified into exclusionary discourse conventions and practices" (this volume, chapter 12).

Step 3: *Define Key Elements of Your Threshold Concept*

In this section, we lay out specific characteristics of writing that could also be easily applied and adapted for other disciplines. Specifically, we identify five questions to ask when considering what does or does not make a particular piece of writing in a discipline and present illustrative examples to further highlight our points.

1. What level of context is being provided?
2. What terms and concepts are being used?
3. What are the key frameworks (e.g., theories, paradigms, perspectives)?
4. What are the key writing conventions (e.g., phrases, pronoun types)?
5. What narrative position does the writer take?

1. WHAT LEVEL OF CONTEXT IS BEING PROVIDED AND WHY? In thinking about what makes a particular piece of writing gerontology, we were immediately drawn to the notion of context, described here as the details necessary for the perceived reader to make sense of a given piece. For example, the context provided by a gerontologist writing for an audience of psychologists likely differs from the context a psychologist provides for an audience of gerontologists. Consider the following opening sentences from two different age-related articles, both published in 2015.

> Around the world, the older population is growing rapidly. By the year 2050, estimates predict that the global over-65 population will nearly triple. Given these near-universal demographic trends, the issue of how societies across the globe will view, treat, and accommodate their aged is gaining worldwide attention. (North and Fiske 2015, 993)

> Ensuring economic security and meeting the health and long-term care needs of older people are major challenges associated with population aging. In addition to taking a problem-focused approach to address these serious challenges, we must also take a solution-focused approach, a social development approach. (Gonzales, Matz-Costa, and Morrow-Howell 2015, 252)

In the first excerpt, which comes from *Psychological Bulletin*, the authors orient the reader to changes in population aging as a way to establish the context for their later argument since it is likely that the readership of this journal is not familiar with trends in population aging. In the second example, from *The Gerontologist*, population aging is not explicitly referenced; the writers assume such basic context is not necessary for readers of a gerontology journal. Instead, they go on to specifically address economic security, which may not be familiar to gerontologists. In this respect, neither opening sentence would be effective for their intended readership if interchanged.

2. WHAT TERMS AND CONCEPTS ARE BEING USED (AND WHICH ARE BEING OMITTED)? This includes terms and concepts commonplace in gerontological writing, as well as those that are omitted (i.e., what gerontologists say and don't say.) Consider the following nongerontology excerpt:

> The elderly are the majority of users of many medicines. Although persons aged ≥65 represent only about 13% of the population, they consume nearly one-third of all medications. (Shenoy and Harugeri 2015, 184).

Here, all persons aged sixty-five and over are placed into one group—the "elderly"—a term gerontologists find stigmatizing and offensive. The pronoun "they" further others people over sixty-five, ignoring that the population age sixty-five and over is more heterogeneous than people in younger age groups. We note that although most gerontology journals now require that ageist language be removed, *elderly* is unfortunately still widely used in publications outside gerontology.

3. WHAT ARE THE KEY FRAMEWORKS (E.G., THEORIES, PARADIGMS, PERSPECTIVES)? As in all disciplines, key frameworks and assumptions underlie the ways a specific discipline makes sense of a particular problem or issue at hand. In gerontology, life-span development and the life-course perspective can be found implicitly or explicitly in most gerontological writing. For example, in the Ernest Gonzales, Christina Matz-Costa, and Nancy Morrow-Howell (2015) article excerpted in the illustrative example for question 1, there is an underlying assumption that how people experience later life is influenced by their experiences throughout their lives and by the lives of

people to whom they are linked (e.g., spouses, parents). One must be familiar with the life-course perspective (or the life-span-development model) to reflect the idea that aging is a lifelong process and therefore to write like a gerontologist.

4. WHAT ARE THE KEY WRITING CONVENTIONS (E.G., PHRASES, PRONOUN TYPES)? In our own observations, gerontological writing follows several key writing conventions. These include neutral voice, tendency toward third-person (rather than first-person) pronouns, and tendency to not use the label *gerontologist* when referring to people who study later life since it is often unclear to what *gerontologist* refers (e.g., a person with a degree in gerontology, someone who studies aging, something else). In addition, because social gerontology is a social science, it typically features a sense of scientific distance closer to what one might find in the natural sciences rather than in the humanities and avoids value-laden language. Consider the following two examples:

> One marketing research firm predicted that in 2015, Americans will spend 114 billion dollars on products dedicated to hiding the physical signs of aging on our face and bodies. Our birthday cards convey the same underlying message: I'm sorry to hear you are another year older. (Nelson 2016)

> Ageism, or discrimination based on age, is extraordinarily complex and is often covert. . . . To add to the confusion, ageist remarks may be well-intentioned. For example, an ageist remark can appear on the surface as a compliment (e.g., addressing an older woman as "young lady") when in fact it subtly perpetuates the idea that "old" is "bad." (Gendron et al. 2016, 997)

The first example features first-person pronouns that align the speaker with the reader, a convention that would seem quite out of place in a gerontology journal. It is also direct (abrasive in a gerontological sense) in its message. The second example avoids the use of a speaking pronoun altogether and presents a less emotional example to illustrate its point about ageism. In this way, the issue seems to stand on its own, outside the reach (and potential bias) of the authors. First-person pronouns are sometimes used but only with the same neutral tone as in the second example.

5. WHAT NARRATIVE POSITION DOES THE AUTHOR TAKE? Another consideration is the author's narrative position and tone. In gerontology, key features are polite disagreement and respectful authority. An excellent example of these features can be found in the following excerpt from Martha Holstein and Meredith Minkler (2003) in reference to the very contested paradigm described earlier—Rowe and Kahn's (1997) model of successful aging:

> Time and popularity have not, however, erased our concerns about this paradigm and the associated use of the implicitly normative phrase, "successful aging." Its very simplicity and apparent clarity mask vital differences and many critical dimensions of what may be described as a liminal stage—"the condition of moving from one state to another" (Heilbrun 1999, 35)—under circumstances marked by change and uncertainty. (Holstein and Minkler 2003, 788)

In contrast to the example by Todd Nelson (2016) in the previous section, Holstein and Minkler (2003) provide a very measured tone while offering an important critique of Rowe and Kahn's successful-aging paradigm. Narrative position and tone are also related, in some respects, to vocabulary and context. The words specifically related to gerontology are important, as is the use of non-value or value-neutral language.

Overall, we believe acquiring the components of and proficiency in the gerontological voice can lead to scholarly or professional identity. This conclusion therefore led to our next step in our process: creating assignments that can help students develop a gerontological voice in their writing.

GROWING THE GERONTOLOGICAL VOICE, ONE ASSIGNMENT AT A TIME

As a result of what we learned and explored through the Fellows Program, we further honed our understanding of the gerontological voice by developing assignments in our introductory and advanced graduate-level theory courses. In the introductory course, our goal was to socialize students to the discipline through writing these assignments. At the advanced level, the assignments were opportunities for students to exercise their gerontological voice. Across the two theory courses, the assignments capitalized on CALP's synergy between working toward mastering content and writing in the discipline of, in our case, social gerontology. The assignments also relied on writing as both a component and an outcome of the learning process. We found Krashen and Brown's (2007) reading strategies of narrow reading (i.e., focused reading in a particular area of interest) and utilization of background knowledge helpful in designing several of the assignments. Particularly helpful across all the assignments were Krashen and Brown's (2007) problem-solving strategies, which comprise specific tasks in the writing process (i.e., planning, revision, delayed editing, rereading, regular daily writing, incubation). Krashen and Brown characterize these tasks as "the means by which 'writing makes us smarter' " (3); they also help explain/provide insight into the common adage "writing is thinking." The development of these assignments was also informed by ongoing instruction and consultation from the university's Howe Center for Writing Excellence.

Here we highlight components of the major writing project—the theory project—for the introductory graduate course, Perspectives in Gerontology (GTY 602). The purpose of the semester-long project was for students to explore the development of a gerontological concept of personal interest to them. In step 1, which addressed CALP component 2 (i.e., knowledge of academic content), students identified several concepts or theories they had learned from their previous knowledge or experience related to gerontology. For each concept/theory, they were asked to reflect on how their prior knowledge related to what we had read in class so far and to speculate on what else they needed to know to gain more insight into their concept/theory of interest. Overall, this assignment provided a way for students to reflect on how their past learning and experiences affected their current views and to have ownership in identifying knowledge or skills they lacked.

Steps 2 through 4, which featured writing assignments of increasing length, primarily focused on knowledge proficiency. For example, step 2 involved writing a paragraph explaining why the student chose a particular concept/theory. In step 3, students prepared a one-page summary for three to five articles related to their topic. In step 4, "Looking back/historical influences," students examined the reference list for a step-3 article they thought was most helpful and completed an article-summary matrix. Step 4 emphasized the disciplinary roots of the current concept and allowed students to begin to see how arguments and writing styles in different disciplines vary, even if slightly, from gerontology. Finally, the students used CALP components 1 and 3 for the remainder of the assignment by writing drafts and peer reviewing fellow classmates' work. Although this project relied more on students gaining knowledge than on improving writing, it was an important first step in their graduate experience and complemented another required class specifically in writing, which we discuss in the next section. Overall, students liked the project, specifically the scaffolding aspect, although they recognized building knowledge could be difficult. They also commented on how the iterative process helped them think through ideas and forced them to think critically about each article and its value and contribution to the field.

WRITING COURSE IN THE GERONTOLOGICAL VOICE: A NEW COURSE

In addition to serving as a foundation for individual writing assignments in the theory courses, the concept of the gerontological voice subsequently guided the development of a doctoral course on writing in social gerontology offered for the first time in spring 2019. The three primary objectives of the course were to (1) make the process of writing in social gerontology explicit, (2) give each student the opportunity to develop "good writing" habits, and (3) for each participant to end the semester with either a manuscript or grant application ready, or close to ready, for submission for peer review. A longer-term goal of the course was to create a culture of writing among graduate students in social gerontology. Beginning in the 2020 academic year, the course has been required for all gerontology master's students as well.

Three interrelated techniques guided the design of this course. The first was conversational inquiry (Adler-Kassner and Wardle 2015; Wardle and Downs 2020). Conversational inquiry is a collaborative process in which participants use careful reading and writing as the basis for an ongoing conversation around an open question; it is also an effective way to understand genre as both a reader and a writer. The purpose of the conversation is to analyze and interpret what is presented to generate new knowledge using a consensus-seeking process. The inquiry process is "imperfect, incomplete, provisional (uncertain), revisable and iterative" (Wardle and Downs 2020, 33). Conversational inquiry thus provided a strategy for a semester-long exploration of the open question, "What does it mean to write like a social gerontologist?"

Because conversational inquiry requires careful reading and writing, it is important that students engage in rhetorical reading, which was the second technique that informed the design of the course. As described by Wardle and Downs (2020), there are four elements of rhetorical reading. First, any given text is not a disembodied set of facts. Rather, each text reflects the opinions, perspectives, and voice of the writer(s). Second, how you make sense of a text depends on who is speaking because neither writers nor readers are neutral. Third, readers construct their own meaning of a text based on what they think they know. As such, a text can mean different things to different readers. Finally, the meaning ascribed to a text derives from the reader. Although these ideas are familiar in rhetoric and composition, they are often not made explicit in the social sciences. However, because these ideas were explicit throughout the course, students challenged themselves and each other to read rhetorically, which prepared them for the conversational-inquiry process. It also helped them master the fundamental concept that writing is a conversation, which is essential for successful participation in the peer-reviewed publication or grant-funding arenas, the genre sets targeted in the course.

The third technique that informed the design of the course was Sonja Foss's (2018) model of generic criticism. In this model, "the generic critic seeks to discover commonalities in rhetorical patterns across recurring situations" (179). Thus, generic criticism results in the identification of commonalities that characterize a particular genre. To achieve this goal, Foss identifies four elements that can be used to examine artifacts that comprise a particular genre. The four elements are (1) situation (i.e., the circumstances under which the genre is produced), (2) substance (i.e., the content included in the genre), (3) style (i.e., the form [organization, tone] the genre) takes, and (4) organizing principles (i.e., the essential characteristics that must be present in order for an artifact to represent the particular genre). These four elements of generic criticism provided the framework students used to analyze different genres of gerontological writing during the semester as part of their efforts to answer the question of what it means to write like a gerontologist.

The three-credit-hour course met weekly, and most class meetings were divided into two sections. The objective of the first section was to explore what it means to write like a social gerontologist, making the process as explicit as possible. During the second (workshop) section of each class meeting, students developed their writing habits and worked on their manuscript (the genre chosen by all students). This process could consist of working independently, sharing a particular challenge with the group, and/or soliciting/providing individual peer feedback. At the end of the workshop period, the group typically reconvened to share progress, challenges, and next steps.

The first section of each class focused on a particular microgenre of social gerontological writing that is part of the larger genre (e.g., a manuscript or a grant application) that is part of a genre set (e.g., the publication process, the funding process). Whereas typically a genre analysis is conducted on the larger artifact, subsections of the genre were the target for analysis. Thus, for example, individual weekly topics included the instructions for authors for preparing a manuscript, writing an abstract, an introduction, a methods section, the discussion/conclusion of a manuscript, revisions based on reviewers' feedback, and the cover letter that accompanies a revised manuscript. Corresponding topics for grant applications were originally included in the course; because all students elected to work on manuscripts, more time was spent on the publication genre set. The microgenre approach required students to develop and use their rhetorical reading skills in the in-class genre-analysis sessions that informed the conversational-inquiry process.

Prior to each class, in addition to reading assigned articles about the writing process, students carefully read three to four artifacts from the microgenre for that week. Initially, the instructor chose the artifacts. Subsequently, once students were familiar with the process, they chose artifacts relevant for their writing project. Students came to class with a genre analysis based on the artifacts that used Foss's (2018) elements of generic criticism (i.e., situation, substance, style, organization). During the class discussion, which followed the principles of conversational inquiry, a group genre analysis was completed for each minigenre. Over the course of the semester, this activity resulted in a set of minigenre analyses that, in the aggregate, provided students with a foundation of what it means to write like a social gerontologist, at least with respect to the genre of a manuscript and, to a lesser extent, a grant application. As a result of the workshop sections, they also made progress on their own writing.

Marcia Johnson (2014) identifies two threshold concepts independent academic researchers must understand: developing clarity in writing (i.e., talking to think) and self-efficacy so overcoming barriers in writing is possible. End-of-the-semester course evaluations and reflections revealed students made progress with respect to both threshold concepts. These comments captured the liminal space in which students found themselves at the beginning of the semester. As one student explained, "I know we struggled with the first couple of rounds of the genre analyses, but eventually we picked up momentum. During our struggle, there were moments of silence in class when we were feeling unsure of how to approach its application (totally normal for applying a new tool)." With respect to the course goals of making the process of writing in social gerontology explicit and giving each student the opportunity to develop "good writing" habits, one student indicated the course helped "demystify/be honest about the academic writing process and products." Another student reported, "Dissections of various types of writing (by the genre analysis method) helped to see the structure I can follow in my own work."

With respect to their development as gerontological writers, several students commented specifically on the workshop portion of the class sessions. In one students' words, "I really appreciated that we had time to write in class—this practice encouraged me to focus on the writing I needed to accomplish by creating an intentional community (like our readings suggested!)." Other students indicated the class "create[d] a space where we [and the instructor] can be open and honest about the difficult conversations attached to translating our gerontological knowledge into different forms of writing." Another student proclaimed, "We are pioneers of the genre analysis, and we think we are doing great work together! We discuss about writing as a gerontologist and share what we struggle with and our success." Further alluding to the sense of community that developed over the semester, several students anticipated the experiences of future cohorts of students who would enroll in the course. One student commented, "For future classes, who might not be as 'gelled' as our class was, you might think about . . . opportunities for team-building. I say this because I think a strong relational foundation across students was critical to having the open/honest/tough conversations we had—and to be trusting in others not to have judgment etc." Another student claimed, "I'm excited to see where the next class of students takes it!"

Two students achieved the objective of submitting a manuscript for peer review prior to/within several weeks of the end of the semester; as of spring 2020, these two manuscripts have been published (after one rejection and several revisions). One of these publications is solo authored; the second includes another graduate student and a staff researcher as coauthors. A third student who conducted data analysis and produced the methods and results sections for a manuscript during the semester is in the process of submitting their manuscript (which is coauthored with a faculty member) to a new journal after an initial rejection. A fourth student created two assignments based on the idea of the gerontological voice for the undergraduate introductory gerontology course she was teaching, which served as the basis for a poster presentation at the annual meeting of the Gerontological Society of America and the annual statewide gerontology meeting. In addition, during the semester in which they took the course, the five students also produced three accepted abstracts and one manuscript-length conference submission (that received a student award) for the annual statewide gerontology meeting, and an accepted abstract for presentation at the annual meeting of the Gerontological Society of America.

ONGOING WORK ON THE GERONTOLOGICAL VOICE

In our chapter, we provide our insights into threshold concepts in social gerontology to include our own journey to identify, articulate, and communicate this primary concept—the gerontological voice—to our students, our colleagues, and the field. Although focused on social gerontology specifically, we strongly believe the frameworks, student assignments, and contributions to our field could be easily applied to other disciplines.

We note that when we began exploring the gerontological voice as a threshold concept, we were excited to share our evolving ideas with our students and colleagues; in this chapter the focus is on our students. As we brought our ideas into the classroom, initially via individual assignments in the theory courses and then in the writing course, we increasingly appreciated the usefulness of the gerontological voice as a threshold concept. At the time, we did not realize creating coalitions with students and generating awareness and consciousness through classroom practices are two strategies for second-order/deep change (Kezar 2018; Kezar and Lester 2011; this volume, chapter 3). A third strategy of collecting and using data was useful in assessing students' feedback about the assignments—and the outcomes they achieved. Even as we continued to define the concept, graduate students started using the term *gerontological voice* in the context of their writing and also in their teaching. We considered this a step toward our longer-term goal that the writing course foster a culture of writing, especially among our graduate students in social gerontology.

As part of our ongoing work as scholars interested in helping other gerontologists contribute to gerontology's threshold concept, we recently published an editorial for our discipline's lead journal, *The Gerontologist*, entitled "Writing Like a Gerontologist for *The Gerontologist*" (de Medeiros and Kinney 2020). Here, we make explicit what people writing in gerontology may understand on some level but that many people outside the field who submit academic manuscripts do not. The article identifies and discusses five features that contribute to academic proficiency in social gerontology. The first two, neutral voice and polite disagreement/respectful authority, are discussed earlier in the chapter. The third, beyond the demographic imperative, notes that people in gerontology are well aware of changing demographics, and they should not be included in the text unless to make a specific point. The fourth, context that reflects the heterogeneity of later life, suggests that "gerontological writing explicates myriad factors (internal and external; micro, meso, macro) that contribute to the richness and diversity of what it means to be old" (795). The fifth, "integrated, contextualized theory that builds on prior research to generate new knowledge/insight on aging/late life specifically" points to the need for synthesis and contextualization of key theories (795). And finally, the sixth, "clear description of the framework that advances gerontological ideas," indicates that writing should help move gerontology into the future by emphasizing evolving ideas and perspectives (795). Although we use this specific configuration of features to operationalize the gerontological voice, we hope our work will inform scholars who are working on threshold concepts in other disciplines and provide a framework that can be used to better understand other disciplinary voices.

NOTE

1. We note we have recently published the first article that specifically articulates and makes explicit the key attributes of writing in gerontology (de Medeiros and Kinney 2020).

REFERENCES

Adler-Kassner, Linda, and Elizabeth Wardle, eds. 2015. *Naming What We Know: Threshold Concepts of Writing Studies.* Logan: Utah State University Press.

Baker, Jeannette L. 1959. "The Unsuccessful Aged." *Journal of the American Geriatrics Society* 7 (7): 570–72.

Baltes, Paul B., and Margret M. Baltes. 1990. "Psychological Perspectives on Successful Aging: The Model of Selective Optimization with Compensation." In *Successful Aging: Perspectives from the Behavioral Sciences,* edited by Paul B. Baltes and Margret M. Baltes, 1–34. New York: Cambridge University Press.

Barradell, Sarah. 2013. "The Identification of Threshold Concepts: A Review of Theoretical Complexities and Methodological Challenges." *Higher Education* 65 (2): 265–76. https://doi.org/10.1007/s10734-012-9542-3.

Cummins, Jim. 1979. "Cognitive/Academic Language Proficiency, Linguistic Interdependence, the Optimum Age Question and Some Other Matters." *Working Papers on Bilingualism* 19: 121–92.

de Medeiros, Kate, and Jennifer M. Kinney. 2020. "Writing Like a Gerontologist for *The Gerontologist.*" *Gerontologist* 60 (5): 793–96. https://doi.org/10.1093/geront/gnaa060.

Foss, Sonja K. 2018. *Rhetorical Criticism: Exploration and Practice.* 5th ed. Long Grove, IL: Waveland.

Gendron, Tracey L., E. Ayn Welleford, Jennifer Inker, and John T. White. 2016. "The Language of Ageism: Why We Need to Use Words Carefully." *Gerontologist* 56 (6): 997–1006. https://doi.org/10.1093/geront/gnv066.

Gonzales Ernest, Christina Matz-Costa, and Nancy Morrow-Howell. 2015. "Increasing Opportunities for the Productive Engagement of Older Adults: A Response to Population Aging." *Gerontologist* 55 (2): 252–261. https://doi.org/10.1093/geront/gnv066.

Groundwater-Smith, Susan. 2014. "'Nettlesome Knowledge' and Threshold Concepts: An Afterword." *Waikato Journal of Education* 19 (2): 123–26. https://doi.org/10.15663/wje.v19i2.104.

Havighurst, Robert J. 1961. "Successful Aging." *Gerontologist* 1 (1): 8–13. https://doi.org/10.1093/geront/1.1.8.

Heilbrun, Carolyn G. 1999. *Women's Lives: The View From the Threshold.* Toronto: University of Toronto Press.

Holstein, Martha B., and Meredith Minkler. 2003. "Self, Society, and the 'New Gerontology.'" *Gerontologist* 43 (6): 787–96. http://doi.org/10.1093/geront/43.6.787.

Johnson, E. Marcia. 2014. "Doctorates in the Dark: Threshold Concepts and the Improvement of Doctoral Supervision." *Waikato Journal of Education* 19 (2): 69–81. http://doi.org/10.15663/wje.v19i2.99.

Kezar, Adrianna. 2018. *How Colleges Change: Understanding, Leading, and Enacting Change.* 2nd ed. New York: Routledge.

Kezar, Adrianna J., and Jaime Lester. 2011. *Enhancing Campus Capacity for Leadership: An Examination of Grassroots Leaders in Higher Education.* Stanford: Stanford University Press.

Krashen, Stephen, and Clara Lee Brown. 2007. "What Is Academic Language Proficiency?" *STETS Language & Communication Review* 6 (1): 1–4. http://doi.org/10.5054/TJ.2011.274624.

Land, Ray. 2011. "Threshold Concepts and Troublesome Knowledge." Paper presented at the Threshold Concepts Symposium, Cork, Ireland.

Meyer, Jan H. F., and Ray Land. 2003. *Threshold Concepts and Troublesome Knowledge: Linkages to Ways of Thinking and Practising within the Disciplines.* ETL Project Occasional Report 4. Edinburgh: University of Edinburgh.

Nelson, Todd D. 2016. "The Age of Ageism." *Journal of Social Issues* 72 (1): 191–98. https://doi.org/10.1111/josi.12162.

North, Michael S., and Susan T. Fiske. 2015. "Modern Attitudes Toward Older Adults in the Aging World: A Cross-Cultural Meta-Analysis." *Psychological Bulletin* 141 (5): 993–1021. https://doi.org/10.1037/A0039469.

Rowe, John W., and Robert L. Kahn. 1997. "Successful Aging." *Gerontologist* 37 (4): 433–40. https://doi.org/10.1093/geront/37.4.433.

Shenoy, Premnath, and Anand Harugeri. 2015. "Elderly Patients' Participation in Clinical Trials." *Perspectives in Clinical Research* 6 (4): 184. http://doi.org/10.4103/2229-3485.167099.

Wardle, Elizabeth, and Doug Downs. 2020. *Writing about Writing.* 4th ed. Boston: Bedford/St. Martin's.

7

FOSTERING DEVELOPMENTALLY INFORMED COLLABORATIVE WRITING

Bringing the Team (and the Instructor) across the Threshold

Carrie E. Hall, Jennifer J. Quinn, and L. James Smart
Psychology

The goals of our classes indicate what we think expertise in writing is, and the way we teach indicates how we think writers achieve "expertise."

—Michael Carter

As three experimental (cognitive, social, behavioral neuroscience) psychology instructors who have taught numerous research-methods courses, lower-level courses that prepare students to engage in genre-specific writing, and upper-level courses that utilize and refine genre-specific writing skills, we have a lot of experience teaching writing and thinking in our discipline. We enthusiastically applied to participate in the Fellows Program, thinking we might trade a few ideas, develop some new assignments, and gain additional insight from the writing experts who facilitated the program. Little did we know our participation, and learning about threshold concepts (Meyer and Land 2003; this volume, chapter 1), would upend how we thought about writing in our classes. We spent much of the time walking to and from our Fellows sessions deep in conversation about the paradigm shift we were experiencing and realizing how our own liminal state might be similar to our students'. We said things like, "I feel like I want to redesign my entire course around how writing should be" and "No wonder students are struggling" and even "I'm excited—I haven't been excited about teaching writing for so long." The Fellows Program propelled us toward the realization that our approach to teaching disciplinary writing in psychology must change. In fact, we ourselves encountered several threshold concepts while participating in the program that forced us to reconsider our own conceptions about the purpose of teaching writing. Learning about these concepts

https://doi.org/10.7330/9781646423040.c007

gave us a language to talk about what was bothering us about the way we were currently teaching writing. In particular, the threshold concepts that "writing is a . . . social activity" (Roozen 2015) as well as a "cognitive activity" (Dryer 2015) and that "all writers have more to learn" (Rose 2015) resonated with us and helped us pinpoint where we thought our current methods of teaching writing were unsatisfactory.

Previously, we had approached writing instruction as just that—instruction in how to write effectively, with a focus on mechanics and essentially neglecting idea development (thinking) and orientation to the conversations happening in the discipline (Wardle and Downs 2020). We now realize writing should serve a developmental purpose in that it facilitates growth in one's thinking and perspective on a particular topic, rather than solely communicating knowledge to an (abstract) external audience. Expanding our view of what writing entails and can accomplish, along with how we might teach and evaluate that writing, is necessary to bridge the gap between what we ask students to do and what we expect them to know.

The group term paper, which can take many forms (literature review, empirical [research] manuscript, or grant proposal are typical examples), is a common semester-long assignment in the field of psychology, including in our own courses. Prized for its perceived ability to initiate majors into one of the key writing genres in the field while simultaneously introducing students to the process of working with collaborators, it unfolds in familiar steps throughout the semester. Student groups choose a topic, possibly during the second class session but certainly by the end of the second week, individually written sections of the paper are generated and intermittently revised throughout the semester, and then at some point (often late in the semester) these individual drafts are merged into a group paper. The product of this last-minute cobbling together of individual drafts is often disjointed and does not read like a single voice, as the team members rarely have the time or the incentive to ensure the paper fits together. This divide-and-conquer approach has been repeatedly reinforced since we, as instructors, have not developed strategies to disable or combat this unsatisfactory routine.

Contrast this with the professional writing practice of psychologists. A researcher first reads extensively and starts to dig into potential gaps in the literature. Ideas are then vetted through informal channels and forms with lab personnel, professional peers, and field experts, who often become collaborators on the paper. The researcher then continues to seek peer feedback as the brainstorming process continues and an idea and paper organization start to emerge. Writing a full draft of the paper is one of the final steps of the protracted writing process.

So, although one goal of major-specific curriculum is to prepare students to engage in professional writing in that particular discipline through writing that approximates professional activities (Brown, Collins, and Duguid 1989), students are often held to a more solitary and linear process than professionals in the field actually engage in. Students have the additional burden of needing to develop through a series of threshold concepts, and as a result, students spend most of their time in a messy and sometimes uncomfortable liminal space during the writing process (Meyer and Land 2006). In addition, students move through threshold concepts at different times, and the typical strict march through assembling a paper does not acknowledge or honor these developmental differences. The group members who are furthest along developmentally likely do the bulk of the work, with little interaction with other group members who could benefit from discussion. This, coupled with assessment practices tailored for individual competence (despite the group task), can result in challenges, such as accusations of discarding individual group member's contributions when portions of a paper are developed independently with the expectation of a quick assembly (and a good grade) at the end of the process.

In this chapter, we describe what we learned about student writing in our Fellows sessions and why traditional approaches to teaching genre-specific writing in psychology are often frustrating (for both the student and the instructor). Then we discuss how we are now approaching writing instruction that utilizes a developmentally informed team-based approach. Specifically, we discuss the importance of designing scaffolded writing assignments in a way that supports student development *and* is mindful of instructor workload, including examples of writing assignments and assessment strategies.

ISSUES WITH TRADITIONAL PEDAGOGY OF DISCIPLINARY WRITING IN PSYCHOLOGY

The stated purpose of major writing assignments in psychology courses most commonly centers around preparing students to engage in field-specific writing. Students are taught the mechanics of APA style and the components of each section of the given genre of writing and then are marched through a tightly scheduled linear paper-construction process. However, we argue this looks nothing like the process of writing in our field; in fact, we would not be able to write for publication using this method, and we already know the mechanics. Importantly, the focus on the mechanics, and APA writing style in particular, may also reinforce disciplinary practices that limit diversity of thought and voice (see this volume, chapter 12). Part of the revision we are proposing emerged from the fact that in teaching writing, we are addressing four linked components: idea generation and refinement; communication (written product); the formatting/mechanics (in our case, APA style); and conventions of the field (how professionals interact and share information). Traditional approaches often do not effectively address all these aspects of the disciplinary writing process. We summarize the three main issues with this traditional approach to teaching disciplinary writing in psychology.

Issue 1: *Incongruence among Instructor Expectations, Writing Assignments, and Student Ability*

In an ideal world, we as instructors would accurately gauge our students' readiness for particular scaffolded assignments that progressively advance student learning, allowing students to perform in a manner consistent with our expectations. However, we have all experienced the frustration associated with grading a pile of student papers and realizing (too late) that our expectations are incongruent with the preparedness/ability of our students (mismatch 1). This incongruence between instructor expectations and student abilities often results in frustration for the students as well. Alternatively, we may realize we failed to implement appropriate activities prior to or during the assignment that would have allowed the students to meet our expectations (mismatch 2). This failure often leads to poor performance on the part of the students.

These mismatches among our expectations, the assignments we provide, and the students' abilities are not unique to psychology but represent common design issues that occur in many contexts and can be summed up by the fact that designers (instructors) are not the typical users (i.e., students; Norman 2013). In our context, it is the fact that our thinking (and therefore writing) as professionals bears little resemblance to that of an undergraduate student learning to write for the first time or even graduate students who have mechanical proficiency but are still developing professional-level knowledge.

To use an example from our university, we might assume because students have had ENG 111 (our university's introductory writing course), they have the ability to write a grammatically correct, coherent narrative that justifies their proposed study. Not only does this reveal the large assumptions about what is expected from and covered in ENG 111, but these expectations are in marked contrast to our knowledge that writing competency cannot be achieved in a single course. Given this, students do not typically come in with knowledge on how to synthesize information to make a discipline-relevant argument. ENG 111, though required of all students, is still just one course taught in one department that cannot teach all kinds of writing, especially disciplinary writing. It is important to note that what one considers a coherent narrative that justifies their proposed study is often deeply disciplinary, though that may not be obvious to those who are experts and thus to whom many of the assumptions of the discipline have become automatic. This expectation mismatch (1) leads to the next mismatch (2), in which the assignment is not aligned with student capabilities (the assignment mismatch is the physical manifestation of the expectation mismatch). This results in the final mismatch (3) between what the instructor intends the assignment to accomplish (the learning outcome or goal) and what the assignment will actually assess or require. For example, our common practice of requiring five references for the students' introduction is meant to give the students the ability to support their argument but instead becomes a checking-the-box exercise in which the references may not help the students create a coherent, persuasive narrative (and in many instances does the opposite).

We argue that instructors often fail to take into account the difficulty students experience in this regard and thus set expectations higher than what student writing development suggests is suitable for many students. Expectations outside student development can lead to any number of issues, including disengagement from the process, dismissal of the work/feedback as busywork, and even academic dishonesty when a standard feels impossible to achieve. Instructors can address this issue by attending to the level of development in writing skills students have achieved (which may vary as a result of course level) and tuning writing-related expectations and requirements toward stretching that development and not toward achieving writing perfection.

Issue 2: *Overutilization of Individualized Approaches and Assessment*

Research and writing in psychology are fundamentally collaborative. Single-author papers are rare and in decline (Henriksen 2016; White, Dalgleish, and Arnold 1982), and thus the development of effective collaboration skills is key in order to be successful in this field. In contrast, the typical research paper course assignment requires individual completion and individual assessment in an attempt to ensure each student is both contributing and developing the requisite writing skills. Unfortunately, writing individual assignments within a group project does not authentically approximate the collaborative process that unfolds when professionals in the field write together. Thus, these assignments not only fail to model ways of thinking and doing within the discipline that Hunter and Tse (2013) advocate for but they also prevent students from experiencing the numerous benefits collaborative writing affords each individual student (see section below). Recognizing and implementing team-based learning and assessment best practices into our instructional writing practices addresses concerns about individual participation and skill acquisition, while also developing effective and transferable collaboration skills.

Issue 3: *Overemphasis on Polished Final Product*

The purpose of writing in the field of psychology is primarily to develop and communicate new ideas. Writing in coursework should support the development of the skill base needed to do that effectively. After our participation in the Fellows Program, we realized the typical progression of the term paper does not support this developmental process. In fact, we experienced this disconnect firsthand as we spent a semester reading, discussing ideas, and getting feedback before we even started working on this chapter. It seems obvious that we could not have proposed a chapter topic in the first week of the Fellows Program, gathered our resources over the next two weeks, split up the writing, and then pasted together the results to deliver to the editors. It is comical to consider such a process in our professional lives, yet this is exactly what we often ask students to do. The commonly required quick identification of a paper topic followed by a laborious paper-construction process often required of students does not actually practice or support the skills needed for writing in our field.

Instead, writing can support the development of these skills when it is utilized in more authentic ways, such as in brainstorming sessions, short topic summaries, and email exchanges. Writing can then be later used to communicate the ideas once students have completed the scaffolded topic exploration and topic-development process (i.e., the thinking). The communication of new ideas can only happen at the end of the process once existing work has been explored and new ideas considered. It is easy to see how this might occur during the final 20–30 percent of a course in contrast to current practices, in which exploration is typically cut short and followed by a long and laborious paper-construction and revision process that never feels satisfactory or complete (for students or instructor).

By reversing this division so the exploration and idea-development phases are extended and the formal paper-writing phase is compressed, students gain more authentic skill building in the writing strategies psychologists actually use. During extended topic exploration and idea development, students gain repeated experience communicating and reflecting on what they think the state of research in a certain area is and what the interesting gaps in knowledge may be, all with the rapid and on-going feedback afforded by effective teams. The compressed paper-writing phase may necessitate the sacrifice of some final polishing; however, we argue that the value of the edits typically made in final drafts (i.e., APA style corrections, grammar corrections, etc.) is much less important than the value gained from an emphasis on topic exploration and idea development—in which deep learning and critical thinking occur.

THE DEVELOPMENTALLY INFORMED TEAM-BASED SOLUTION (DITBS)

We have developed a multifaceted approach to address these three issues directly. Our developmentally informed team-based solution (DITBS) consists of four elements. First, we utilize a developmental approach to situate expectations and assignments within students' current skill level. Then we utilize a team-based assignment structure in order to teach collaborative writing, which affords numerous benefits to individual students. The team-based assignments then are carefully crafted so the focus is on the early stages of writing (e.g., brainstorming, idea refinement, etc.) and, finally, the assessment process honors this process-not-product focus. In the next section, we discuss each of these elements in detail, including specific examples of each.

DITBS Theoretical Element: Using Kellogg's (2008) Theory to Design Scaffolded Assignments That Support Student Writing Development

Students, and indeed all of us, are writers (thinkers) in development. As instructors, we can find it easy to forget the perspective of a novice writer. Our reading of Ronald Kellogg's (2008) discussion of the development of writing ability during the Fellows Program was pivotal in the shift in how we think about student writing because of Kellog's focus on discrete stages. A fundamental shift must take place in the learner. Framing writing development as moving through a series of shifts akin to threshold concepts was illuminating, as we realized students cannot just do more of something or be told how to do something in order to move to the next stage. Instead we must design assignments around the stage students are in, such that they can practice and solidify skills they have just acquired and also start to develop the foundation for the skills that will move them into the next stage.

Kellogg (2008) proposes three main stages of writing development. The primary constraint that eases and allows movement from one stage to the next is that we have limited working memory. In fact, automatization as a component of expertise has been observed more generally, and it is no different for the writing process (Gobet and Simon 1996). As parts of the writing process become automated, we become able to handle progressively more complicated components of the writing process. For example, expert writing involves awareness of one's audience's perspective and maintenance of that awareness throughout. However, perspective taking while writing is an advanced skill (Kellogg 2008), and most students in our classes (as well as some of their instructors) have not yet mastered it (Moran 2013). Like adjusting the radio while driving a car, perspective taking while writing may feel easy to those who have automatized aspects of both actions, while it may feel overwhelming and clumsy to those still developing those skills.

Gaining this understanding of the relationship between limited working memory and our students' ability to engage in the writing process was pivotal to our realization that, at times, we were asking students to write in ways they simply cannot yet perform. Components of writing that may seem simple to experienced writers may consume large amounts of cognitive-processing resources for novice writers, and our writing assignments/expectations/assessments should reflect that. Learning to write is not simply receiving clear instructions that one then follows. Instead, writing development involves important changes in cognitive processing that take time, practice, and automatization. Specifically, we realized we should design writing assignments in ways that ask students to practice the specific skills that must be automated that then free up working memory and allow students to start to move to the next stage.

The typical form and function of writing in each of Kellogg's (2008) stages, and the challenges inherent in each due to cognitive-processing limitations, are summarized below (also see figure 7.1).

Knowledge-Telling Stage (Zero to Ten Years of Writing Practice)

Typically, children and adolescents are in this stage, in which comprehension is the main struggle. Students at this level have difficulty with concrete perspective taking such that they have a difficult time comprehending how a specified Other would understand the text and instead focus on explaining a topic from their own perspective. The vast majority of college students are past this stage.

Knowledge-Transforming Stage (Ten to Twenty Years of Writing Practice)

In this stage, some of the mechanics of writing have been automatized, which frees up some working memory for additional tasks. Writers in this stage use writing as a tool to clarify what they think and what they want to say through their writing. Whereas writers in the knowledge-telling stage are simply reporting what they know about a topic, writers in the knowledge-transforming stage hold both the text they are working on and their own thoughts and reactions in working memory. In this way, the process of writing, and one's reaction to the text, can influence how one thinks about the topic and motivate text changes in a cyclical process. Writers in this stage expend considerable effort identifying gaps and inconsistencies in current knowledge through evaluation of, and synthesis across, multiple sources. Most college students, graduate students, and some faculty are in this stage.

Knowledge-Crafting Stage (Twenty-Plus Years of Writing Practice)

The knowledge-crafting stage is reached mostly by people who write professionally. Professors may have reached this stage, but students (undergraduate or graduate) generally have not. In this stage, text is written while taking into account the perspective of the hypothetical reader, which is only possible because the automatization of the prior writing skills frees up working memory that can be devoted to maintaining the second perspective in mind while also engaging in the process of both writing and reflecting on one's own thoughts and reactions to the text. These expert writers often struggle with effectively communicating with novice or lay audiences through their writing.

Therefore, designing developmentally informed writing assignments for college students is imperative. Given that most college students are somewhere in the knowledge-transforming stage, either just barely or solidly, writing assignments should be designed to allow students to practice and automate the related skills. The primary new ability in this stage is being able to think about both the text and one's own reaction to it and thus engage in a back-and-forth process in which writing and thinking impact each other. However, this skill is not yet automated within the knowledge-transforming stage, and it is still consuming large amounts of cognitive resources. Thus students need to practice this skill until it is not so resource intensive. Examples of the types of tasks that

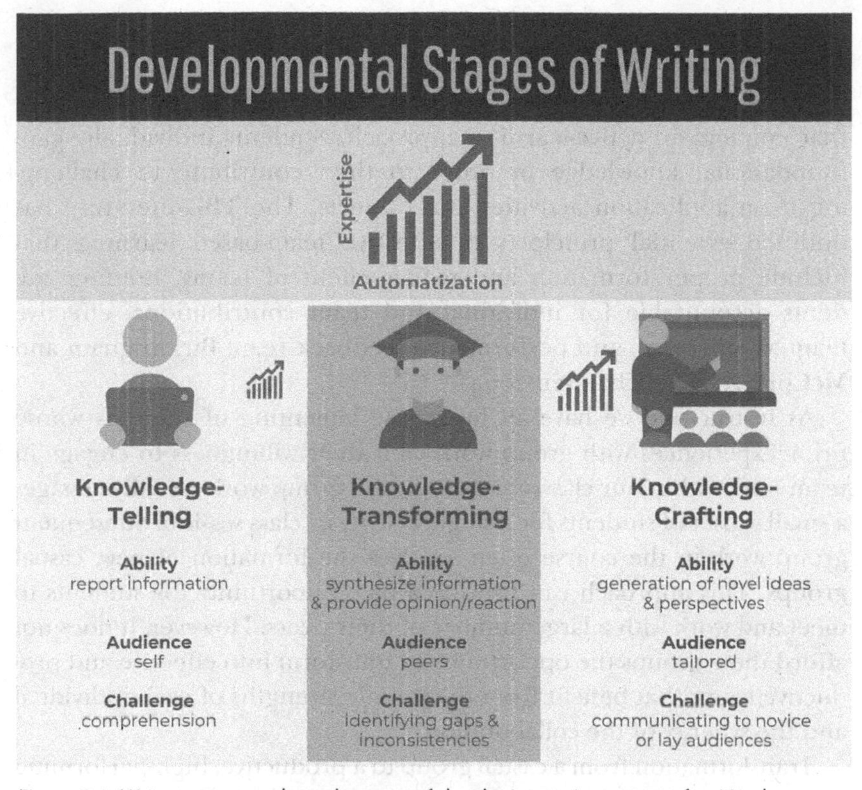

Figure 7.1. Writers progress through stages of development. As aspects of writing become more automatic, authors are increasingly able to engage more complex tasks and consider the intended audience, leading to increased writing expertise.

prompt this back and forth between writing and thinking include asking students to brainstorm ideas about a topic, categorize different types of information (perhaps results from research articles), develop an outline or idea cloud based on new information, and list what we don't yet know about a particular topic.

However some students may become stuck during these tasks. Because students are at different levels within the knowledge-transforming stage, completing these assignments in teams allows students to receive and provide real-time feedback at a pace (perhaps several times a minute) that simply cannot be matched by an instructor. Students in well-developed teams tend to contribute at a high level, constructively challenging each other's ideas, engaging in spontaneous debate, and participating in consensus decision-making. In the next section, we discuss how to use teams to facilitate individual development through collaborative writing.

DITBS Strategic Element: Harnessing the Power of Team-Based Learning in Collaborative Writing

Team-based learning (TBL) is an evidence-based teaching strategy that employs an active-learning approach. Students individually gain foundational knowledge in order to then contribute to challenging team application activities and projects. The TBL literature has outlined essential principles of effective team-based learning that include proper formation and management of teams, holding students accountable for individual and team contributions, effective team assignments, and performance feedback (e.g., Birmingham and McCord 2004; Michaelsen 2004).

As instructors, we have all heard the lamenting of students whose prior experiences with group work taint their willingness to engage in team work within our classrooms. Typically, group work casually engages a small subset of students for a single activity or class session. Subsequent group work in the course often involves the formation of new, casual groups. This approach can provide a nice opportunity for students to meet and work with a large number of their peers. However, it does not afford these groups the opportunity to transform into effective and productive teams that benefit from the unique strengths of each individual and the synergy of the collaboration.

Transformation from a casual group to a productive, high-performing team requires time along with carefully scaffolded, challenging activities to promote trust, knowledge acquisition, and skill building (Fink 2004). Evidence suggests team development occurs in stages that differ along several dimensions, including goal orientation, familiarity, level of contribution, task difficulty, and conflict-resolution strategies (Birmingham and McCord 2004; see figure 7.2).

In psychology, writing a research paper (e.g., literature review, manuscript, grant proposal) is one of the most challenging assignments students are required to complete and, as such, is a highly suitable opportunity for student groups to develop into productive, high-performing teams. Developing the ability to work productively in a team proves valuable for future performance in the workplace, where collaboration has become the norm. On the flip side, we argue that using a team approach as a tool for teaching disciplinary writing within psychology yields numerous benefits to the individual student that could not be actualized within an individualized writing approach. The team approach can have several benefits for both engagement and writing and are detailed in the following sections.

Casual **Group**	VS.	High-Performing **Team**
Commitment to individual goals		Commitment to team goals
Casual familiarity		High level of trust
Willingness to offer individual ideas		Willingness to challenge each other's ideas
Single, easily-accessible task		Scaffolded, challenging tasks
Democratic voting		Consensus-building discussion and decision-making

Figure 7.2. Casual groups and high-performing teams differ in the way they work in a number of important ways: level of engagement, work processes, and task difficulty.

Benefit 1: Frequent Feedback on Individual and Group Performance

Instructors can incorporate multiple drafts into assignment scaffolding and check in on teams while they work in class in order to give students frequent feedback. However, the speed and frequency of feedback that occurs in real-time, moment-to-moment team interactions cannot be matched. Students in a team have different strengths and areas for growth, and as they work through ideas together, they can give each other instant feedback that fosters individual and team development. The role of instructor feedback shifts to areas where the entire team (or class) is struggling, which makes it more focused and impactful. Even then, students on the team may not evenly take in the feedback, and again students can refine their understanding of the feedback through discussion within the team.

Benefit 2: Inspiring High Level of Individual Effort

While group work often leads to social loafing (Latané, Williams, and Harkins 1979; Simms and Nichols 2014) due to the lack of individually identifiable contributions, and thus accountability, team-based work leads to social facilitation. Team assignments are innately structured in a way that preserves identifiable contributions, as the focus is on the process. A key component of team process is the degree to which each group member feels capable of, valued for, and motivated to make contributions, and as a result, the degree to which they actually do contribute. Within the team framework, a "perfect" paper written by one group member is not a success. Redefining success in terms of inclusive contribution and engagement, as opposed to the final deliverable, means the contributions of each team member are key for success, even if they are not the best writer, the best researcher, or the best editor in the group.

Benefit 3: Increased Access to Resources

Teams can benefit from the resources individual team members have access to. Individual students have varying academic and personal backgrounds that uniquely inform team efforts. In fact, formation of diverse teams is a central tenet of the TBL approach (Birmingham and McCord 2004; Michaelsen 2004). In addition, team members may have differential access to software or other technology, established relationships with others who have advanced statistical or library skills, templates for genre-specific writing (e.g., a poster template), or other practical resources. Bringing these intellectual, experiential, and material resources together both benefits the team and underscores the importance of each group member.

Benefit 4: Team Development

As a team develops through carefully scaffolded and challenging tasks for which they need to rely on each other to fully accomplish the task, they get to know each other and their relative skills and strengths (Harrison, Price, and Bell 1998). As this knowledge becomes more detailed and individuals become more confident in their team members' efforts and reliability, team members begin to naturally rely on, learn from, and trust one another (McAllister 1995). This trust naturally leads to safety within the team, where ideas can genuinely be challenged and subsequently revised. Utilization of the full complement of skills and strengths held by the team allows for high-level performance not realized by casual groups that tend to operate more on a technically equal framework (e.g., we all type one-fourth of the paper, we all create a figure, we all find four resources, etc.).

Benefit 5: Spontaneous Debate and Consensus Decision-Making

Casual groups tend to make decisions via either democratic voting or by agreement with the first option suggested. Neither of these methods of decision-making promote cognitive development or actually even require students to interact; if the individual responses were known, we argue that a computer algorithm could make the same decision the group would likely produce. On the other hand, teams that have developed trust and a sense of each other's skills and strengths engage in spontaneous debates about the merits of ideas, rather than simply choosing an option via social rules akin to who arrived at the four-way stop first. This tendency to engage in spontaneous debate then creates space for individuals' ideas to be revised, synthesized, and ultimately transformed into a team perspective, which allows the team to engage in decision-making via consensus.

Benefit 6: Frequent Challenging of Ideas

Teams are much more likely than casual groups to engage in constructive conflict. Constructive conflict occurs when ideas are discussed in terms of their merit, as opposed to being influenced by outside factors such as who contributed the idea, the desire to avoid conflict, feeling personally attacked by disagreement, and so forth (Wolfe 2010). When constructive conflict happens, team members benefit from the experience of their ideas being challenged and learning to effectively challenge the ideas of others. Without feeling defensive, team members are pushed to consider alternatives and to think through implications they might not have considered individually. We argue that this type of moment-to-moment volleying of ideas and critiques is incredibly beneficial for cognitive development in that students are cued to consider other perspectives and assess how their argument is received by others, all with real-time feedback.

DITBS Practical Element: Allowing Adequate Time/Emphasis for All Phases of the Writing Process: The Deep-Dive Approach as an Exemplar

The activities of team writing provide a number of benefits we believe provide students with the skills to write in a manner more aligned with how we as professionals communicate in psychology. These activities can be implemented in many ways; we would like to highlight an exemplar approach called the "Deep Dive." The Deep Dive process (Moen 2001; Norman 2013) is an approach to innovation and creativity in product design tailored to team idea development. It was first developed by the IDEO company in the late 1990s (Kelley 2001). It typically involves multiple stages, starting with observation and proceeding through synthesizing, then visualization, followed by prototyping and finally implementing (Moen 2001). For purposes of collaborative writing, we suggest labeling these phases as *brainstorming*, followed by *organization* and *idea refinement*, then *drafting* and *revision* (where formal writing begins), and finally *dissemination*. What is different about this approach is that the formal-writing stage that typically begins very early and occupies a majority of the entire writing process for a class assignment now occurs much later and is no longer the primary focus. The team is encouraged (required) to allocate extensive time and effort to exploring a topic, synthesizing information, identifying gaps, and generating/refining ideas before worrying about the formal mechanics of writing and polishing a product.

Brainstorming

Brainstorming is not a new idea and has been shown to be an essential part of the team process (Wolfe 2010). What is different about the brainstorming phase in a deep-dive process is that it is purposefully extended over a longer period than typically given. Students are required to spend a significant period of time just generating ideas/questions/hypotheses without editing or constraining. The goals are to (1) generate a large number of items and (2) ensure every team member contributes a sufficient number (e.g., each team member should produce at least ten ideas). This time frame should be scaled to the scope of the project; for a semester-long project, we suggest at least two class periods devoted to brainstorming. As part of this phase, teams are explicitly instructed to be verbal and visual; writing at this stage is necessarily informal, incomplete, and messy and likely includes written words but also sketches, diagrams, and doodling (as it aids in the thinking process). Students are also encouraged to wait at least one day after the brainstorming phase before beginning to organize and refine. This time allows team members to share and reflect on ideas/perspectives before committing to a specific topic. The instructor's role at this stage is to encourage thinking and idea generation and to prevent students from settling on an idea/solution too quickly (or at all). These ideas can be jotted on large sheets of paper or in individual notes and do not need to be complete or consistent. In fact, students should avoid details at this point, as details will result in fewer ideas being generated and potentially lead students to commit to an idea prematurely before exploring all options. This process can be frustrating for students, particularly at earlier developmental stages, because it does not allow for simply reporting the "right answer," and, unfortunately, the "right-answer" approach has been overwhelmingly reinforced in their education up to this point.

Organization and Idea Refinement

In the organization phase, teams work to identify potential themes across the ideas generated during brainstorming; these themes are then used to form potential topics for research papers/projects. At this point, a cyclical process of idea refinement ensues in which teams disperse and each team member gathers additional information relevant to the identified theme(s); then the team reconvenes to discuss and evaluate the new information contributed by each team member. With each successive pass through this cycle, the team is increasingly challenged to wrestle with the new information to determine its consistency (in terms of both the broader literature and the current perspective of the team). Constructive conflict (Wolfe 2010) is likely to arise at this stage as the team debates competing ideas in an effort to build consensus needed to revise the team perspective. At this stage, the instructor's role is to provide mediation (often by providing prompts for teams to think about and discuss) and additional resources as needed by individual teams.

Drafting and Revision

Now the drafting/revising process can begin. Team members can write individually, but their contributions are compiled into a shared document all members can see, comment on, question, and edit continuously throughout the drafting stage. This collaborative writing process is different from more typical divide-and-conquer approaches in that teams have already established their ideas together, agreed on an organization and sources, and cycled through several rounds of refinements—firmly establishing the team perspective. Though each team member may generate specific sections of text, the other team members are deeply involved both through their prior contributions and through ongoing editing and rounds of peer review within the team. During this part of the process, the instructor can view the shared document and provide support, but the team is still the driving force. To guide further progress, the instructor may use subtle prompts such as "How might we . . . ?" or "Can you tell me more . . . ?" language, as this allows students to correct, clarify, or expand their ideas while retaining agency and limiting defensiveness on the part of the writers. The team may cycle through peer review followed by revisiting the literature (to address gaps, inconsistencies, etc.), at which point the team reconciles the new information with their prior text and revises the draft. This cycle repeats until the team does not find gaps, inconsistencies, or other triggers to revisiting the literature. At certain points in the class, a draft is due to the instructor, who can then provide feedback appropriate to the progress stage of the draft. The benchmarks for earlier drafts are different from subsequent drafts (see figure 7.6 for an example of a state-of-the-draft rubric).

Dissemination

In the field of psychology, researchers/scholars are expected to disseminate their ideas to the broader community within the discipline and, increasingly, to lay audiences. Typically, this dissemination is accomplished through the publication of manuscripts and, to a lesser extent, books. In addition, professionals in psychology typically present their ideas at specialized conferences in the form of talks or posters. Obviously, it is beyond the scope of any course to yield student publications, but it is typical for students to present their work at the end of a course, and in psychology this display generally takes the form of a talk or poster. We strongly encourage this final step in the writing process since it allows teams to share their ideas and progress with other teams and the instructor. The timing of this step is somewhat arbitrary in that it is based on external semester timelines rather than the state of the project. Given this, teams may present work at different stages of completion. However, all individuals should demonstrate their full engagement in the team process through their deep familiarity with and understanding of the project (e.g., ability to answer questions about the project). Thus, the final course deliverable becomes evidence of full engagement with the project ideas and their development, as well as the team-writing process, rather than a fully realized final product.

Adopting this developmentally informed team-based solution to writing instruction necessitates changes in how we evaluate performance, moving from absolute assessments of a final product to progress-based assessments throughout the process. This shift can seem daunting, but we believe committing to this process will itself have a normalizing effect. We need to relax (or preferably discard) the assumption that students will be professional-level writers after a single course. Instead the goal should be to give students ample opportunity to practice disciplinary thinking and writing in a developmentally conscious, challenging yet supportive environment (Ambrose et al. 2010), along with some valuable strategies they can use in future opportunities to practice their professional writing. The next section provides strategies and tools for assessing student writing in this way.

DITBS Evaluative Element: Using Process-Focused Assessment of Collaborative Writing

Traditionally, the primary goal of assessing student written work has been to determine whether students have successfully learned genre-specific writing. However, such grading often relies on a rubric that reduces genre-specific writing to a list of easily quantifiable metrics, such as number of APA style mistakes; number of sources used; whether the sources are the correct type; whether each required section is present; quality of transitions; grammar/spelling/typos; organization of ideas. However, we argue that this type of summative assessment does not capture the process each individual and the team worked through in order to arrive at the final product. A "quality" final product that was primarily written by one student with little-to-no interaction with the rest of the group would get a high score on this type of rubric but actually would not have successfully taught students how to engage in genre-specific writing or collaboration; a team of coauthors in psychology would not function in this way. Through the Fellows Program, we have become convinced that the entire writing process (from brainstorming through dissemination), and the progress made throughout, is what should be the primary focus of assessment rather than the quality of the final written product. In order to support team development through both individual and team accountability (Sibley and Ostafichuk 2014), formative assessments throughout the process should occur at both the individual and team levels. Here we provide several example methods for assessing the collaborative writing process while honoring both individual and team contributions.

CRISP Tables

Individual methods of assessment may focus on individual or team assignments as long as the individual contributions are identifiable. Individual assignments might focus on preparing students to actively engage in upcoming team discussions. For example, after reading a review article in the team's chosen topic area, individual students use CRISP tables (see figure 7.3) to record information from the article they found to be critical, relevant, interesting, surprising, and worth including in the team project. Such an assignment goes beyond asking students to summarize the information they read—summaries can be written without much cognitive involvement and perhaps without reading the entire article. Instead the CRISP table prompts students to evaluate and react to information presented in the article prior to the team meeting to discuss the article. This facilitates individual preparedness and willingness

Name: ______________________
Team #: __________ **Team Topic:** ______________________
Review paper full reference (APA style):

****

CRISP Table

C = Critical information to guide team topic
R = Relevant to team topic
I = Interesting idea/approach
S = Surprising (worth discussing with team)
P = Project (would like to see this incorporated into the team project – e.g., a particular methodology)

For each of the columns, add a bulleted list of critical, relevant, interesting, surprising, and project ideas. You will likely be able to identify at least 2-3 for each column.

C	R	I	S	P

Figure 7.3. CRISP table used by students to prepare for team discussion of a review paper from the literature. The CRISP table increases individual accountability and provides a product for assessment of individual contributions.

to contribute to the team discussion. Typically, it also promotes practice in considering multiple perspectives within team discussions.

Paper Survey

The Paper Survey (see figure 7.4) also asks students to individually process their reading prior to participating in a team discussion of the paper. Students are asked to personally reflect on an empirical research paper and then are prompted to consider specific relationships between the paper and their team project. These possible relationships include whether the paper might contribute to the team's development of their project background, methodology, future directions, and so forth. This reflection pushes students to process the information deeply in that it does not allow for a simple binary judgment of whether the paper is on a topic relevant to the team project. Instead, students are asked to consider one type of relationship, then consider another type of relationship, and so on, which allows them to practice the type of thought and writing-feedback loop central in the knowledge-transforming stage.

Name: ____________________
Team #: ________ **Team Topic:** ____________________
Empirical paper full reference (APA style):

****

Paper Survey

Respond to each statement below according to the following rating scale:

1 = very much agree
2 = agree
3 = neither agree nor disagree
4 = disagree
5 = very much disagree

Fill in the blanks providing your reasons for your ratings.

	Statement	Rating
1.	I enjoyed reading this paper.	
	Reason:	
2.	This paper provides relevant background for the team project.	
	Reason:	
3.	This paper may provide useful methodology for use in the team project.	
	Reason:	
4.	This paper provides some ideas for future directions/follow-up experiments.	
	Reason:	
5.	This paper references other papers that will be useful for the team project.	
	Reason:	
6.	I agree with the authors interpretations of their findings.	
	Reason:	

Figure 7.4. Paper survey used by students to prepare for team discussion of an empirical paper from the literature. The survey encourages individual reflection on specific aspects of the paper prior to the team discussion.

Color-Coded Brainstorming Sessions

Making individual contributions visible is key in terms of assessing the process the teams engage in. For example, without identifiable individual contributions, a process in which one student does the bulk of the work with little input from other students is indistinguishable from a process in which every student contributes. An effective method that makes individual contributions visible at the time of assessment, but also to the team members during the process, is to ask students to color code contributions by team members. During brainstorming tasks, this coding can be done easily with different colored Post-it notes stuck on a large sheet of paper or on the wall, or different ink colors for writing on a large sheet of paper (see figure 7.5). This approach can easily be adapted for online classes using different-colored text boxes or fonts.

In terms of assessment, an expectation can be set for how many total ideas must be generated and the minimum number per team member. Contrast this to the traditional approach of assessing a submitted topic or other product in which the process the team used to generate the

Figure 7.5. Team brainstorming session in which students make contributions on Post-its and in writing using assigned individual colors

submitted item cannot be determined and thus assessment cannot account for engagement in the full process.

State-of-the-Draft Rubrics

Throughout this chapter, we make the case that the process should matter more than the final product for a number of reasons. With a focus on the process, strong team performance requires the participation of every team member. However, with a focus on the final product, strong team performance only necessitate participation by the most skilled team member(s). Assessment of drafts must be congruent with messaging about the importance of the process, otherwise students (rightfully) lose trust in the approach. Joanna Wolfe (2010) suggests first articulating to students what "state" their draft is in (early, middle, late) and then providing feedback congruent with the state of the draft. This takes the pressure off the most skilled group member to simply create or take over the editing of the final product in order to get the best grade possible. Instead, everyone's participation is crucial and does not negatively impact the team grade even if they are not as skilled yet.

See figure 7.6 for an example of a state-of-the draft rubric that differentiates among an early, middle, and late draft and points students

"Early Draft"	"Middle Draft"	"Late Draft"	Instructor Comments
Narrative is incomplete, does not sufficiently address Incident/Design problem (Description, Analysis (e.g., Norman's action cycle; Vicente's HT ladder), "Solution"). Format (length/language) is not appropriate for project. Few members of team have contributed/ fulfilled their agreed upon roles	Narrative is complete and addresses some key aspects of Incident/Design problem (Description, Analysis (e.g., Norman's action cycle; Vicente's HT ladder), "Solution"). Format (length/language) is appropriate for project but may not be accessible to broad audience. Most members of team have contributed/ fulfilled their agreed upon roles	Narrative is complete and explicitly addresses all aspects of Incident/Design problem (Description, Analysis (e.g., Norman's action cycle; Vicente's HT ladder), "Solution"). Format (length/language) is appropriate for project and accessible to broad audience. All members of team have contributed/ fulfilled their agreed upon roles	
Next Steps: Strongly consider revision, making sure to address deficits in content and formatting. Reviewing project overview/ course content recommended. Revisions should be done in consultation with the team and instructor.	**Next Steps:** Possible revision, check for details that need to/should be added. Check language to ensure that an intelligent but non-expert can understand your project. Continue to communicate with team/instructor as appropriate.	**Next Steps:** Think about possible outlets for this project. Who would benefit from this information? Would there need to be revisions to accommodate potential audiences. Continue to communicate with team/instructor as appropriate.	

Figure 7.6. Sample state-of-the-draft rubric for a course in human factors; note there are both content and process benchmarks.

toward the next steps based on where the current draft is. Note there is no judgment; it is not bad to be at an early-draft stage. Instead, the rubric clarifies for students why the draft is in that state and how to move it along to the next state.

CONCLUSION

As we document in this chapter, significant issues make teaching discipline-specific writing in psychology challenging. In particular we identify three issues that emerged as we participated in the Fellows Program: (1) incongruence among instructor expectations, writing assignments, and student ability; (2) overutilization of individualized approaches and assessment; (3) overemphasis on a polished final product. We propose a developmentally informed team-based approach to writing capable of addressing each of these challenges, with its focus on collaboration and the creation of high-performing teams. We believe collaborative writing can be a highly effective mechanism for helping each individual student progress in their professional-writing competency. Our proposed solution is in line with how professional writing in psychology occurs, with adequate time (and reinforcement of effort) allocated to all aspects of the writing process, from brainstorming, through idea generation and refinement, drafting and revision, and ultimately to dissemination. This approach is necessarily accompanied by a change in how writing is assessed, moving away from individual competencies and product benchmarks toward collaborative, process-oriented assessments.

The team-process and assessment sections highlight the benefits of implementing a team-based writing-development approach and how that might be assessed differently from traditional "finished-APA-paper" assignments. This approach addresses logistics but still leaves the issue of how we move students forward in their writing development. Often the intangible or "soft" aspects (argumentation, perspective taking) of writing are difficult to teach in courses in which the emphasis has been on getting the mechanics of "APA style" (Ishak and Salter 2017; Moran 2013). The emphasis on APA style can provide the structure of writing (and provide an easy means of assessment) but not necessarily the meaning/understanding of writing (as an analogy: infant babbling typically has the structure of the to-be-learned language without itself being meaningful). This myopic focus on APA style can create artificial constraints on how material is presented and inherently produce writing that averages across different writing styles and perspectives to achieve "objectivity." This focus is problematic in that the processes we are suggesting in this chapter depend on the inclusion and value of multiple perspectives. Vrinda Kalia (this volume, chapter 12) reminds us we must consider the known implicit biases that operate among individuals within diverse teams. Such biases influence unspoken value judgments regarding individual contributions, potentially undermining the benefits of the collaborative approach. Instructors have a responsibility to remain cognizant of these issues and carefully monitor the team processes, perhaps by making these issues explicit within the classroom, in an effort to guard against these biases.

Prior to participating in the Fellows Program, we would have approached updating the writing assignments in our classes very differently. We might have talked about how to increase student motivation or accountability. We would have considered areas in which students still make mistakes on the final draft (usually APA style) and designed additional scaffolding, and perhaps a quiz, to make sure they are getting all the details on these conventions. Our updates to our writing assignments would have focused on ways to refine the final draft of the paper, to get closer to the A+ paper.

However, after learning about the developmental stages of writing and threshold concepts, we now realize these small adjustments would not create real change. Instead we discovered meaningful change comes from aligning our writing assignments with the developmental stage of writing our students are most likely in and then focusing our assignments on introducing and reinforcing (through practice) the threshold concepts related to that stage. In particular, our recommendations incorporate the threshold concept that "writing is a . . . social activity" (Roozen 2015) while still focusing on accountability. The state-of-the-draft rubrics honor the threshold concept that learning to write is a continual activity without an endpoint (Rose 2016). Finally, adjusting expectations to be in line with student abilities and limited working-memory capacity were crucial in addressing the threshold concept that "writing is a . . . cognitive activity" (Dryer 2015). Team-based writing became an effective strategy to facilitate engagement with these threshold concepts; without the developmental approach and the threshold concepts we incorporated, our team-based approach would likely just be more group work that does not actually meet students' needs or promote deep learning.

There are a number of challenges going forward. Developmental approaches are intended to foster skill acquisition over time, certainly in longer timeframes than a single course or semester. Though we can take a common approach across our own courses, it will take a considerable effort to implement systematic change across the departmental curriculum. Until there is a systematic implementation of the developmentally informed team-based approach, students in our courses may have some adjustment pains as they navigate new and different expectations and processes. For example, students may initially have a difficult time understanding the focus on the state of the draft as a genuine approach to improving their work at whatever level they are at versus focusing on how to get to the "top" level (spoiler: there is no top level).

We assert in this chapter that the use of team structures and processes can help build these "soft" but professionally relevant writing skills. Our approach, which allows more time to be devoted to idea generation, refinement, and consideration of multiple perspectives will promote the development of transferable skills necessary to communicate effectively in psychology and beyond.

REFERENCES

Ambrose, Susan A., Michael W. Bridges, Michele DiPietro, Marsha C. Lovett, and Marie K. Norman. 2010. *How Learning Works: Seven Research-Based Principles for Smart Teaching.* San Francisco: Jossey-Bass.

Birmingham, Carolyn, and Mary McCord. 2004. "Group Process Research: Implications for Using Learning Groups." In *Team-Based Learning: A Transformative Use of Small Groups in College Teaching, edited by* Larry K. Michaelsen, Arletta Bauman Knight, and L. Dee Fink, 73–93. Sterling, VA: Stylus.

Brown, John Seely, Allan Collins, and Paul Duguid. 1989. "Situated Cognition and the Culture of Learning." *Educational Researcher* 18 (1): 32–42.

Carter, Michael. 1990. "The Idea of Expertise: An Exploration of Cognitive and Social Dimensions of Writing." *College Composition and Communication* 41(3): 265–86.

Dryer, Dylan B. 2015. "Writing Is (Also Always) a Cognitive Activity." In *Naming What We Know: Threshold Concepts of Writing Studies, edited by* Linda Adler-Kassner and Elizabeth Wardle, 71–74. Logan: Utah State University Press.

Fink, L. Dee. 2004. "Beyond Small Groups: Harnessing the Extraordinary Power of Learning Teams." In *Team-Based Learning: A Transformative Use of Small Groups in College Teaching,* edited by Larry K. Michaelsen, Arletta Bauman Knight, and L. Dee Fink, 3–26. Sterling, VA: Stylus.

Gobet, F., and H. A. Simon. 1996. "Recall of Random and Distorted Chess Positions: Implications for the Theory of Expertise." *Memory & Cognition* 24 (4): 493–503.

Harrison, David A., Kenneth H. Price, and Myrtle P. Bell.1998. "Beyond Relational Demography: Time and Effects of Surface- and Deep-Level Diversity on Work Group Cohesion." *Academy of Management Journal* 41 (1): 96–107.

Henriksen, Dorte. 2016. "The Rise in Co-authorship in the Social Sciences (1980–2013)." *Scientometrics* 107 (2): 455–76.

Hunter, Kerry, and Harry Tse. 2013. "Making Disciplinary Writing and Thinking Practices an Integral Part of Academic Content Teaching." *Active Learning in Higher Education* 14 (3): 227–39.

Ishak, Shaziela, and Nicholas P. Salter. 2017. "Undergraduate Psychological Writing: A Best Practices Guide and National Survey." *Teaching of Psychology* 44 (1): 5–17.

Kelley, Tom. 2001. *The Art of Innovation: Lessons in Creativity from IDEO, America's Leading Design Firm.* New York: Currency/Doubleday.

Kellogg, Ronald T. 2008. "Training Writing Skills: A Cognitive Developmental Perspective." *Journal of Writing Research* 1 (1): 1–26. https://doi.org/10.17239/jowr-2008.01.01.1.

Latané, Bibb, Kipling Williams, and Stephen Harkins. 1979. "Many Hands Make Light the Work: The Causes and Consequences of Social Loafing." *Journal of Personality and Social Psychology* 37 (6): 822–32.

McAllister, Daniel J. 1995. "Affect- and Cognition-Based Trust as Foundations for Interpersonal Cooperation in Organizations." *Academy of Management Journal* 38 (1): 494–504.

Meyer, Jan, and Ray Land. 2003. "Threshold Concepts and Troublesome Knowledge: Linkages to Ways of Thinking and Practising within the Disciplines." ETL Occasional Report 4. Edinburgh: University of Edinburgh. http://www.etl.tla.ed.ac.uk/docs/ETL report4.pdf.

Meyer, Jan H. F., and Ray Land. 2006. "Threshold Concepts and Troublesome Knowledge: Issues of Liminality." *Overcoming Barriers to Student Understanding,* 19–32. New York: Routledge.

Michaelsen, Larry K. 2004. "Getting Started with Team-Based Learning." In *Team-Based Learning: A Transformative Use of Small Groups in College Teaching, edited by* Larry K. Michaelsen, Arletta Bauman Knight, and L. Dee Fink, 27–50. Sterling, VA: Stylus.

Moen, Ron. 2001. "A Review of the IDEO Process." https://rwjf.org/content/dam/web-assets/2001/10/a-review-of-the-ideo-process.

Moran, Katherine E. 2013. "Exploring Undergraduate Disciplinary Writing: Expectations and Evidence in Psychology and Chemistry." PhD diss., Georgia State University. https://scholarworks.gsu.edu/alesl_diss/24.

Norman, Donald. 2013. *The Design of Everyday Things*. Rev. and expanded ed. New York: Basic Books.

Roozen, Kevin. 2015. "Writing Is a Social and Rhetorical Activity." In *Naming What We Know: Threshold Concepts of Writing Studies*, edited by Linda Adler-Kassner and Elizabeth Wardle, 17–19. Logan: Utah State University Press.

Rose, Shirley. 2015. "All Writers Have More to Learn." In *Naming What We Know: Threshold Concepts of Writing Studies*, edited by Linda Adler-Kassner and Elizabeth Wardle, 59–61. Logan: Utah State University Press.

Sibley, Jim, and Pete Ostafichuk. 2014. *Getting Started with Team-Based Learning*. Sterling, VA: Stylus.

Simms, Ashley, and Tommy Nichols. 2014. "Social Loafing: A Review of the Literature." *Journal of Management Policy and Practice* 15 (1): 58.

Wardle, Elizabeth, and Doug Downs. 2020. "Participating in Conversational Inquiry about Writing." In *Writing about Writing*, 54–79. Boston: Bedford/St. Martin's.

White, Ken D., Len Dalgleish, and G. Arnold. 1982. "Authorship Patterns in Psychology: National and International Trends." *Bulletin of the Psychonomic Society* 20 (4): 190–92.

Wolfe, Joanna. 2010. *Team Writing: A Guide to Working in Groups*. Boston: Bedford/St. Martin's.

8

GIVING WORDS TO WHAT WE SEE

Threshold Concepts in Writing Art History

Annie Dell'Aria, Jordan A. Fenton, and Pepper Stetler
Art and Architecture History

INTRODUCTION

The work of art history is accomplished almost exclusively through words, rather than charts, tables, or graphs. The process of translating what is seen to written analysis is the most fundamental task of the discipline. Yet it is difficult to articulate and externalize the role of writing in art history to students. As scholars and teachers of art history, we came together through the Howe Faculty Writing Fellows Program to discuss how our students enter the liminal space of art history. Our goal was to develop strategies to help our students overcome their uncertainties about how or why to articulate the appearance and meaning of what they see. Our students often assume what they see—in a work of art or in the everyday world—is self-evident and universally understood. Engaging students in the process of writing art history requires them to work through key threshold concepts that define the discipline and transpose the necessary attentiveness, time, and patience required in looking closely at art and interpreting it through written language.

In this chapter, we explain how we help students gradually develop a complex understanding of the gaps in translation between vision and writing, the conditioning of art and its experience by historical and cultural circumstances, and the ability of art and visual practices to withstand multiple, productive forms of interpretation. By passing through these threshold concepts, students become aware of how the skills of art historical analysis extend beyond the world of art to the training of more discerning twenty-first-century citizens. The broader takeaways in this chapter are scaffolding course assignments, being transparent with the intended outcomes of assignments with your students, and having meaningful, long-term dialogues and conversations with your immediate colleagues. Such conversations help identify threshold concepts and

https://doi.org/10.7330/9781646423040.c008

develop meaningful strategies to better engage with them, especially with core disciplinary classes taught on a rotational basis. The Fellows Program offered us a formal space in which to actively engage in weekly discussions about curriculum improvement that went well beyond any informal conversation about teaching or syllabus sharing we have had in the past.

We were unfamiliar with research on threshold concepts before the Howe Faculty Writing Fellows Program. While the study of threshold concepts has been transforming the pedagogical approach to higher education for decades, it has made little headway into the field of art history (Loeffler and Wuetherick 2012). The Fellows Program gave us the time to study how our students progress through our curriculum. When do students seem to struggle with particular conventions and concepts? When do they begin to master them? In order to develop the answers to these questions, we had to reflect on how we teach writing and how we write and think as art historians. Through our conversations, we discovered a greater need to be honest and transparent with students about the style and format of writing art history and why these conventions have been established. We also learned about the importance of being transparent with our students when assigning written prompts. This level of transparency helped students better understand the overall goals and intended outcomes of assigned work. We feel such openness fostered a level of appreciation in our students when they started to better understand why various assignments were indeed assigned.

The art and architecture history program at Miami University is relatively small (five full-time faculty) but geographically and temporally broad in academic focus. Our challenge as Fellows was to identify threshold concepts that emphasized a journey of learning and development, rather than privileging one methodology or frame of interpretation. Even a statement as broad as "art is a language," suggested as a threshold concept of art history by Elizabeth Loeffler and Brad Wuetherick (2012), privileges one system of meaning over another. Expectations for how art makes meaning develop differently in various cultural and geographic contexts. Therefore, we found privileging any one frame of interpretation often meant privileging a European-American perspective. Despite the clear need to be sensitive to interdisciplinary differences—how, for example, interpreting an object made in Nigeria in the nineteenth century can look vastly different than the ways of interpreting a twenty-first-century video projection—consistent disciplinary practices emerged. Through our many conversations, we realized we all want our students to learn to reflect on the language they use to write about art and on the perspective they take when interpreting it.

In what follows, we explain the three threshold concepts we developed for our program as Howe Faculty Writing Fellows. These threshold concepts motivate how we teach a global art history. In the following three sections, we describe the development and teaching of three threshold concepts that form the core of our 200-level writing-intensive course all three of us teach, albeit in our own, nuanced ways. We see that these three threshold concepts are imperative for not only learning the basics of writing in art history but also succeeding in more advanced, upper-level art historical courses.

In general, we expect students to pass through these concepts in the order we discuss them below, but due to the messy, nonlinear nature of learning, this order is not universal. We also acknowledge that each threshold concept can be approached with various degrees of complexity and that each might never be fully mastered or passed through. Ultimately, we want our students to gain an increasingly complex perspective on these concepts and a fuller understanding of why they are so essential to the discipline of art history and to the study of human culture more generally. The first threshold concept addresses immediate connections between looking and writing, shaping an approach to the translation between these realms before more interpretive challenges are addressed in the other two threshold concepts.

THRESHOLD CONCEPT 1

It is not easy to write what you see. If seeing establishes our place in the world, art history is a tool to make sense of the visual world in which we all live.

We came to our threshold concepts by reflecting on two things: what our students struggle with the most about the disciplinary practices of art history and why we have dedicated our professional careers to the idea that the study of art history is essential for the development of more conscientious citizens in the twenty-first century. Our approach to teaching writing aims to find a balance between disciplinary writing (acknowledging that all writing is disciplinary and it is not possible to teach writing in general) and communicating the value of writing about art to the values and goals of a liberal arts education. To strike this balance, we emphasize that becoming more careful, scrutinizing interpreters of the visual will make our students better twenty-first-century citizens.

One of the first discussions we had as Writing Fellows focused on identifying the tasks and assignments our students find most challenging and addressing what preconceptions about practices of looking they might have internalized that caused them to struggle. We noticed students underestimate the patience and time it takes to look closely at a work of art. They expect meaning from visual information to be transparent and immediately clear. Students also assume what they describe is apparent to everyone else. If vision is a shared sense, then description seems unnecessary and redundant. While we did not study the motivations for these assumptions among our students in any formal way, we surmised that their visual habits and expectations are shaped by our current screen culture. Capitalist marketing practices cultivate immediate consumer responses, and social media practices are based in clicking on, sharing, and commenting on visual information. While our current screen culture promises our students what some have called "visual literacy," it also instills a demand for immediacy and instant gratification. In contrast, art historical interpretation demands a slower pace.

The process of looking and translating what we see into words takes time. This alone is a troublesome concept for students in the twenty-first century, who have a seemingly ingrained understanding of the instantaneousness of our digital world. In our introductory courses, students must traverse a gap between the consumption of visual information in their everyday lives and what is expected in the disciplinary practice of looking, writing, and interpretation. Writing assignments at the introductory level aim to confront students with the idea that looking is a temporally unfolding process. The noninstantaneous nature of looking informs the threshold concept we developed—that looking and writing are not synonymous practices.

Our next task was to develop class activities and assignments that help students interrogate their own visual habits and compare those habits to what art history is asking them to do. We realized we needed to have more explicit conversations with students about the relationship between looking and writing. We were excited to have conversations with our students about the value of art history to the twenty-first-century world. This was an opportunity to define art history as a way of seeing and experiencing the world instead of the memorization of historical names and dates, which is all-too-often the task our students associate with the discipline.

To initiate such a conversation, students might read art historical texts that model such a discussion on looking. Michael Baxandall (1985) begins his book on the practice of writing art history by stating, "We do not explain pictures, we explain remarks about pictures" (1). Baxandall, an art historian who connected practices of seeing to cultural circumstances in ways that are now fundamental to the discipline, unknowingly coined a fundamental threshold concept of art history. When students read the introduction to his *Patterns of Intention* in our course, Writing and the Visual Arts, they initially find Baxandall's dissection of statements about art to be cumbersome and tedious. Baxandall complicates the translation between looking and writing by inserting an intermediary step. Writing about what is seen is a process of interrogating how and why something is seen. Why, for example, do interpretations of works of art shift and change over time? Why does a work of art mean one thing for a seventeenth-century viewer but mean something entirely different in the twenty-first century?

For Baxandall, the simplest descriptions of any work of art are complex. The words the writer chooses to describe a work of art say as much, if not more, about the discursive identity of the writer than about the work of art itself. As exasperating as they might find Baxandall's meta-analysis of analysis, the text demonstrates to our beginning students that what art historians mean when they talk about description is anything but straightforward. Describing works of art involves choices, and those choices are informed by the unique circumstances of the writer. Another way of thinking about this is that description in art history does not aspire to reproduce a work of art in any comprehensive way. It aims to draw a reader's attention to what might be overlooked and redirect the perspective from which a work of art's meaning might be understood. It leads the student to engage with the process of teasing meaning from looking. A path of research and interpretation might be implied in the way students choose to describe it.

Giving students the opportunity to become accustomed to the slower pace of art history helps them notice the gap between looking and writing. We cultivate an awareness of this gap through writing. For instance, in an in-class activity, a student describes a work of art projected on the classroom screen to a partner who is facing away from the screen and is unable to see the work of art. Then the partners reverse roles. From this exercise, which also serves as a preliminary form of peer feedback and review, students notice two things. First, they have described the work differently from their partner, and these differences imply different meanings and interpretations that could be developed about the work of art. Second, precise description requires a shared disciplinary vocabulary.

The second assignment asks students to spend an uncomfortable amount of time in front of a work of art they choose at the Miami University Art Museum. This approach was inspired by a paper the art historian Jennifer Roberts gave at Harvard University in 2013 (Roberts

2013). Roberts asks her students to write a research paper based on an analysis of a single work of art. To prepare for the paper, students are expected to spend at least three hours looking at the work of art in person. We do not require the full three hours, but we do spend a full class period (an hour and twenty minutes) in the art museum rigorously studying our individual selection, and we ask students to return to the art museum at another time for at least thirty minutes to observe on their own. Students keep a temporal log of their observations so they can reflect on how new observations open up over time. Students usually find the process foreign and tedious, but they are often surprised by how their observations change. With so much time for reflection, the activity helps students challenge their own observations. The writing assignment emphasizes reflection on the process of looking and forces students to understand looking as a process. From these written observations, students are then asked to reflect on what research questions they might pursue about the work of art they have studied, suggesting there is a certain limit to what knowledge can be gained from visual observation alone.

We designed these introductory-level assignments to raise our students' consciousness about the practice of looking and to make them aware of the challenges of translating that practice to writing. We have found that having a conversation centered around a key text, implementing the practices of looking we want our students to attempt, and then asking them to reflect upon how those practices increase their sensitivity to the close, sustained, and patient looking art history demands prepares them to both write insightful descriptions and develop meaningful interpretive inquiries for research. It also provides a space to compare this kind of looking to the practices they are more familiar with as members of the screen culture of the twenty-first century. Through this comparison, their own habits can be dislodged from the naturalized behavior of capitalist looking, making the familiar seem liberatingly less so.

THRESHOLD CONCEPT 2

All art is conditioned by historical and cultural circumstances. Art history endeavors to understand these circumstances or contexts in order to explain the crucial role art occupies in humanity. The contexts that produced the work of art help art historians contextualize why art matters.

Students struggle with the complex relationship between looking and writing. Interpreting and drawing conclusions about what they see is usually the next challenge students face. Often our students see art as open to the interpretation of the viewer and their evaluation of its quality (judging art as good or bad). These misconceptions are, once again, most likely grounded in the easy manipulation and circulation of images in the twenty-first century. In contrast, we want our students to generate art historical interpretations grounded in knowledge and research about specific cultures and historical events relevant to a work of art. Engaging context, our second threshold concept, is thus foundational to any art historical analysis, as well as to understanding any work of art or artistic intent.

Understanding context is crucial for grasping the ways humans and the environment breathe life into works of art. That life or energy is also contingent on the personhood of the individuals who privately, publicly, or collectively create or engage with said works of art. Those individuals, and often the broader environment, bring with them their own experiences, perceptions, forces, and ideas that forge a layered and thus myriad of contextual frames that all artists tap into. And as people engage or perform differently, and at different times, with an artist's piece, especially over the changing lifespan of a given work, the public context and thus interpretation of art are in a constant state of flux. The importance of context is not unlike how art historians understand this as a crucial threshold concept. If we take the notion of context even further, it provides a perfect frame for understanding the role, importance, and layered challenges in teaching context to beginning art history students.

While identifying the importance of context is easy for students, understanding that various contexts do not stand on their own but usually overlap, and even change over time, is more difficult to grasp. As a challenge for teaching context, it further ebbs and flows through time and space as people interpret works of art from different time periods or from different perspectives. This latter aspect of teaching context is crucial for bridging the gap between the threshold concepts of looking and writing and the last concept discussed below, multiple frames of interpretation. Context is thus the glue that, when properly applied, can seamlessly fuse together the challenges of looking and writing while helping students position their discussion in the broader discourses that frame their selected topics. Understanding context as a mediating analytical tool provides yet another messy facet to teaching the importance of context in art historical writing.

For students, the fact that art is never understood by its visual appearance or form alone is challenging. Contextual analysis helps to start to overcome this misconception and guides students in how to analyze and make arguments with art. A basic goal of art history is to place a work of art within its historic, religious, political, economic, and aesthetic contexts. Only by unpacking the circumstances that give rise to a work of art is one able to communicate how art matters and how its meanings change through time and place.

A writing assignment developed to hone the ability to conduct contextual analysis serves as a mechanism to help students understand this second threshold concept. Building from the visual-analysis paper (described above), this assignment asks students to return to their local art museum to select another work of art from an entirely different area of the world and made for a different purpose than the first piece selected for the formal analysis. In this way, the selected artworks for this paper include one made for museum or gallery display and a second that appears to be made for a ritual, performance, or festive event. In most cases, but certainly not all, this assignment presents students with the difficult task of comparing a Western work of art to another from Africa, Asia, Oceania, or Native America (see chapter 9 for teaching the threshold concept of Otherness in a course on the latter). After selecting the additional object for the assignment, during a class held at the local museum, students formally analyze it, being sure this time to employ the process of closely looking to stimulate questions for the contextualization of the object.

The assignment's specific aim is to have students contextualize both objects and then compare and contrast the contextual aspects of the works of art. The assignment requires students to engage with at least two contextual frames that bring together both pieces, essentially asking them to produce a cross-cultural analysis. For example, a paper could compare the political or religious contexts of both pieces, discussing their similarities and differences, while still addressing the artistic, albeit from a more ideological or spiritual context. By this time in the class, the various contexts typical to art historical analysis (politics, religion, society, culture, education, economics, aesthetics, etc.) have been engaged with through course readings, class discussion, and in-class activities.

Another layer to this writing assignment is that it requires research. In order for students to analyze and compare two appropriate contexts for comparison, students must engage with the literature written on the selected objects, artists, cultures, or related fields. With this in mind, we make it a point to assign a specific number of peer-reviewed sources (in this case five). Class meetings, discussions, and required readings running parallel with this assignment are designed to help students properly conduct research, effectively engage with scholarly literature, and learn how to paraphrase important ideas, curbing the tendency to insert long passages of quoted material into their text.

As part of our efforts to be more transparent with students about the writing process, we have conversations in class about the styles and conventions of writing for different audiences. We demonstrate these differences by reading texts written for a variety of different audiences and talking about the different stylistic choices. We realized that when we make assignments, we should specify the audience for which they should be written. For the context-and-comparison assignment, we ask them to consider the audience for this paper is a group of art historians and museum curators who are developing a cross-cultural thematic art-museum exhibition based on the objects and contexts students selected to explore. The goal of the paper is to convince this group of scholars to select pieces for the thematic show. We find this task helps mitigate the stress associated with students struggling to develop their own tone and prose with persuasive and argumentative writing.

In the end, this assignment, scaffolded from the visual-analysis paper previously discussed, helps students grapple with how contexts are layered and temporally situated and how they overlap and change over time. Students also start to understand that not all relevant contextual information must be included in the written narrative. The use of footnotes is stressed in this assignment to help students understand that structure and flow sometimes relegate important yet secondary information to the margins of the text. We see that by engaging with a purely contextual analysis, students become more comfortable with constructing a broader framework for understanding how to effectively analyze works of art as primary sources and not something simply appreciated.

The last point is where this assignment shines: framing contextual analysis as a threshold concept in Writing in the Visual Arts helps students navigate the messiness of supporting persuasive styles of writing with art historical analysis. Before the Fellows Program, we noticed this assignment did not fully achieve its intended goal. Let's face it, this assignment is not all that glamorous for undergraduates—it's rather dry, boring, and frankly dull. However, we understand that honing the ability to place a work of art in its proper context, whether historic or contemporary, is key for learning how to successfully analyze art. After the Fellows Program, we started to realize that for an assignment like this one to be successful, taking a step back from it to explain to students the intended aim is crucial. In other words, among the many lessons of the Fellows Program, we learned the importance of an honest and transparent discussion with our students about how a seemingly mundane assignment like this one is meant to bring together the effective skill of deeply looking, contextual analysis, and the interpretation of art—essentially the three threshold concepts of writing about art history reinforced in one assignment. That level of honesty helps students understand the outcome of this assignment is not meant to stand on its own or be a polished publishable paper. Rather, the context-and-comparison assignment enables students to start to bridge the gap between deep looking and interpretive analysis.

The context-and-comparison assignment is thus a useful mediator between formal analysis and the more in-depth research paper meant to be the culmination of undergraduate art historical skills. While context may be the easiest of the three threshold concepts to grasp, it may be the most important for helping students overcome the daunting ability to move beyond the typical art-as-good-or-bad paradigm. If done correctly, contextual analysis in the field of art history helps one become familiar with how to use art to support persuasive writing. Returning to Goldsworthy's statement about how context breathes life into a work of art, if undergraduates start to embrace the idea that contextual analysis is indeed the life blood of art historical analysis, they take one step closer to entering the thresholds of the discipline.

THRESHOLD CONCEPT 3

> *Art historical writing involves multiple frames of interpretation and—perhaps more importantly—the ability to hold multiple frames in suspension at the same time while producing an original argument. While there is no one right interpretation of a work of art, some interpretations and scholarly arguments have more quality or staying power than others.*

Our third threshold concept acquaints students with scholarly discourse, and it most explicitly develops our students' growing confidence as art historians. As Writing Fellows, we discussed our concerns with our students' lack of confidence in their research and interpretations. Even our most advanced students often seemed to struggle to position their own scholarly arguments in relation to a larger body of scholarship about works of art. We needed to have a conversation with our students about how to assert their scholarly voice. Kenneth Burke (1941) famously describes rhetoric as entering into a room where a conversation is already in place, listening to that conversation, becoming a part of it as more people enter and leave the room, then leaving with the conversation going just as strong (110–11). When writing in art history, this problem is arguably compounded. Not only is the conversation in the room in full swing, but it is a terribly snobbish affair: speakers move confidently within a fancy art museum, pointing to paintings and sculptures with confident familiarity and a critical eye while name dropping, using unfamiliar vocabulary and terms from other languages, creating a cultural mystique that can intimidate almost anyone just entering the room. We seek to make this room, and the "unending conversation" of art history itself, more inviting for students and accepting of new voices.

Shepherding students through this threshold is particularly difficult, as it both builds upon and destabilizes the surefootedness gained from moving through the first two. A convincing scholarly argument hinges on clear visual analysis and the ability to contextualize works of art, but it can also point to different conclusions and readings based on those findings, dislodging meaning from any singular description or contextual filter. Art history itself becomes discursive, and art objects enter into different narratives and theories of the world. Research papers shepherd students through this difficult threshold concept, and our approach to it is informed by our own reflections on scholarly writing. In other words, we learned that teaching writing in art history involves honest and open conversations with our students and colleagues about the messiness of writing. We began showing students drafts of our own work and sharing with them our own frustrations and challenges with this tedious yet rewarding process.

The term paper, a point of dread for many students, should not be something completed in a flurry of work at the end of the term but rather the product of thoughtful engagement, drafting, feedback, revision, and collaboration throughout the semester. While students at this point have the foundation of the first two threshold concepts, constructing a scholarly argument still involves a shaky and unstable process, and we support this process through scaffolding. Scaffolding is adaptive and distinguished from one-time feedback, instead entailing "a reciprocal feedback process" that "enables the learner, over time, to be able to work with the task, content, or idea independently" (Renninger and List 2012, 2923). Our scaffolded approach involves demystifying scholarly writing and creating supportive space for students to work through messy ideas. We do this through multiple ways throughout the term: (1) we ask students to complete active reading assignments that ask them to annotate and mark up scholarly readings digitally or on paper, prompting them to learn art historical writing through example; (2) we point students toward internal and external resources and cultivate an encouraging environment for research inquiry; and (3) we build multiple stages of experimentation, feedback, revision, and celebration into the final paper process. In all, we seek to find ways to embrace the messy stages of writing and the liminal nature of threshold concepts while still scaffolding projects that can (ideally) stand on their own.

The scaffolded research paper asks students to begin working on their final paper early in the term, creating low-stakes assignments along the way to encourage accountability and provide supportive feedback (Dell'Aria 2016). In our classes, we work closely with staff at the Wertz Art and Architecture Library, who provide orientations at the library that are built into our syllabi and individual consultations with students upon appointment. We find that instructors should not assume students are acquainted with library resources, both physical and virtual, and walking them through how to locate materials, think of relevant keywords, and navigate the stacks is worth at least one class session. Holding a class in the library also allows students to begin their research process early, working through potential topics and ideas and seeing what is available.

After wading through some initial research at the library on general topics of interest related to the class, we ask students to write a research proposal with a preliminary bibliography. This two-paragraph assignment outlines their research question and primary methodologies. Students then read their proposals aloud in a roundtable discussion in class. This activity both provides early instructor and peer feedback and cultivates a community of research early in the semester. Students revise their proposals based on feedback and continue to support each other throughout the term through formal activities and informal class discussion.

As students dive into their topics, they are encouraged to widen their research. We sometimes require students to bring in three books they've checked out from the library for a "Research Show-and-Tell" activity. They swap books and each student is asked to locate relevant passages for their partner using the index, table of contents, chapter headings, and skimming and scanning. This activity both requires students to conduct research beyond digital resources and develops multiple reading skills relevant to research in the humanities. An annotated bibliography assignment a bit further into the term asks students to step back and summarize their findings and sketch out a draft thesis statement. We ask them to not only summarize each resource in their annotations but also to indicate how each resource will be relevant to their research question and possible argument.

Relating each source to their argument begins to move research through the third threshold—each book or article is not only a source of information or stand-alone argument but is also now part of a developing argument produced by an informed writer. Feedback at this point addresses gaps in research, as well as the nascent scholarly argument emerging in the draft thesis statement. Peer and instructor feedback evaluates draft thesis statements against the following questions, adapted from the IU Bloomington Writing Tutorial Services (Indiana University, n.d.):

- Does it take a stand?
- Does it justify the discussion?
- Does it express one main idea?
- Is it specific?

These guidelines help structure feedback and evaluation throughout the drafting process. Students anticipate that their thesis statement will evolve and change. Periodically asking them to take a step back and evaluate their argument—and incorporate peer feedback and readability—ushers them through multiple stages of revision.

Once students acquaint themselves with scholarly argumentation through reading and begin to chart their own pathways through frames of interpretation in their research, they next must develop their own arguments. This is perhaps the most daunting task we ask them to undertake, one that involves a great degree of uncertainty. To this end, we ask students to write drafts early and often, rewriting and revising along the way. We sometimes like to model this process by showing screenshots of our own messy scholarly works in progress. Though David Wood, Jerome S. Bruner, and Gail Ross (1976) argue that modeling is an important part of scaffolding as "an 'idealization' of the act to be performed" (98), we contend that modeling messiness and vulnerability are just as important. Having students read Anne Lamott's (1994) essay "Shitty First Drafts" from *Bird by Bird* when they begin their first rough drafts sparks discussion about our own approaches to drafting and the writing process. Students first produce an outline of their paper and a draft of two pages (which can be from anywhere in the paper) and receive feedback from two peers and the instructor. We also encourage students at this stage to work with consultants at the Howe Center for Writing Excellence and to make appointments during office hours.

In the final weeks, students complete full drafts and deliver presentations, moments when supportive and pointed feedback are essential. These drafts may include notations where students will build out an idea further or need to fact check, but they at least attempt to complete the argument. In addition to feedback from us, we build in time for peer feedback, which we argue reinforces critical reading skills and further

*Paper Author:*____

*Reviewer:*____

Abstract:
- After reading through the paper, summarize the argument in one succinct paragraph. Write an abstract for the paper.

Thesis:
- Is this argument clearly stated and are you convinced by it? Does it take a stand/justify the discussion/express one main idea? Is it specific?

Organization:
- Do you feel this paper was clearly organized?
- Do you have suggestions for arranging material differently, as a reader?

Evidence:
- Are the sources used effectively and cited properly to advance the argument?
- Assess the quality of the research sources used. Are they scholarly? Are there places they should look to help shore up the argument more?
- What holes do you see in this argument and how might the writer address them?

Revisions:
- What are your main suggestions for revisions?

Presentation:
- What visual and textual evidence would need to be included for the oral presentation?

Figure 8.1. Sample Peer-Review Template

cultivates a supportive environment. As part of a robust worksheet for peer evaluation (see figure 8.1), we ask students to write an abstract for their peer's paper. The author realizes whether or not their core idea comes across to a reader. This exercise moves students from considering a paper's overall takeaways to more granular usage of evidence and language, pointing to modes of revision and strategies for presentation.

We find building time for student presentations into the course schedule is a valuable way for the class to share their progress, and we encourage students to formulate their arguments well before the final due date. When possible, we structure class presentation days as miniconferences, which creates buzz and encourages students to find connections between papers and participate through question-and-answer sessions. When class size prohibits this kind of scheduling, our colleagues have created poster presentations in which students present to each other in small groups. In both instances, the research project is not simply something the professor and no one else reads but is part of an ongoing conversation happening throughout the term.

In the final revision stages that accompany or follow presentations, we begin to address polish and presentation, having worked through ideas in messy stages and "shitty first drafts." We want to encourage the production of clear, error-*light* final papers that could be sharable to a wider audience. To this end, we find value in creating brief in-class workshops that break down common problems we see in papers and allow students to ask questions in class. We do not assume students know how to insert footnotes, format margins, or follow disciplinary citation protocol, so we both demonstrate these skills in class and point the students to useful resources. These steps, which many instructors might balk at incorporating into class time (at the expense of content-related lecture or discussion), both take up less class time than expected and result in lower stress for students and more readable papers for instructors.

Throughout the research, writing, and revising process, we ask students to write informal reflections, which provide space for metacognitive understanding that extends what we learn in an art historical context to their broader studies. We also create opportunities for students to share their work with a wider audience through our capstone exhibition (for which students write all gallery material and curate a show at the Miami University Art Museum), our student journal *Effusions*, and symposia and conferences. By approaching the term paper as an opportunity to move through this third threshold concept, students become more prepared to enter their thoughts and ideas into the "unending conversation" of art history.

CONCLUSION

We believe higher education should "teach for deep learning and critical thinking that is transferable across contexts and that will enable learners to be productive and innovative citizens in a democracy," as is stated forcefully in chapter 1 of this volume. One of our main responsibilities as art historians is to make our students aware of the role visual practices play in being productive and innovative citizens. Learning art history is an opportunity to tear vision away from the dominant practices of consumption and ideological control that characterize the neoliberal university, as described by the editors of this volume. Most important, learning art history denaturalizes students' own visual habits and practices, opening them up to scrutiny and critique and making possible a richer and more patient human experience. As experts in the discipline, we often feel uncomfortable shifting our emphasis away from the precise and specific acquisition of knowledge about works of art (and we have not abandoned this entirely). However, we have found asking our students to interrogate their own practices of looking and interpretation makes art history relevant to all twenty-first-century viewers.

REFERENCES

Baxandall, Michael. 1985. *Patterns of Intention: On the Historical Explanation of Pictures.* New Haven, CT: Yale University Press.

Burke, Kenneth. 1941. *The Philosophy of Literary Form: Studies in Symbolic Action.* Baton Rouge: Louisiana State University Press.

Dell'Aria, Annie. 2016. "The Scaffolded Research Paper." *Art History Teaching Resources,* June 4. http://arthistoryteachingresources.org/2016/06/the-scaffolded-research-paper/.

Indiana University Bloomington Writing Tutorial Services. n.d. "How to Write a Thesis Statement." Accessed September 15, 2020. https://wts.indiana.edu/writing-guides/how-to-write-a-thesis-statement.html.

Lamott, Anne. 1994. *Bird by Bird: Some Instructions on Writing and Life.* New York: Pantheon.

Loeffler, Elizabeth, and Brad Wuetherick. 2012. "Exploring Threshold Concepts: An Example of a Threshold Concept in Art History." *Bridges* 11 (1): 7–9.

Renninger, K. Ann, and Alexandra List. 2012. "Scaffolding for Learning." In *Encyclopedia of the Sciences of Learning,* edited by Norber M. Seel, 2922–26. Boston: Springer.

Roberts, Jennifer L. 2013. "The Power of Patience, Teaching Students the Value of Deceleration and Immersive Attention." *Harvard Magazine,* November–December. https://www.harvardmagazine.com/2013/11/the-power-of-patience.

Wood, David, Jerome S. Bruner, and Gail Ross. 1976. "The Role of Tutoring in Problem Solving." *Journal of Child Psychology and Psychiatry and Allied Disciplines* 17 (2): 89–100.

9
TEACHING GLOBAL ART HISTORY
Otherness as a Threshold Concept

Jordan A. Fenton
Art and Architecture History

INTRODUCTION

During the spring semester of 2019, I participated in the Faculty Writing Fellows Program along with two of my art historical colleagues at Miami University, Annie Dell'Aria and Pepper Stetler.[1] As art historians we were particularly interested in learning how to more effectively teach writing to our students. The previous chapter is a collaboratively authored essay that looks closely at teaching threshold concepts of writing in art history. As the program developed, and as an art historian of African art, I began to merge my interests in developing pedagogical strategies for writing with the difficulties of teaching my introductory course on the arts of Africa, Oceania, and Native America to predominantly US students. In Fellows, I started to realize that the idea of Otherness, the core principle I use to endeavor to deconstruct the layers of cultural bias that comes with this material, was indeed a threshold concept.

In the narrative that follows, I provide a self-reflexive, first-person narrative of my journey of rethinking my teaching of diverse worldviews and ways of thinking that many US students may never have engaged with if it wasn't for globally-oriented general education requirements. Regardless of the nature of the class one is teaching, this chapter offers thoughts on helping students actively engage while avoiding the tendency of telling students what they need to know. I also consider how being transparent with assignment outcomes builds trust, that scaffolding is a valuable teaching tool, and finally, how writing is an effective means of thinking for students as they navigate the challenges of learning threshold concepts.

https://doi.org/10.7330/9781646423040.c009

OTHERNESS AS A THRESHOLD CONCEPT

The US education system has historically privileged Western narratives in its approach to art and culture, as well as in most other academic fields. For example, one art history course I currently teach, ART 162: African, Oceania, and Native America (hereafter AOA), was previously known in the field as "Primitive Art," "Tribal Art," or more recently by the acceptable, yet still Eurocentric, designation, "Non-Western" Art. Even the popular title "Global Art" is misinformed, vague, and limiting. These labels are based on longstanding forms of misconception lingering from colonialism and other exploitive moments in history. Most students come to the subject matter with prior knowledge and cultural assumptions that make the threshold concepts of the course—particularly the notion of Otherness—distinctly troublesome. In this chapter, I consider the ways the threshold concept of Otherness in art history is challenging for students. I offer specific pedagogical strategies that have been more and less helpful in assisting students as they move through the liminal space around this concept. This chapter also reflects on how the Writing Fellows Program helped me significantly rethink and change how I teach the threshold concept of Otherness.

One of the goals of the AOA course is for students to encounter their Western biases inherent in the study of "non-Western" art and culture. In doing so, a learning outcome is that students develop a broader understanding of the ways cultures from around the world produce, employ, and conceptualize what the West has conventionally labeled *art*. In the broadest sense, teaching students predominantly raised in the West the ways that expressions such as *ritual process, hair, tattoo, dress, clothing, performance,* and *masquerade* (along with *paintings, sculptures,* and *architecture*) are all conventionally defined as "non-western" art is not the primary challenge. In fact, instilling a broader perspective to myriad connotations of art is not as difficult as one might suspect. I have found most students enrolled in this type of class are new to art and have a fluid and open definition in lieu of the typical confines of the art historical canon, that precious list of artworks and artists that has long defined the discipline, which of course has favored Western art since the beginning. The hardest challenge I have observed for students is not the classic "What is art?" paradigm but how to honestly and self-reflexively engage with their cultural biases that hinder objective learning. And this is where the threshold concept of Otherness is most present.

When learning about cultures and their art from parts of the world that may seem as distant as Africa, Oceania, and Native America, most students cannot help but fall prey to the constructed differences they have grown up with. Think about how most Americans only hear about Africa through news stories and other media, which project the continent as a place where poverty, disease, and political instability thrive,[2] not to mention that many still perceive Africa as a country and not the large, diverse continent that it is. We are all familiar with those highly curated, tear-jerking television commercials about the starving children of Africa who are too weak to even swat away the hundreds of flies scattered across their bodies and faces. These, like most news stories about the continent, are unfortunately believable constructed narratives that unequivocally invite misconception. How can one possibly look objectively at the arts, rituals, and other cultural expressions of underrepresented groups when such flawed constructions immediately fill one's mind? And this is what my students are up against when enrolling into AOA. These commercials, like most news stories about the continent, are constructed narratives that feed misconception. And these are the blinders with which most see and understand AOA cultures when first enrolling into this course.

Sociologists have taught us that cultural, ethnic, gendered, and class identities are constructed by the broader social structure in which we all live, which is where the notion of Otherness lies. Sociologist Zygmunt Bauman (1993) demonstrates that Otherness is a foundational way society constructs the conventionally accepted identities that underlie societal categories. Otherness is therefore a culturally constructed bias that reinforces how aspects of society establish difference between people of diverse backgrounds, class status, religious affiliation, appearance, and even interests. In other words, Otherness is that knee-jerk reaction that happens when some choose to focus on seeing apparent differences rather than who someone actually is.

Much of the Otherness engaged in AOA stems from the European colonization of Africa and Oceania, as well as ongoing settler and reservation tensions in the United States. During colonialism, the construction of the colonial Other, and the lecherous fascination with the exotic Other, became staples for the way colonized populations were perceived in the past and are still perceived in the present.[3] Some of the most alarming moments that forged Otherness were showcased in the highly curated, live expositions of colonized people literally placed on public display that were common during Universal Expositions or World Fairs.[4] The historical construction of the Other during Western colonialism was therefore a product of imperialistic power plays in competition for the vast raw resources of Africa and Oceania. This was also the case during the early settlement of America, and such preconceptions and false narratives were only increased as forced removal acts, reservation life, and

Westward expansion materialized. The rhetoric of Otherness established during these forms of colonialization, reinforced by the racist pseudoscience of evolutionary theory, ensured that anyone beyond the West was positioned as naturally inferior.

Clearly there is a well-entrenched, multidisciplinary historiography of Otherness. I, however, do not delve deeply into it in this entry-level class. I made this mistake in my earliest version of this course. I have found it much more helpful to approach the messiness of this concept by making it relatable by tracing historic misrepresentations still apparent in the contemporary culture younger generations experience. To foster meaningful, objective, and enriching learning experiences, the threshold of Otherness must first be acknowledged, and, if at all possible, even breached. Once armed with an objective understanding about African, Oceanic, and Native American art and culture, students are able to approach the broader world with more awareness and ethical reason.

As I endeavor to aid objective learning in my AOA course, the basic framework of my teaching is devised around postcolonial perspectives and awareness. Over the years, I have learned that to effectively reach as many students as possible, tempering the delivery and heaviness with which I critique Western misrepresentation is imperative, however. N. Martin Nakata, Victoria Nakata, Sarah Keech, and Reuben Bolt (2012) demonstrate that approaching teaching Indigenous topics through a strict lens of anticolonialism could come across as an attempt to change the way a student thinks, ultimately undermining the entire learning process (121). I confirm that how one goes about teaching AOA art and culture can rub students the wrong way and that in teaching sensitive topics, one's pedagogical approach is often more important than the actual content covered in the course.

Given that everything these days seems to be hyperpoliticized, and that many students do not have the basic introductory knowledge to negotiate their own cultural bias, the goal of teaching Otherness becomes a slippery slope, and when it is not facilitated through an inquiry-based model, students quickly inject what they know—which can often result in politicizing course material. I share an honest student comment from a 2019 student evaluation confirming the benefits of my inquiry model. The student wrote, "I looked at the topic and expected to be bored out of my mind, and I also kind of expected some Liberal propaganda. What I really got was a complete change of heart and the opportunity to learn about something I would've otherwise ignored." This student evaluation came after fresh revisions I implemented in the course upon completion of the Fellows Program.

In the Fellows seminar, I started to realize that my early focus on telling students what they needed to know about how best to understand the complexity of Otherness was a misstep. While I certainly identified this complexity in earlier iterations of the course, it was not until the Fellows Program that I gained the confidence to change from a content-focused class to fostering a more sensitive, empathetic approach to teaching Otherness. The Fellows Program helped me embrace that in teaching students hard-to-grasp concepts, it is okay for learning to be transparently messy, hard, and challenging. I came to realize that when students are encouraged to embrace the messiness, and to think self-reflexively about the material and learning process (not unlike what the facilitators of the Fellows Program instill in us faculty), students are able to better grasp threshold concepts like Otherness.

In the realm of teaching Indigenous Australian studies, I return to the ideas Nakata et al. (2012) propose: in their words, "Students might be more disposed to understanding the limits of their own thinking by engaging in open, exploratory, and creative inquiry . . . while building language and tools for describing and analysing what they engage with" (121). My newer, post-Fellows iteration is similar to this model in that I now encourage students to discover and come to terms with their bias on their own, using discourse, writing, and lecture as a way to spark an invested interest, while avoiding at all costs an authoritative tone telling my students how and what to think. Prior to these changes, early versions of the course did not utilize in-class work and writing assignments that brought out self-reflective consideration. My revised approach is more about creating a space to help my students discover their own individual bias and those of broader Western society. Indeed, fostering a sense of self-reflexive relatability with course content while applying writing as a way to think through and put in practice course teachings has shown to be a successful model. Even though this approach focuses on teaching global art history, my hope is that the proposed strategies prove useful for thinking about how to successfully foster learning experiences when students must first come to terms with their own cultural bias, a challenging task that many topics/courses well beyond global art history and broader Western society contend with.

COURSE SCAFFOLDING IS KEY!

The course in question, ART 162: Africa, Oceania, and Native America, is an entry-level class capping at 150 students. It also counts as an option for Miami University's liberal education curriculum. Consequently, students from all divisions, programs, and majors enroll in this class. In fact, since 2017, I have noticed that many students come to this class without any prior coursework or even experiences with art, art history, Africa, Oceania, or Native America. In many ways, this is truly an introductory course to art and to cultures from around the world. In most cases, whether students are aware of it or not, they bring cultural biases—what I term *Otherness*—to a class that explores cultures of the world that were displaced, marginalized, and drastically misunderstood long before the lifetimes of the students enrolled in it and that continue to be marginalized in these students' lifetimes. It is safe to say that at the start of the class, many students struggle with objectively seeing and approaching these cultures and their art. I have found that the careful scaffolding of this course, in terms of the week-to-week framework and even how assignments build from one another, is an effective means to help students overcome their lack of experiences and knowledge with global worldviews.

To approach the struggles associated with students having to come to terms with their own Otherness, the course framework is divided into three blocks. Each block spans approximately five weeks, and all three sections of the course include a writing assignment and a separate multiple-choice exam. The first is the Oceanic content, followed by the African block, and then the course finishes with our examination of Native American art and culture. Each block or section builds from the last. For example, the Oceanic block focuses on delving into the concept of Otherness as we learn from selected case studies of the diverse expressions of this region. During these first five weeks, great care and attention are paid to repeatedly approaching the barriers preventing objective learning. Lecture, watching in- and out-of-class films, assigned readings, writing assignments, and honest discussion of all these formats are used throughout these first five weeks. This framework is repeated in the next two blocks.

The first five weeks serve as an extended introduction to Otherness, while the next block engages more thoroughly how to apply the art historical tool of contextualization. In this way, with the Africa block, the importance of teaching how to contextualize art takes center stage. In AOA, the threshold of Otherness is of course still reinforced in this second part of the course; however, students start to understand that broad contextualization of creative expression (a hallmark of what art history does broadly, discussed in chapter 8 of this collection) is a successful method in curbing cultural bias. For example, when the nuance or background information of a given work of art or an expressive event is understood, the mystique that once clouded comprehension dissipates. In other words, learning ways to contextualize the material goes a long way in deconstructing Otherness. The last section of the class brings together the two previous approaches, as attention turns to Native America. I save Native America for last since it is the most sensitive and follows a very different type of colonial history than that of Africa and Oceania.

At about week ten, when we start Native America, students are more apt to combine an honest self-reflexive assessment of their own cultural bias with an increased interest for broad contextualization. This helps students better confront how broader US society has seemingly swept under the proverbial rug relations with First Nations or even a basic knowledge of their histories and cultures. I have found that at this point in the semester, students are better equipped to engage with the problematic label of "Native Americans," the fallacy of Thanksgiving, why many are still instructed to dress up as Indians and Pilgrims to reenact the controversial holiday in kindergarten class, and last, how problematic sports logos and mascots across the nation perpetuate long-standing forms of misrepresentation.

These topics are closer and more sensitive to the lives and lived realities of US students, and facilitating honest discourse around them, with as much varied student contribution as possible, can be quite challenging. This is precisely why, before our Native American block, the class endeavors for ten weeks to work students up to understanding and approaching the ways Otherness has long created problems for objective learning about diverse cultures of the world, even if some of those cultures are not as geographically distant from the United States as others. I have found that scaffolding the course in this way goes a long way to helping students overcome issues of sensitivity and the general lack of knowledge that comes with AOA. Even further, from my experiences, scaffolding works best when the teacher is completely transparent with their students as to why the course structure and assignments are designed in the way they are. That level of transparency provides yet another layer of instruction, albeit a meta one, that students appreciate.

TELLING IS NOT TEACHING

In past versions of this course, I placed too much emphasis on lecture materials as a way to approach objective learning. I, perhaps naïvely, trusted that the cases and content embedded in lectures were enough to help students understand the ways Africa, Oceania and Native America are misrepresented in mainstream Western education. After some experimentation and willingness to modify my own approach, I discovered that an effective way to initiate the learning process was to help students confront culturally ingrained Otherness by helping them relate to the material, or at least relate to the ways they have been taught very little about these places in the world. In other words, telling them about the messiness of Otherness took a back seat to enabling them to experience just how much their cultural biases affect objective learning. Whatever the nature of the class at hand may be, the principles of not relying on telling but instead helping students actively engage are important to teaching threshold concepts in any discipline.

As I developed my approach, I soon realized facilitating honest, in-class discussions about students' previous engagements or experiences was a way into helping them approach the threshold of Otherness. Some cases in point happen within the first two weeks of class. For example, on the very first day, even before we engage the syllabus, I take to the chalkboard, asking the class to share a word or phrase that first comes to mind when they hear the words "Africa," "Oceania" and "Native America." Without fail, every semester I employ this exercise, the class offers the typical stereotypical labels: *tribal*, *primitive*, *rural*, *pure*, *poor*, and *traditional*, just to name a few. We pick a few to unpack, discussing how such terms misrepresent and problematize these areas of the world (as well as most people living beyond the purview of the West).

We then turn attention to student responses that were more objectively appropriate. From semester to semester, these are often *diverse*, *marginalized*, and *misunderstood*. I return to those who offered these contributions, asking them to further explain and elaborate based on their knowledge and experiences. I find this activity extremely helpful since it demonstrates that some in the class are ready to take on Otherness. Another positive outcome, happening on the very first day, is that students who may struggle with the concept of Otherness hear from peers and not just the professor. While I certainly embraced this strategy before, it was not until the Fellows Program that I trusted myself to let go even more of closely controlling the scope and points during broad discussion, in so far that I started to lean more heavily on those students ready to take on Otherness, asking them to clarify their points and experiences further. I started to notice this activity helped those caught on the very first day in the messy and liminal spaces of the concept.

From that exercise, again before even turning to the syllabus, I move to another quick activity, asking the class to honestly raise their hands if they had a meaningful engagement with any aspect of African, Oceanic, or Native American culture prior to coming to college. When the entire class observes that more than 90 percent of the students in the room haven't, something magical happens: I manage to pique interest by making the material relatable on the very first day. To further drive the point to my students, I ask them to consider if even in their college experience they have had a meaningful engagement. When only a handful of others join the group of raised hands, the point is collectively taken.[5]

In teaching something as diverse as African, Oceanic, and Native American art and culture, or perhaps any topic traditionally beyond the realm of Western knowledge, having students openly acknowledge with each other at the very start of the course that they are often taught very little about these places in the world helps foster a palpable gauge of relatability that keeps students hungry for more. Although I did not plan for this, something else quite charming resulted in starting the semester this way: a class of about 150 students becomes much more at ease with openly sharing ideas despite such a large class size.[6]

Heading into day two of the class, I now start to mix lecture with discussion based on our first assigned reading. The lecture starts to arm students with an understanding of the historical antecedents that laid the groundwork for the types of Otherness students often bring to a class. After our first lecture that seeks to broadly engage with how the colonial past, the highly problematic, yet once accepted, evolutionary theory, and historical exploitation of Africa, Oceania, and Native America forged the rhetoric of Otherness, we turn attention to our first assigned reading, "The Body Ritual Among the Nacirema," by anthropologist Horace Minor (1958).

With this brilliantly brief piece of writing, students unsuspectingly read a parody about American culture (Nacirema is "American" spelled backward). The article provides our first encounters with how important writing is to our learning process, especially as we consider the language and ways written discourse on cultures beyond that of the writer are framed. In turning to discuss the lessons embedded in this article, some students are very well aware of what is about to unfold while others are completely credulous—part of the article's dazzling charm. In trying to extend our analysis of the Nacirema as long as possible, before someone gives away the witty satire of the piece, I purposely facilitate a slow-paced discussion. I ask, "Where are the Nacirema located?" After some answers about how the location was vaguely described as North America, somewhere between Canada and Mexico, I follow up with, "What are some behaviors of the Nacirema?" The small majority of students who closely read the article understand my intent and continue to play along while the unsuspecting offer their observations.

The discussion that ensues brings out how life for the Nacirema is obsessed with a ritual lifestyle aimed at overcoming the belief that the human body is ugly. Student participants offer how every morning the Nacirema enter the shrine room, bowing their heads before a charm box and font to purify their faces with ritually cleansed holy water. Others say most are obsessed with the mouth and seek out "holy mouth men" when the need arises to exercise the "evils" of the mouth. Some students are fascinated by how the Nacirema subject themselves to great pain: men lacerate their face almost daily while women bake their heads. Many other observations are shared with a building chorus of chuckles murmured throughout the room. At this point the broader class is starting to see the trick. Usually at this moment, a student starts to defend the Nacirema, or the opposite happens, a student cautiously offers, "Isn't this about us Americans"?

I allow these comments to fester before I ask, "What is the punch line of the article" or "What is Nacirema spelled backwards?" Depending on the group, reactions are usually a combination of raucous laughing out loud, exasperated expressions of oh!, or looks of wide-eyed embarrassment. After a long pause to allow the pedagogical trick to be fully realized by the entire class, we return to our previous discussion and spend time carefully unpacking how the author facilitated his ruse. Great care and time is expended in discussing how the morning shrine room and font are a bathroom with sink, the "holy mouth man/woman" is a dentist, evils of the mouth is the American fetish of dentistry, lacerating the face is simply shaving, and the ovens baking women's heads are indeed old-fashioned hair dryers at salons. In short, the Nacirema help create a fun and interesting space to relate more to the notion of Otherness.

After the deception is fully exposed, we turn attention to how Minor (1958) was writing to the field of anthropology, reminding his peers during the late 1950s of the importance of cultural relativity. The discussion of the Nacirema thus precipitates introducing an idea that will model how we will endeavor to confront the challenges of Otherness. Cultural relativism, the anthropological method to the scientific study of culture, becomes our crutch to curb Otherness as we check our cultural bags of misconception at the door.[7] Although we discuss how impossible it is to completely curb subjectivity, the point is well taken that an objective approach to Otherness must be realized if we are to be successful moving forward with the course.

I find it necessary to delineate the above exercise because I have come to understand that in some cases, at least for the way I teach the Nacirema, the performance or delivery of the content is often more important than the content itself. Telling them the point of the Nacirema reading would simply not have the same learning effect as experiencing the moment when many finally realize they have been tricked (even though some are very well aware). I therefore employ the lessons in the article as pathways for students, who are already at different levels in grasping the concept of Otherness, to collectively help each other reach the doorstep of this threshold. Infusing the content with meaningful humor and fun is an additional bonus that helps build a palpable level of rapport during the first week of class. When dealing with sensitive issues such as Otherness, or its closely related cousin white privilege, forging classroom trust, a sense of togetherness, and relatability to the limits of knowledge is absolutely critical for delving deeper into course content.

While I have always used the three aforementioned learning exercises since I developed the course, another important lesson I learned from the Fellows Program is to provide enough time to allow the intended outcomes of the above exercises to sink in. Before the seminar, I often gave more time to lecture and telling my students what they needed to know. The Fellows Program freed me from what I always seemed to instinctively fight: that individual impact of the lessons and exercises are far more important than trying to cover what is canonically expected of us. This lesson was pivotal, and the above descriptions of how I performatively and painstakingly tease out the lessons embedded in Nacirema are reformulated versions of previous attempts. In short, the Fellows Program helped me reconfigure how I make use of precious class time, making sure to allow the learning process to take shape even if that means sacrificing content for the unquantifiable time it takes for students to reach the doorstep of a threshold concept.

WRITING AS A STRATEGY FOR LEARNING

The lessons embedded in the Nacirema exercise further help students grasp the way one's language or terminology, especially when written, may construe objectivity. Describing a dentist as a "holy mouth man," for example, reinforces preconceptions that likely lead to the interpretation of Otherness. This is not unlike the use of the typical non-Western catch-all constructions of "Shaman" or "Witch-Doctor." Such labels conjure misplaced imagination and therefore leads to Otherness. Why we insist on these labels instead of simply referring to them as ritual specialists is baffling. The barriers of language when reading and writing about diverse cultures often precipitate notions of Otherness. The ability to identify and interrogate problematic language used to describe diverse cultures of the world enables students to start to explore how analyzing written discourse, and engaging in the process of writing, can help students confront Otherness more directly.

Being open and transparent with my students about the intended outcomes of assigned writing assignments was yet again another lesson I learned from the Fellows Program. Fellows helped me better understand what I already knew about myself: that writing is a way of thinking and learning. Until this experience, I never thought to break down the process of writing in an entry-level class the way I started to after participating. I quickly learned that honest, self-reflexive discussions about the importance of writing, and its messy process, with my students helped students understand how writing is an important learning strategy to overcome culturally ingrained bias. Writing soon became one of the best ways to assess learning outcomes for this course. After discussions with my students about the importance of writing, and how to embrace the frustrating process writing sometimes cultivates, as a way to think through course material, I noticed a broader level of honesty and buy-in I had rarely seen in papers in prior semesters.

Writing assignment 1 (see figure 9.1) is a case in point. This assignment was devised as the first attempt to apply course teachings by identifying and analyzing traces of Otherness and misrepresentation in a museum displaying "global art." As the assignment makes clear, I assign students to go to our local University Art Museum and analyze the Global Perspectives Gallery, asking students to engage with both the success and the limitations of the display of African, Oceanic, and Native American art. Since art, art history, and attending art museums are new to many enrolled in the course, I host a class in the museum that serves as the springboard for starting the assignment. Prior to our meeting in the museum, we critique a couple of highly problematic displays of African and Oceanic art, providing examples to reflect on as they themselves search for Otherness in their home museum.

A major goal of writing assignment 1 is to help students realize Otherness is all around them. The process of analyzing the exhibition and writing it up provides the necessary space to think through and directly engage with the widespread reach of Otherness. Many are also quick to share just how shocked they were to find traces of misrepresentation in their home institution. It is important to state that in no way does this assignment pick on or target the museum or exhibition. It helps students apply what they learn in class, that even in the most honest attempts at engaging with "global art" and culture, Otherness is

General: *Write a 2-page (double-spaced) paper in response to the presentation of African, Oceanic, and Native American art in the Global Perspective Gallery.*

With this assignment, I ask all to critically consider what we have addressed thus far in class as you assess, analyze, and interpret this exhibition. Be sure not to be vague with your discussion; be as specific and detailed as possible with your examples. The point of this assignment is to analyze if there are elements of misrepresentation in our "home" museum.

Be sure to focus on the Africa, Oceanic, and Native American displays, spending a good portion of time in the exhibition analyzing how the museum presents "Global" art to you.

Requirements:

- Consider the overall scope of the exhibition (read the intro label for this). Does it facilitate or hinder an understanding of the exhibited material? What are the successes and limitations of the way in which African, Oceanic, and Native American arts are presented to you? Does the display do a good job in teaching Ohio-based audiences about the art and cultures exhibited?
- Consider the issue of context (or lack thereof) by analyzing how and if art works are contextualized. Does this exhibition help or hurt in contextualizing cultures new or unfamiliar to Ohio-based audiences?
- How are time and history presented in regards to African, Oceanic, and Native American cultures?
- Do you detect elements of Otherness and misrepresentation in the exhibit? Briefly consider the way this exhibition is presented to you versus others in the museum. Are there differences? What do these differences communicate?

Figire 9.1. Writing Assignment 1: Analyze an Exhibition at Miami's Art Museum

often present even without signs of malicious intent. This is an important idea we revisit later with the final writing assignment.

One of the most important lessons of this assignment is that students explore the importance of contextualization and how it is a successful way to lessen misrepresentation and Otherness. Another important lesson instilled with the assignment is that no matter how hard a given museum tries, art employed in the context of African, Oceanic, and Native American cultures, given the ritual and performative qualities, for instance, will always be decontextualized to a certain extent. This sets up just how difficult it is to present an objective and culturally appropriate exhibition on "global art" in Western museums, thanks in part to conceptual and methodological distance.

General:

In response to our discussion on the Global Perspective Exhibit, most agreed AOA art (Africa, Oceania, and Native America) lacked context. With this assignment, return to Miami's Art Museum and their Global Perspective Exhibit and choose one African object and develop 3 different strategies to better contextualize your chosen object. With this assignment you will create a PowerPoint meant as a digital proposal to be pitched to the Museum. PowerPoints should include carefully composed text and images. Graphics, video, and voiced narratives are welcome.

Requirements:

- Visit the Global Perspective Exhibit once again and select one African object.
- Conduct preliminary library research into your chosen object to understand the object's functions, meanings, symbolism, and uses. You can also use class materials.
- Develop 3 different ways/strategies to better contextualize your chosen object for museum viewers (be creative with this—what would you like to see!)
- Create a PowerPoint presentation of at least 5 slides, but no more than 10 slides, with your 3 ideas to better contextualize the object, better convey its use, meanings, function, aesthetic value, etc. to Ohio-based audiences.
- Format of PowerPoint: at least one slide should introduce your object (with image); at least one slide should be used for each contextualization strategy; and finally, one slide should be your bibliography.

Library research:

- 5 peer-reviewed sources must be used and listed in bibliography. This includes books as well as articles via our library databases (most of these are peer reviewed but not all so be careful. Hint: *African Arts* journal is a great peer-reviewed source available).
- With this assignment, as with all assignments and exams, academic integrity matters. Books, images pulled from the web, images scanned from books, and videos must be properly cited. You are to cite your sources using the *Chicago Manual of Style* (author/date) format.

Figure 9.2. Writing Assignment 2: Thinking Context, beyond the Static Object

In response to the overwhelming acknowledgment of the lack of context students observed in the exhibition, I devised assignment 2 (see figure 9.2) to provide an opportunity to correct what most found problematic. It is important to state that at this time in the semester, we are well into the African block and are already trying to hone the learning tool of contextualization when looking at culturally diverse art. Assignment 2 thus provides a nice pedagogical segue from assignment

1 and the focus of introducing Otherness in the previous block. With assignment 2, students are asked to correct the identified limitation by going back to the exhibition and picking one African object to focus on. With that work of art, students are asked to conduct research and develop three contextualization strategies that attempt to break down the barrier of misrepresentation.

Readers will notice this assignment requires research, and the final outcome is a digital poster presentation rather than a formally written paper. In changing the format of the assignment to a type of proposal whose audience is intended to be the museum, students become empowered to spark change. Students have often remarked how they enjoyed this assignment and that it fosters a more positive reaction than the difficult realization engendered by the first writing assignment.

The assignment is also meant to introduce students to the rigor of art historical research. During class, I take time to address how to conduct successful research, and although I omit it here, I provide a list of sources and explain how to properly cite sources in the assignment prompt. In the end, assignment 2 helps students put into practice how to deconstruct Otherness with carefully considered contextualization strategies while also briefly introducing them to the more advanced skill of art historical research (see chapter 8 for more on art historical frames of interpretation).

Assignment 3 returns students to a two-page written format that brings together the two separate themes of the previous assignments as students explore and research the controversial issue of Native American mascots in US sports. At this time in the course, and with our previous introductions to Otherness and the important lesson of contextualization, students are now ready to take on a more delicate topic for undergraduates. Assignment 3 (see figure 9.3) asks students to select a sports mascot or logo that portrays Native American culture and interrogate the ways it visually and performatively produces Otherness.

The core of the exercise asks students to consider if the selected mascot or logo is a twenty-first-century representation of the problematic phrase *noble savage.* Noble savage was an early construction steeped in Otherness when Europeans and Americans encountered Indigenous populations. In the late eighteenth and early nineteenth centuries, it was quite common for Americans to refer to Native Americans as "savages" who lived "noble" lives thanks to an alleged "pure" and "uncivilized" lifestyle. As we engage in class with examples from American pioneer artists such as George Catlin, students can see that early depictions by Western artists of Native Americans misrepresented them in

General:

Write a 2-page (double-spaced) paper that makes the case that Native American mascots/logos are a twenty-first-century iteration of the "noble savage."

Requirements:

- Pick only **one** problematic mascot to analyze within this paper. High-school mascots/logos are an option.
- In your own words, define noble savage and connect this idea to the topic.
- Analyze the visual aspects of the mascot/logo. In what ways are the visualizations problematic and riddled with stereotypes? If you chose an example that changed its mascot/logo (as with our very own institution), be sure to compare the new version to the old.
- Analyze the performative aspects of the mascot/logo. With this, you will need to search for performances of the actual mascot or descriptions of a performance. Do also understand the performance of a mascot/logo can extend to fans "dressing up." In what ways are these forms of "playing" and "dressing up" manifestations of the noble savage?
- Cite sources properly and include a bibliography. Use the *Chicago Manual of Style* (author/date) format. You may include images as part of your paper.

In-depth research is not required for this assignment. I am more interested in your analysis of the visual and performative aspects of mascots/logos. However, since I am asking you to find a performance, do be sure to cite things properly, especially if you choose to conduct a little research. It is recommended that you find the words or thoughts on this issue from those who identity as First Nation.

Figure 9.3. Writing Assignment 3: Mascots and Misrepresentation

highly stereotypical ways. Students are therefore tasked to consider the ways contemporary sports mascots and logos are an extension of the visual rhetoric suggested by the construction of the *noble savage*.

Assignment 3 builds from a class in which we delve exclusively into the topic of mascots and misrepresentation. We start by closely examining the infamous Florida State University Seminole logo and mascot, spending time discussing and unpacking videos of the mascot performing and Florida State promotional films supporting the institution's use of this mascot and logo. Assigned readings detailing other cases of problematic uses of Native American mascots add to the conversation. Inevitably, a student offers that our institution, Miami University, once had a problematic mascot and recently changed it to honor the relationship the university has with the Myaamia Nation of Oklahoma, who are not only officially represented on campus but are also the ancestral owners of the land on which the university was built. Such contributions nurture a type of self-reflexive discussion that brings the entire class back to the notion of Otherness.

At this point in the class, most are ready and willing to self-reflexively explore the complex nuances surrounding the issues of mascot representation in the US sports industry at a more honest and earnest level. In prior versions of the course, before I participated in the Fellows Program, I did not successfully implement this assignment. My earlier iterations of this assignment and related class activities, mostly lecturing on the history of this topic, fell flat because I did not provide a space for students to contribute and talk through all the layers of their thinking about this topic. As a result of the Fellows Program and our workshop-like approach with our teams, I brought that type of informal group-work exercise into this lesson.

After I revised my delivery and framework of this lesson, I was quite floored by the collection of papers I received. After assessing them, and thanks in part to implementing the many changes I learned from the faculty seminar, I was quite humbled by the honesty with which most approached the writing assignment. I could see that as a result of my willingness to embrace a more self-reflexive, transparent, and patient learning process, not unlike the method I had engaged in during my participation in Fellows, most students were either at the door of Otherness or even knocking it down! In fact, many papers ended with self-reflexive statements about how the writers were injected with a sense of pride in being able to grapple with and identify their own cultural bias as they engaged with the culture of US sports mascots.

TEACHING THRESHOLD CONCEPTS: AN ONGOING PROCESS

Not unlike how academic discourse is an ongoing dialogue, the Fellows Program reinforced what most readers of this volume already know: that teaching, too, is an ongoing process of revision and engagement. And more often than not, that process needs support through meaningful faculty-level seminars and workshops. The Fellows Program taught me that taking a step back from the *content* of the course to highlight the *processes* of learning for students can create a level of classroom rapport and buy-in most educators crave. In other words, students often need help to understand *how to learn* and not always *what to learn.* It is important to point out that in no way did I mastermind this approach. I learned that revising failed attempts, as well as sacrificing course content to make time for teaching the processes of learning, is important.

Teaching as an ongoing process has taught me that designing assignments that effectively engage students while being transparent with the aims and outcomes guides them through liminal learning spaces. The willingness to be self-reflexive and revise or overhaul my courses remains crucial to the success of AOA. And while I always stressed the importance of Otherness in past versions of the course, it was not until the Fellows Program that I realized I needed to have transparent, truth-telling moments in class, breaking down for my students that Otherness is in and of itself a threshold concept that might not even be fully understood with this class alone. This level of honesty with my students helped me achieve something I had never successfully done before: allowing an aspect of the learning process to be palpably on view, not unlike an impossible challenge students become piqued by and eager to best.

NOTES

1. I thank the editors of this volume for a wonderful faculty seminar and their insightful comments on earlier drafts of this chapter. I also thank my art history colleagues, Annie Dell'Aria and Pepper Stetler, for their support, thoughtful ideas, and teamwork during the Fellows Program.
2. See Keim and Somerville (2018) for an excellent and general source on US misconceptions about Africa.
3. In the realm of literature, Edward Said (1978), credited as a founder of postcolonial studies, published his landmark book, *Orientalism,* a critique of the way the Western world perceived the Middle East as "The Orient." Said's challenge to Eurocentrism, although critiqued for politicizing Middle Eastern studies, has become required reading in the field of art history for his analysis of how Western artists have long portrayed "The Orient" in stereotypical, romantic, and exotic ways. Although Said was interested in Western perceptions of the Middle East, his ideas certainly extend to understanding Otherness in broader global art history.
4. These displays are also rightly referred to as "Human Zoos." Indeed, as Raymond Corbey (1993) demonstrates, the colonial Other was objectified through the lenses of the erotic and the savage, compelling the millions of European middle-class spectators that viewed these events to position the "civilized" and "progressive" West in stark contrast from the "rest" (341–43). For a broader view of the "West versus Rest" idea in relation to non-Western art in the context of Western museums, see Sally Price (1989); from the perspective of the issue of authenticity in relation to the African art, see Sidney Kasfir (1992).
5. Although AOA is a 100-level course, since it counts as an option for Miami's liberal education requirements, many choose to take it during their sophomore, junior, or even senior year. In terms of class composition, sections of AOA are filled with students from all levels and ranks.

6. If I sense that the group is shy or that there is some trepidation with talking in front of a large group, I break them into smaller groups to discuss, asking them to return to the larger group to share ideas. Either way, the aim remains the same: get them talking about the material on the very first day.
7. Founded by anthropologist Frans Boas and his students in the late nineteenth century, cultural relativism is an objective approach to studying culture from a neutral point of view. It rejects all value judgments and seeks to understand culture from the tenets of that culture and no other. Even though cultural relativism has changed over the years, many anthropologists still make use of it in undergraduate classes as an example to promote objective learning. For more on how cultural relativism has been interpreted in anthropology since the turn of the twenty-first century, see Michael Brown (2008).

REFERENCES

Bauman, Zygmunt. 1993. *Modernity and Ambivalence.* Cambridge: Polity.

Brown, Michael F. 2008. "Cultural Relativism 2.0." *Current Anthropology* 49 (3): 363–83.

Corbey, Raymond. 1993. "Ethnographic Showcases, 1870–1930." *Cultural Anthropology* 8 (3): 338–69.

Kasfir, Sidney L. 1992. "African Art and Authenticity: A Text with a Shadow." *African Arts* 25 (2): 41–53, 96–97.

Keim, Curtis, and Carolyn Somerville. 2018. *Mistaking Africa: Curiosities and Inventions of the American Mind.* New York: Westview.

Minor, Horace. 1958. "The Body Ritual Among the Nacirema." *American Anthropologist* 58 (3): 503–07.

Nakata, N. Martin, Victoria Nakata, Sarah Keech, and Reuben Bolt. 2012. "Decolonial Goals and Pedagogies for Indigenous Studies." *Decolonization: Indigeneity, Education and Society* 1 (1): 120–40.

Price, Sally. 1989. *Primitive Art in Civilized Places.* Chicago: University of Chicago Press.

Said, Edward. 1978. *Orientalism.* New York: Pantheon Books.

10

MATTERS OF INTERPRETATION

Locating the Thresholds of Historical Thinking

Erik N. Jensen
History

In my class on nineteenth-century European history, I regularly assign the Henrik Ibsen play *A Doll's House* as one way to explore how gender shaped and constrained behavior in bourgeois households. In our class discussions, students think about the ways in which the character Nora manages to exercise power within Norway's system of laws and social conventions, as well as how that system fundamentally binds her. Students point out moments in the play when Nora uses the prevailing norms of gender to her advantage and, momentarily at least, exercises power, which we define for the purposes of the discussion as the ability to effect a desired outcome in a specific circumstance. We compare this play to other documents about middle-class society at the time that also show individuals negotiating paths within systems of power that included not only laws and military force but also familial expectations and language itself. As we were concluding one of these discussions several years ago, a student raised his hand with an exasperated request: "I appreciate what we're doing here, but now can you just tell us how it really was?"

His desire to have me just tell him "how it really was" reflects the expectation of so many students in our classrooms. It stems not only from an innate preference for certainty over uncertainty but also from a learned response to how history has so often been taught to us since our first exposure to the subject. When I told my barber at a recent haircut what I did for a living, she responded, "Oh, that was my worst subject in high school. I was never any good at remembering dates!" I'm still not, I thought to myself. Our department did once print t-shirts that read "Historians are never without a date," but we almost always have to look dates up. My barber's understanding of what history is and does, though, echoed that of the student who raised his hand. It associates history with a single, definitive narrative that we commit to memory because that is precisely

https://doi.org/10.7330/9781646423040.c010

what so many of our history courses have asked us to do. Even some of my third- and fourth-year majors cling to the idea of history as an uncontested narrative of the past, a straightforward telling of "how it really was."

Our first challenge as history teachers, therefore, is to help students understand that interpretations of the past vary from historian to historian, depending on the questions we ask; the sources we use; and the perspectives, training, and experience we bring to our practice. Historians construct the past. Theories and methodologies guide us in that construction, but we select and interpret our evidence through necessarily subjective lenses, and then we submit those interpretations to our fellow historians for critique. "How it really was," in other words, is a matter of debate, and most historians reject the premise. Only after our students have understood this central feature of the discipline—that all history is, explicitly or implicitly, an argument about how best to represent the past—can we encourage them to pose questions, seek evidence, craft arguments, and join the ongoing *debate* over how it was. As I argue in this essay, until students master this first threshold concept of the historical discipline—that all utterances about the past contain an inherent argument—they cannot think and practice like an historian.

In arguing for the precedence of one threshold concept before the others, I diverge from Peter Davies and Jean Mangan (2007), for instance, who discourage a scaffolding approach to threshold concepts. "These relationships" between the various concepts, Davies and Mangan write, "are better viewed as a web than a hierarchy, because there is no fixed requirement for one threshold to precede another" (724). When Jan Meyer and Ray Land introduced the notion of the "threshold concept" in 2003, however, they used the metaphor of a "portal" to convey its function, and I find this metaphor especially apt for history (11). It evokes the image of a student moving through a doorway from a preliminal understanding of history to a deeper comprehension of it, somewhat akin to an epiphany. The term *threshold concept* itself, moreover, reminds me of the phrase "threshold of revelation" that playwright Tony Kushner (1991) uses to describe the flash of clarity achieved by two of his characters in *Angels in America.* I only wish I had had such dramatic revelations during my history training, but I do remember growing ever more aware that the different interpretations of the past I was reading reflected the different subject positions from which historians wrote them. Only with this realization that we historians continually construct new pictures of the past did I understand that history has ways of thinking and practicing specific to our discipline. Only then did I perceive that I even had thresholds to cross.

Although historians construct a vision of the past through our individual lenses, a number of disciplinary sensibilities and practices provide the parameters within which fellow historians judge one another's constructions and debate one another's arguments. Particular historical interpretations only gain currency in our field when historians support them with evidence and present them persuasively. The ability to interpret historical evidence persuasively, in turn, can call upon a whole host of sensitivities historians hone over a lifetime of practice, but I start my students with the "five C's of historical thinking" that the historians Thomas Andrews and Flannery Burke (2007) outline ("Introduction"). Students might master these five intertwined threshold concepts in any order or all at once: context, contingency, complexity, causality, and change and/or continuity over time. These "shared foundations of our discipline," Andrews and Burke argue, "stand at the heart of the questions historians seek to answer, the arguments we make, and the debates in which we engage" ("Introduction"). These foundations, though, rest upon the base of our students' having first understood that history entails subjective interpretation and debate, hence my added sixth C, *contestation*, preceding the other five. Together, these six threshold concepts enable our students to begin to think and practice like historians.

In the remainder of this chapter, I first survey two studies that examine the challenge we face in disabusing our students of the belief in a single historical representation of "how it really was," a challenge we can inadvertently magnify through our own teaching. I then propose some approaches that might aid our students in crossing this first threshold, such as calling attention to the ongoing debates that have reshaped historical understandings and practices since the emergence of the discipline itself. I also propose some assignments and approaches that encourage our students to look for the arguments being advanced by other historians. After discussing ways of assisting our students across that first threshold, I explore how to incorporate Andrews and Burke's "five C's of historical thinking" into assignments that help our students make their historical arguments more persuasively. Although this section draws its examples from honors theses, which only around 10 percent of our majors undertake, I have also adapted the exercises in the past to nonhonors courses involving a selected set of sources and taking less than a semester to complete. I conclude with a few thoughts on how the intellectual growth that comes with crossing disciplinary thresholds might continue to serve our students beyond graduation, even if they never engage professionally with the discipline again in their lives. History departments—and so many others within the academy—must address this question much more directly than we have so far, in light of declining enrollments and justifiably pointed questions from debt-saddled parents and students who have trouble seeing the value of certain college degrees in today's economy.

CROSSING THRESHOLDS AS TEACHERS

Two recent studies suggest the difficulties we ourselves have in conveying the contestability of history to our students, as well as the difficulty they have in accepting it. In their article "A Tale of Two Thresholds," historians Arlene Diaz and Leah Shopkow (2017) point out how few secondary-education majors in their classes emphasized the role of debate in history, a particularly telling observation since those students would themselves go on to teach the subject. Diaz and Shopkow suggest several reasons for this omission: the way high-school social-studies classes teach history; the way colleges often unconsciously replicate that teaching; and a broader set of assumptions that so many people (such as my barber) have about what it means to do history. From at least the time US educators began folding history into the new high-school curriculum known as "social studies" in the 1920s, Diaz and Shopkow write, they have tended to promote "a notion of history as a single-stranded narrative, which students are to memorize, an idea profoundly at odds with how historians see their discipline" (230). College classes often impart that same impression. In particular, students perceive lectures as masses of information to accept and absorb, even though we might intend for students to engage just as critically with our lectures as they would with any other assigned text. Highlighting our own positionality in the classroom, Diaz and Shopkow suggest, could help students understand "that historians actually construct history through the process of making claims" and then empower students to begin doing the same at a junior level (235).

Such self-reflexivity is easier said than done, however. Part of the challenge stems from the fact that we, as historians who are deeply immersed in our discipline's competing interpretations, might see contestation as such an obvious feature of our field that we forget to communicate it to students and to address how troublesome they might find it. In "The Value of Troublesome Knowledge," Linda Adler-Kassner, John Majewski, and Damian Koshnick (2012) analyzed whether and how the classroom instruction and writing assignments in a first-year American history course aligned with the discipline's threshold concepts. Instructors had the most difficulty, the three authors found, when it came to consistently communicating to their students that "history consists of multiple competing narratives," each of which can have elements of broad disciplinary acceptance and acute disciplinary contestation (4). In fact, the three pointed to moments when they perceived the instructors to be directly contradicting the idea that multiple competing narratives coexist in the discipline. For instance, the authors note that when instructors told students that an historian's principal task is to study change over time, this message negated the existence of a vast scholarship that argues instead for continuities over time, and it overlooked the vigorous debates in the discipline over whether purported turning points should really be seen as such. The definitiveness with which one instructor made this pronouncement, moreover, unconsciously undermined the idea that historians regularly debate the aims of the discipline itself.

In another instance, the three authors question the appropriateness of an instructor's comment that history courses serve an important role in the undergraduate curriculum because such courses teach "essential information." This value-laden judgment, Adler-Kassner, Majewski, and Koshnick (2012) argue, also strayed from history's central threshold concept: students "need information and facts . . . to write persuasive historical narratives, but elevating particular facts and particular narratives as 'essential' calls into question the notion of competitive historical narratives." That degree of adjectival scrutiny strikes me as paralyzing, but I do agree with their larger point that we often present history in a way that students perceive as objective, definitive, and beyond debate. If all statements about the past inherently make an argument about it, which I believe they do, we must continually remind our students that our own statements in the classroom make arguments, too. The phrase "essential information" poses no contradiction to history's central threshold concept as long as students understand it as a rhetorical element within an implicit argument about the past that the instructor is seeking to advance at that moment. Instead of deleting the word *essential* from our teaching vocabulary, therefore, we might instead use it to engage students in a debate over what they deem essential to our understanding of the past and thereby model precisely the value that our discipline places on argument. The study by Adler-Kassner, Majewski, and Koshnick points to our need to explicitly frame even our course's content as a thesis statement about periodization, geographical connections, and significance, which students can then question and even contest.

My own attempt to convey such "troublesome knowledge" to my students frequently stumbles over my "troublesome teaching," however, just to riff on education scholar David Perkins's (1999) wonderfully evocative term. I catch myself in class referring to the "uncovering" of history, for example, as though history already exists in incontrovertible form, like a statue under drapery, awaiting its unveiling. I also catch myself concluding classes with an historical lesson that we can draw from an event, even though I know doing so confers on my hindsight an analytical power, and on my foresight a forecasting power, that neither deserves. The teachability of any historical moment depends—as with everything in our discipline—on the perspective and sensibilities of the historian.

The most troublesome aspect of my history teaching, though, is my tendency to imply the inevitability of historical progress. I lean toward optimism in general, and I often find myself tracing for my students the genealogy of especially laudatory headlines in a manner that veers toward teleology—such as when I connected recent victories for queer rights to fin-de-siècle German social and cultural developments. Don't get me wrong—I firmly believe we can trace the recent gains for sexual minorities in the United States and elsewhere in part to initiatives that first emerged in Germany a century ago. I should present this to students as my interpretation, however, and I must remind myself this story is not necessarily over. Societies can grant rights, and societies can take them away. Moreover, perceived achievements in any one area do not prove that history moves in a progressive direction, as Hegel argues, nor, unfortunately, that the arc of the moral universe will bend toward freedom, as Martin Luther King so movingly declared.

My own troublesome teaching notwithstanding, I have found some approaches that help students see "history as something created by historians as part of a contested intellectual discourse," as Diaz and Shopkow (2017) write, "in which narratives and perspectives simultaneously satisfy disciplinary notions of truth and are in competition with each other" (232). For starters, I share with students how my gradual awareness of debates within the field reshaped my understanding of the discipline's truth claims. That awareness began in my junior year of college, at the latest. One of my classes had assigned a book on Nazi Germany that bore the subtitle *Problems and Perspectives of Interpretation*, and in it, the historian Ian Kershaw outlined a slew of incompatible and even diametrically opposed historical analyses of that period and regime. The fact that respected historians could advance such divergent interpretations opened my eyes to what now seems obvious: disparate experiences, academic milieus, and personal sensitivities had shaped these historians' perspectives.

I share another example from my undergraduate education in the late 1980s, too, by way of illustrating how fundamentally historical interpretations can change within a generation. I clearly remember learning back then that the institution of slavery in the United States would have disappeared anyway with the advance of capitalism if the Civil War had not ended it first. The historical consensus at the time asserted that the two were incompatible, and I dutifully scribbled down that idea in my notebook as an uncontested fact. Less than two decades later, however, a new generation of historical scholarship began to turn that notion entirely on its head. Slavery and capitalism were not only compatible, most historians now argue, but indeed centrally intertwined. That is the historical consensus at the moment, and this tectonic shift in the scholarly terrain exemplifies the force, as well as the presence, of different perspectives and competing interpretations.

HISTORICIZING HISTORY

Because similar shifts have occurred regularly in our discipline, I incorporate historiography into my classes as a means of calling attention to the history of debates that have engaged the field for nearly two centuries now. Historicizing history helps students see the narratives about the past that they are reading now within a long disciplinary tradition of challenging and challenged interpretations. Moreover, it shows that historians have a long record of borrowing ways of thinking and practicing from other disciplines, each instance of which has, in turn, provoked debate within the profession. When Leopold von Ranke started advancing his notion of archive- and document-based history in the 1820s, for instance, he was appropriating the methodologies of philology and using them to challenge existing approaches at the time to writing about the past. Over the course of the nineteenth century, many historians looked to natural scientists as models for how to conduct scholarly study. Just as scientists searched for the causes of natural phenomena, historians did the same for political phenomena. The "polyhistor"—the widely read renaissance man who had earlier animated eighteenth-century salons with his encyclopedic knowledge—gave way to source-oriented and narrowly focused research scholars, who likely observed the sparkling wits from afar (Osterhammel 2014, 8).

Almost immediately, though, historians began contesting what constituted a source and what deserved a focus. Karl Lamprecht sought to redirect historians' attention in the 1890s, for instance, toward cultural and economic forces as a corrective to what he saw as the discipline's blinkered commitment to political history and the lives of great men. He promoted the pursuit of underlying "regularities" at work in society, suggesting a broader shift in focus from changes over time to continuities. Lamprecht's approach generated heated debate and influenced the later French structural approach to history known as the "Annales School." These historians ascribed important roles to climate, landscape, and "mentalities," and they wrote histories of regions over long stretches of time. The Annales School pushed historians toward new sources, such as wills, marriage certificates, and conscription records, which then provoked entirely new sets of questions that inspired a generation of social historians in the 1950s and 60s. My summary here gives the orderly appearance of a dialectic, but these competing approaches did not necessarily move the discipline of history in a "progressive" direction, in the Hegelian sense, or in any discernible direction at all. Nor did later approaches ever truly supplant earlier ones. Instead, competing schools have simply multiplied the possible ways of doing history, making more methodologies and theories available for researchers to employ as their individual experiences and sensibilities see fit.

The debates over the various approaches continue to multiply, too. Some of the most vehement disagreements over how we do history have emerged since the 1990s, when a number of historians took a linguistic turn by borrowing insights from linguistics and semiotics to interrogate not only the role ideologies and assumptions played in the creation of historical documents but also the role they continue to play in our own engagement with the documents. Our politics, our biases, and our very words affect what we consider historical in the first place and how we go about historicizing it. By this point in class, some students look dejected and others frustrated. Even I start to question my existence and what it all means. So, I conclude my brief excursion through the history of history by telling a joke that circulated at the end of the Soviet era. A man calls into Armenian Radio (it's always Armenian Radio!) with a question: "Is it possible to foretell the future?" The host replies, "Yes, no problem. We know exactly what the future will be. Our problem is with the past: that keeps changing" (Judt 2005, 830).

TEACHING STUDENTS TO THINK (AND WRITE) LIKE HISTORIANS

Beyond just talking about how debates around competing interpretations are central to historians' ways of thinking and practicing, though, I have also designed assignments that focus students' attention on the arguments historians make. Students who love history are often drawn to the proverbial "trees," the little details or anecdotes in a monograph, but these assignments prompt them to look for the "forest." My favorite such assignment—deceptive in its simplicity—is one I first encountered in graduate school, and it entails asking students to summarize the central thesis of a chapter or book in one sentence of fifty words or less. In order to nudge students in the right direction, I also tell them that the first two words of their summary should be "[author's last name] argues . . ." Otherwise, as I have discovered from experience, they too often submit argument summaries that tell me what the book is about rather than what it argues. After "[last name] argues," students have up to forty-eight additional words at their disposal to complete that sentence as fully as possible. The exercise gets students into the habit of reading like historians and tuning in to the specific agenda of the historian they are reading.

By way of illustrating the exercise, I share with students a pair of example responses, one of which demonstrates reading like an historian and one of which does not. The examples came from a class that focused on turn-of-the-century Europe, and the students read an article on artistic modernism whose argument they then had to summarize. A seemingly direct approach to summarizing the article might be, "This article summarized the characteristics of modernism, how it came about, and whether or not it has ended." That example conveys the topic of the article, but it says nothing about what the two authors see as Modernism's characteristics or how the movement arose or when it came to an end. A far more substantive and argument-focused approach would be, "Although the article acknowledges the diversity within artistic modernism, it argues that the movement is defined by common characteristics like the questioning of 'human life as a sequence' and 'history as an evolving logic,' and that it reached its high point between 1890 and 1930." That response, in a tight forty-five words, demonstrates an ability to read like an historian and describe the forest. The word limit also encourages students to write like historians—and like journalists, lawyers, and policy professionals, too—in that all these professionals face word limits on the book reviews and articles they write for journals and edited volumes. I have a word limit on this essay here.

If recognizing an argument often challenges my students, recognizing a debate can downright mystify them. This stems in large part from our tendency to conceive of a debate as a formally structured exchange of clearly opposing viewpoints, perhaps even as an altercation or a war of words. History certainly does not lack for those, and when I first taught an Introduction to Historical Inquiry class, I picked the most prominent, heated, and obvious academic altercation that had just engulfed my own field of German history: the one between historians Christopher

Browning and Daniel Goldhagen. Those two scholars worked with the same archival sources, but they drew markedly different conclusions. Browning's 1992 book *Ordinary Men* argues that a number of social and cultural factors contributed to individual German police-battalion members' decisions to kill Jews, decisions in which deep-seated anti-Semitism only sometimes played a role. Goldhagen's 1996 book *Hitler's Willing Executioners* looked at the same postwar depositions and court testimonies of those former police-battalion members and came to the opposite conclusion. He asserts that "eliminationist antisemitism" played the central role, and he excoriated Browning for having ostensibly downplayed it. The ensuing debate—in its scale, directness, intensity, and media attention—demonstrated disciplinary contestation in spades.

By picking this particular controversy as my example of a historical debate, however—so fervent and far reaching that it rapidly spawned its own body of scholarship—I had unintentionally suggested to my students that most historical debates looked like it. I was unconsciously communicating to them that they did not need to look for differences in approaches, assumptions, or conclusions between different historians working broadly in the same area because those differences would hit them over the head. In fact, though, very few historical debates look like the one that played out between Browning and Goldhagen, and very few differences between historians hit us over the head. Most historians do not explicitly state, or themselves even always recognize, the array of debates in which their work engages. When it came time for students in that class to situate their own research projects within the historical debates they would engage, they were flummoxed. Their research areas had no debates, they told me. It gradually dawned on me that I had unwittingly conditioned my students to see a debate only in the presence of multiple pointedly critical exchanges between two historians. The absence of such led them to believe that broad consensus, if not complete agreement, prevailed.

If we understand debate not as a war of words but instead as a discourse stemming from individual perspectives that result in different emphases and implications, however, then debate occurs whenever we bring two or more historical works together around a particular question. The ability to limn such subtle tensions and contestations requires multiple semesters and many different research projects to hone. By way of introducing students to the presence of contestation in the first place, though, I now select far more understated and inconspicuous historical debates than the one that raged around the willingness of Hitler's executioners. Students might, for example, instead read Mark Schantz's 2008 book *Awaiting the Heavenly Country: The Civil War and America's Culture of Death*, in which Schantz argues that a widely shared notion of the "Good Death" contributed to a "culture of death" in antebellum America and gave rise to the rural cemetery movement that laid out such soothingly bucolic exemplars as Mt. Auburn in Cambridge, Massachusetts, and Spring Grove in Cincinnati. I then pair this with Drew Gilpin Faust's *This Republic of Suffering: Death and the Civil War*, also from 2008, in which Faust argues spiritual doubting shaped people's understandings of death as much as believing did, and in which she traces a different culture emerging in the United States around cemeteries that focused on enormity, grief, and the specter of the unidentified dead. Students analyze the myriad ways the two authors diverge from one another in their interpretations and conclusions, even though neither mentions the other by name.

These lessons that help students recognize arguments and tease out debates do not seek resolutions to those historical disagreements, nor do they even ask students which approach they find more convincing, although many volunteer an opinion on their own. Instead, to paraphrase Diaz and Shopkow (2017), the lessons help students to mediate contested material (237). Or, as Peter Seixas, the founding director of Canada's Centre for the Study of Historical Consciousness, has expressed it, history classes do not necessarily seek to resolve scholarly conflicts but instead to understand their genesis (236). Our students think and practice like historians only after finding their way into the conversations where that thinking and practicing take place.

Once students have crossed this first threshold and recognized that historians make arguments, they can begin to tackle the threshold concepts that will help them to frame arguments of their own. Sometimes, this can entail compelling students to make an argument, giving them no other choice but to make an argument. I learned this lesson during my first semester as a teaching assistant in graduate school. The professor under whom I taught had posed the following essay question for the midterm exam: Why did the revolutions of 1848 happen? This seemed, on the face of it, a perfectly good question for eliciting historical thought. After all, it contained the magic word "why." In actuality, however, the question simply prompted students to provide an undifferentiated laundry list of postulated causes for the revolutions that they had heard in lecture or read in the textbook, all of which the students dutifully framed under the capacious thesis statement, "The revolutions of 1848 happened for lots of reasons, including . . ." They made no argument about the relative importance of the reasons or about their geographical variation across Europe because the question did not induce them to do so. Disappointed by the essays, we TAs crafted a revised question for the students that explicitly asked them to argue for the importance of one set of causes or another, posed in the form of a thesis statement: "Political demands for democratic rights and equality under the law played a greater role in spurring the revolutions of 1848 than did demands for social equality and national self-determination. Do you agree or disagree, and why?" Although it constrained students' scope for argument, that question had the great advantage of at least compelling them to make one. Given the discipline's newness to these learners, the question provided the guide rail they needed as novice historians.

THRESHOLD CONCEPTS AND "THE FIVE C'S OF HISTORICAL THINKING"

Guide rails constrain experienced historians, too. Although we have the freedom to argue anything we want, those arguments will likely persuade no one—and certainly not our fellow historians—unless they demonstrate our ability to think and practice like historians. In "What Does It Mean to Think Historically?," Andrews and Burke (2007) highlight key threshold concepts that inform how we gather evidence, interpret sources, and frame arguments. They also grapple with how to cultivate those sensibilities in the classroom, how to "communicate habits of mind we and our colleagues had developed through years of apprenticeship, guild membership, and daily practice" to our students ("Introduction"). To do so, Andrews and Burke have adopted an approach that focuses on what they call the "five C's of historical thinking," referring to the concepts of context, contingency, complexity, causality, and continuity/change over time as "the shared foundations of our discipline" that "stand at the heart of the questions historians seek to answer, the arguments we make, and the debates in which we engage" ("Introduction"). Andrews and Burke acknowledge that historians differentially emphasize these five Cs, depending on our subjective inclinations, but they underscore the idea that "persuasive explanations of historical events and processes based on logical interpretations of evidence" entail adherence to these concepts in some fashion ("Causality"). Sensitivity to the five Cs lends credibility to an historical argument. That does not necessarily mean the argument will garner any agreement at all, but it increases the likelihood the argument at least enters the historical conversation.

Context strikes me as the most important and the most challenging of the five Cs since it includes the context in which we ourselves are doing history. It requires asking ourselves, in the words of the poet Adrienne Rich (1991), "Where do we see it from?" Histories of the modern Middle East or of state power written in the years right after September 11, 2001, for example, could not avoid addressing the context in which they were produced, just as historians of disease writing in the current moment will do so through the prism of the COVID pandemic. We cannot escape the discursive context circulating around us, which shapes not only how we answer historical questions but also the questions we deem worthy of asking at all. That context includes much more than news headlines and current events. Gender, for example, has shaped everyone's experience and acts therefore as an agent in producing knowledge, as well as an agent in structuring the historical experiences about which that knowledge is produced.

Historians have an easier time writing about the context in which historical actors operate than the one in which we do, but students can find even the former process troublesome. Students often reflexively place the historical actors in the students' own shoes, interpreting past actions by the prevailing standards in the students' world. Andrews and Burke (2007) help their students understand the function of context by pointing to its necessary role in helping viewers understand the *Star Wars* films. The words that scroll across the screen at the very beginning give context. They enable viewers to make sense of what they are about to see. I point to an even more historic example of context in my history classes than the George Lucas franchise. Karl Marx (2008) neatly encapsulated the importance of understanding context near the start of his 1852 work *The Eighteenth Brumaire of Louis Bonaparte* when he wrote, "Men make their own history, but they do not make it just as they please; they do not make it under circumstances chosen by themselves" (15).

Context assists in discerning meaning, as we know from our encounters with unfamiliar words or efforts to learn a new language. Indeed, context plays an especially important role in historical investigations that examine how societies have deployed particular words or terms to frame perceptions, shift blame, and motivate action. One of my honors students, for example, is currently exploring how the French selectively deployed the term *collaboration* in the immediate aftermath of the Second World War to deflect recriminations away from the French men who had aided Germany in administering tyranny and onto the French women who had conducted romantic relationships with German occupiers. France's postwar context of shame, guilt, and perceived emasculation is critical to her project's showing how the French defined collaboration in particular ways in the late 1940s to excuse the actions of male administrators—who ostensibly shielded the nation from the far worse effects of direct German rule—while condemning the actions of those women who had engaged in "horizontal collaboration" with the enemy.

Contingency, the next of the five Cs, can prove more difficult than context to define, and yet, paradoxically, easier for students to grasp. "The core insight of contingency," Andrews and Burke (2017) write, "is that the world is a magnificently interconnected place. Change a single prior condition, and any historical outcome could have turned out differently" ("Contingency"). Students commonly understand contingency as the operating principle behind "what if . . ." historical questions. Students' keen interest in such questions likely explains why they pick up the concept so quickly, especially the military-history buffs who enjoy zeroing in on the contingency of a particular officer's decision or change in weather during a decisive battle. Many military historians tend to downplay contingency, however, and instead attribute the outcomes of wars to deeper structural forces, such as population and economic size. At the same time, we often overlook contingency in our analyses of broader social and economic developments, such as the civil rights movement and the Industrial Revolution. Moreover, as Andrews and Burke remind us, social groups and state actors often seek to underscore or minimize the role of contingency in the public's understanding of many historical developments in an effort to aggrandize certain leaders or foster myths of national destiny.

Students grasp complexity fairly easily, too, the fourth of our five Cs. They generally enter my classes with a sense that historians tell a more nuanced story about the past than the simplified depictions that permeate our popular culture and political discourse. That sense has often motivated them to take a history course in the first place. Complexity has actually attracted media attention lately as an historical concept, too, and not just for its ability to complicate Hollywood narratives and campaign slogans. The approach known as "Big History"—which has generated a lot of buzz over the past decade, thanks partly to the backing of Bill Gates—has argued for the tendency of all systems, whether natural or humanmade, to grow more and more complex over time, a tendency Big Historians trace back over 13 billion years to the Big Bang itself. The concept of complexity also counteracts our impulse to derive oversimplified morals or lessons from an oversimplified past. The writer and English professor Rae Yang (1997) rejects such oversimplifications in her memoir

Spider Eaters, the turbulent account of her coming of age during China's Cultural Revolution, a period she criticizes but also refuses to condemn out of hand. As she wrote in copies of her memoir during a book signing immediately after visiting one of my classes, "Let us make the oversimplified history complex again." In addition to Yang's plea for complexity, the expansive intent of her message has always impressed me, too. The "us" in this historical enterprise included everyone in the humanities—herself in English, me in history, and all the students who had just read her.

Complexity can go too far, though, and students sometimes overcomplicate rather than oversimplify their narratives, in which case a greater attention to the last two Cs—causality and continuity/change—can guide writers of history toward a better balance between conveying the inherent complexity of the past, including its inevitable contradictions, and crafting a clear historical argument. Causality and continuity/change go hand in hand and lie at the heart of the historian's enterprise. In my own field of German history, for example, much of the scholarship focuses on explaining the rise of Nazism. Some historians emphasize centuries-long continuities in German militarism, popular anti-Semitism, and authoritarian mentalities to account for its rise. Others point to specific changes in German society and politics, whether the jolting process of economic and social modernization at the end of the nineteenth century or the Great Depression in the early 1930s, as the causal explanation for Hitler's to coming power. In both cases, an attention to causality and continuity/change give necessary form and direction to their narratives and focus them on marshaling evidence to persuade readers of the validity of their claims.

The assignment that best teaches and, at the same time, demonstrates a student's ability to think and practice like an historian—to activate the five Cs of historical thinking and engage in the sixth C of contestation—is an independent research project or senior thesis. Such a project always begins with a question, which I require students to write out lest they settle for a fuzzy plan to merely "look at" something in their research. When an excellent honors student of mine several years ago initially told me that his thesis would "explore the evolving physical ideal for American men in the last half of the twentieth century," for example, I pressed him for a specific question he planned to answer. He came up with something much more focused and attention grabbing: "Why did popular notions of male beauty change from Burt Reynolds in the 1970s to Brad Pitt in the 1990s?" Framing it as a question helped him justify the significance of his project to our understanding of the histories of gender, commodified beauty, and celebrity culture. It also helped him better target his search for sources. Perhaps most important, posing his thesis topic in the form of a question helped this student figure out which scholarly conversations he was engaging in, how his approach was different, and what he was contributing to the field.

Even when students pose their project as a question, they struggle to figure out the historical debates with which their work engages. Most often, the difficulty stems from students' tendency to think too narrowly, looking only for books and articles written on their exact project. Having students make a Venn diagram can broaden their thinking and coax them into considering related historical debates that intersect at least partly with their own, even if not exactly. When a former honors student wrote her thesis on the question of how the controversial 1996 Indian-Canadian film Deepa Mehta's *Fire* changed the public conversation in India around LGBTQ rights, her project stood at the intersection of a Venn diagram that included the following historical conversations: the history of religious politics in India, especially the Bharatiya Janata Party, a right-leaning Hindu nationalist party; a history of the LGBTQ movement in that country; a history of the Indian press; and the history of cinema in India, including film's role as a political catalyst. This student's project contributed to all these historical debates, even though none of the works she discussed in her historiography section once mentioned the *Fire* controversy and nearly all of them predated it. She nevertheless convincingly argued that her thesis on that controversy shifted historical understanding of how the Indian press shaped public opinion and how cinema catalyzed political activism.

Once students have pulled all these various strands together, they are doing history. Maybe they even feel the rush of having crossed a threshold of revelation akin to that of the two characters in *Angels in America*. At the very least, they have the satisfaction of having consciously inserted themselves into a scholarly discourse. They have the gratification of carefully building on the work of previous historians, acknowledging that they stand on the shoulders of giants but also confident that this perch affords them a new vantage point from which to notice different things. They have learned the methodologies that guide them toward making sense of what they are noticing, too. They can support their observations and conclusions with evidence that they have situated in its context by having inquired into its goals, its intended audience, and its possible interpretations at the time. Finally, these students have connected that evidence back to their larger argument about the past. They are thinking and practicing as historians. Or at least that's what I'm arguing. As an historian, I'm open to debate.

FINAL THOUGHTS

I want to conclude this essay by addressing the value of such thinking and practicing even to those students who will never do historical work in any capacity again in their lives, neither voluntarily nor professionally. Although I have just finished arguing that history has a set of threshold concepts specific to it as a discipline, I also believe that the exercise of mastering those genre-specific practices—and the awareness that different disciplines have their own modes of thinking in the first place—sensitizes our minds to a broader array of approaches. It makes us more intellectually nimble. "Good writing" entails an adherence to conventions specific to a particular disciplinary genre, but we can all teach our students, regardless of our field, the value of rhetorical dexterity. We can all teach the importance of thinking about one's audience and the purpose of one's writing.

Such reflective thinking about approaches, audience, and purpose will serve our students well throughout their lives, from their careers to their civic engagement to their dating apps. In fact, such mental dexterity may be the most valuable trait a college graduate can possess on the job market. In his article "What Is College Worth?," Jonathan Zimmerman (2020) acknowledges the growing number of students flocking toward the "employable" majors in business and the health professions, but he cautions that "it's hardly clear that the careers that students imagine for themselves when they choose these majors will even exist in the future." Instead, liberal arts educations, especially when combined with distribution requirements that encourage students to toggle between different disciplinary concepts, cultivate the cognitive flexibility that may just enable these students to adapt better to whatever their futures may hold.

REFERENCES

Adler-Kassner, Linda, John Majewski, and Damian Koshnick. 2012. "The Value of Troublesome Knowledge: Transfer and Threshold Concepts in Writing and History." *Composition Forum* 26. http://compositionforum.com/issue/26/.

Andrews, Thomas, and Flannery Burke. 2007. "What Does It Mean to Think Historically?" *Perspectives on History (The Newsmagazine of the American Historical Association)*, January 1. https://www.historians.org/publications-and-directories/perspectives-on-history/january-2007/what-does-it-mean-to-think-historically.

Browning, Christopher R. 1992. *Ordinary Men: Reserve Police Battalion 101 and the Final Solution in Poland.* New York: HarperPerennial.

Diaz, Arlene, and Leah Shopkow. 2017. "A Tale of Two Thresholds," in "Threshold Concepts and Conceptual Difficulty." *Special issue, Practice and Evidence of Scholarship of Teaching and Learning in Higher Education* 12 (2): 229–48.

Davies, Peter, and Jean Mangan. 2007. "Threshold Concepts and the Integration of Understanding in Economics." *Studies in Higher Education* 32 (6): 711–26.

Faust, Drew Gilpin. 2008. *This Republic of Suffering: Death and the Civil War.* New York: Vintage Books.

Goldhagen, Daniel Jonah. 1996. *Hitler's Willing Executioners: Ordinary Germans and the Holocaust.* New York: Knopf.

Judt, Tony. 2005. *Postwar: A History of Europe Since 1945.* New York: Penguin.

Kushner, Tony. 1991. *Angels in America: A Gay Fantasia on National Themes, Part One: Millennium Approaches.* New York: Broadway Play Publishing.

Marx, Karl. 2008. *The Eighteenth Brumaire of Louis Bonaparte.* Cabin John, MD: Wildside. First published in 1852 in *Die Revolution* under the title "Der 18te Brumaire des Louis Napoleon."

Mehta, Deepa, dir. 1998. *Fire.* New Delhi: Kaleidoscope Entertainment. Film.

Meyer, Jan, and Ray Land. 2003. "Threshold Concepts and Troublesome Knowledge: Linkages to Ways of Thinking and Practising within the Disciplines." *ETL Occasional Report 4.* Edinburgh: University of Edinburgh. http://www.etl.tla.ed.ac.uk/docs/ETLreport4.pdf.

Osterhammel, Jurgen. 2014. *The Transformation of the World: A Global History of the Nineteenth Century.* Translated by Patrick Camiller. Princeton: Princeton University Press. First published in 2009 by C. H. Beck under the title *Die Verwandlung der Welt.*

Rich, Adrienne. 1991. "Here Is a Map of Our Country." In *An Atlas of the Difficult World: Poems 1988–91.* New York: W. W. Norton.

Perkins, David. 1999. "The Many Faces of Constructivism." *Educational Leadership* 57 (3): 6–11.

Schantz, Mark S. 2008. *Awaiting the Heavenly Country: The Civil War and America's Culture of Death.* Ithaca: Cornell University Press.

Yang, Rae. 1997. *Spider Eaters: A Memoir.* Berkeley: University of California Press.

Zimmerman, Jonathan. 2020. "What Is College Worth?" *New York Review of Books,* July 2. https://www.nybooks.com/articles/2020/07/02/what-is-college-worth/.

SECTION 3

THE CHALLENGES OF SYSTEMIC CHANGE IN FIELDS AND DEPARTMENTS

11
INTENTIONALLY INTERDISCIPLINARY
Learning across the Curriculum in Latin American, Latino/a, and Caribbean Studies

José Amador, Elena Jackson Albarrán, and Juan Carlos Albarrán
Latin American, Latino/a, and Caribbean Studies

INTRODUCTION

Interdisciplinary area and ethnic studies programs like Latin American, Latino/a, and Caribbean studies (LAS) offer the potential for transforming students' relationships to their communities, institutions, and themselves. Yet the very interdisciplinary nature of the program can render it invisible to students trying to navigate a curricular structure laden with distribution requirements. Those of us teaching within the program from different, or multiple, disciplines then face the challenge of simultaneously defining the program's goals, conveying the value of interdisciplinarity, delivering new and unfamiliar content, *and* assessing student outcomes. This chapter's authors tackled these issues in the semester-long Howe Faculty Writing Fellows Program, which provided us the space and critical framework to identify LAS's threshold concepts and closely examine and revise our curricular structure so it aligned more closely with the logic of our discussions. By meeting with faculty across other disciplines, our LAS cohort was able to identify shared goals and challenges, but perhaps more important, to more cogently define the parameters of what makes our program unique. The process delivered a clarifying result: by rethinking the courses offered at different levels of the curriculum *from the perspective of the students* most likely to encounter those courses at different stages of their college career, we were able to streamline our written-assignment structures to make our interdisciplinarity more legible to students—not as a messy and undisciplined approach to the study of a region and its diaspora but rather as an intentional and necessary feature of the LAS program that evokes the field's historical *ethos* of diversity and inclusion.

https://doi.org/10.7330/9781646423040.c011

In this chapter, we first outline the forces that gave shape to the study of Latin America in the United States and the resulting epistemological challenges inherent in our program's history. Second, we characterize the particular interdisciplinary composition of LAS at our university and the way our program fits into the larger intellectual mission of a Miami University degree. Third, we introduce some features of our curricular design, including specific assignment products and outcomes, that have allowed us to mobilize the challenges outlined above into optimal outcomes for students.

A BRIEF HISTORY OF THE CONVERGENCE OF LATIN AMERICAN STUDIES AND LATINO/A STUDIES

At Miami University, as in many centers for higher education in the United States, Latin American Studies and Latino/a studies have been absorbed into a larger unit, in this case, the new Department of Global and Intercultural Studies. As a field that explores the localized and transnational experiences of diverse populations in the hemisphere, the program is both uniquely aligned with the university's mission of inclusion and diversity and well positioned to address the changing demography of the student body. However, the field's multidisciplinary and interdisciplinary perspectives are not easily recognized by students or the institution. The implications of this illegibility are multilayered. Bias for discipline-based knowledge calls into question both LAS's academic legitimacy and the possibility of developing coherent curricula. While we recognize moving beyond this bias is challenging, our work as HCWE Fellows convinced us it was a project worth pursuing if it generated an innovative curriculum that upheld the inaugurating principles of both Latin American Studies and Latino/a Studies and challenged traditional narratives through different ways of knowing. We drew on these founding principles as we envisioned creating an effective learning environment for students. For this reason, it is important to situate the place of these fields in institutions of higher learning and review the historical trajectory that led to the emergence of each.

Programs whose research and teaching bridge Latin American Studies and Latino/a studies have become a prominent feature in the US academic landscape. However, collapsing the trajectories of Latin American Studies and Latino/a studies into an academic unit or program ignores the specific political circumstances that led to their development and the fact that there is no unified corpus of work that encompasses the heterogeneity of Latin America and its peoples and the complexity of the Latinx experience.[1] How then is it possible to develop coherent curricula without arbitrarily confining it to regional expressions or erasing distinct historical trajectories? How is it possible to define the core values of a Latin American and Latino/a studies program without framing them in terms of an existing canon or indiscriminately fusing—or worse, colonizing—distinct bodies of knowledge? We approached these difficult questions honestly, reflecting on the historically tense relationship between the two fields. We did not just want to clarify our assumptions about our program. We also wanted to provide a model that allowed our students to comprehend the complexity and richness of these interacting fields as they moved through our curriculum.

Latin American Studies emerged in the United States as a result of the geopolitical concerns of the Cold War (Swanson 2014). Despite the rapid rise to prominence of Latin American Studies in higher education in the 1960s, early critiques of its historical origins and role as a field of study included the assumption of the superiority of the knowledge produced in US universities and the influence of US business and foreign-policy interests in scholarship (Mignolo 2003; Salvatore 2016). Still, the authoritarian regimes in Latin America and their systematic human-rights violations triggered a sense of urgency among academics working on Latin America. Latin American Studies increasingly became more attuned to a radical research agenda that linked political and economic issues to diverse social movements that demanded an end to US imperialism, military dictatorships, and racial, gender, sexual discrimination (Alvarez, Arias, and Hale 2011).

In contrast, Latino/a studies emerged from protest politics and the radical ideas of Chicano and Puerto Rican activists and students who demanded specific ethnic studies programs in the late 1960s. While each group mobilized in response to a unique set of grievances, Chicanos and Puerto Ricans benefitted from the broader currents of social protests, including reinterpreting the Black Power movement's concept of nationalism to demand an end to police violence, access to healthcare, increased community control, and economic empowerment (Cabán 2003b; Flores and Rosaldo 2009; Muñoz 1997; Rodriguez 2000). Chicano and Puerto Rican students fought for a curriculum that provided a vision of emancipatory knowledge that called for equal rights, cultural pride, and an end to discriminatory practices. In contrast to the institutional support Latin American Studies programs received across the country, early Chicano and Puerto Rican studies programs faced outright hostility from university administrators. Today, attitudes have changed from initial apprehension to an acknowledgment of the scholarly and institutional import of Latino/a studies in universities (Cabán 2003a).

These independent but interconnected histories of emancipatory politics informed our curricular revisions. Through our participation in the Howe Faculty Writing Fellows Program, we realized we could make meaningful change by focusing on what we do best: cultivating in our students an *ethos* that fosters an understanding of the perspectives, processes, and struggles that connect Latin America and its people and Latinx communities and that allows them to develop into socially conscious and critically informed individuals. This required us to unsettle top-down mandates to privilege sustained, targeted revisions that seek connections and correlations through different levels of the curriculum. Furthermore, we acknowledged we needed to interrupt the idea of making revisions completely disengaged from our students. Thinking about curricular revisions from a student-centered perspective opened the process to the feedback we have received from them over the years; this, in turn, helped us define the possibilities of impactful curricular change. This chapter is interwoven with first-person vignettes taken from our students expressed through exit interviews, student evaluations, social media, and individual written communications. Their experiences informed how we reflect on the history of Latin American Studies and Latino/a studies and how this trajectory portends for the future.

One way we made sure student-centered perspectives informed meaningful change was to situate them within the systems in which they operate, including university policies that have displaced area and ethnic studies programs to the margins in favor of efficiencies. Exploring curricular and course revisions must stem from an awareness of what successful revisions might look like in this context. For programs like LAS with a very small number of core faculty, the challenges of being absorbed into a new, large department like global and intercultural studies are manifold (Cabán 2003a; Hale 2014). First, the specific relationship between knowledge production and the emancipatory politics of both Latin American Studies and Latino/a studies is rendered less consequential under the totalizing frame of global and intercultural studies. Second, the value of Latin American and Latino/a studies as fields is called into question at an institutional level because of the alleged declining demand for area and ethnic studies among students. Finally, the demotion from an independent program to a major within a department resulted in less representation at the council of chairs, less budgetary autonomy, less ability to request tenure-track lines, and less sustained engagement with LAS affiliates in other departments. The causes of these institutional disparities are complex, but they are intricately linked to structural racism.

If these challenges seem daunting, it is because they are. Our conception and praxis of curricular change thus operated within the limits of this uneven institutional system. Hence, we do not pretend to provide transferable blueprints. We are interested instead in illuminating how we enacted change in a specific academic environment in the hope that it helps interested faculty enter into conversations that will lead to changemaking practices specific to them. We also aim to cultivate conversations among individuals leading professional development programs by showing how institutional policies have inequitable outcomes for those teaching and working in these fields and what they can do to support faculty. While we recognize our work as Fellows is specific to LAS at Miami University, we believe it could provide a model of resiliency and innovation for other faculty to follow, especially those in area and ethnic studies increasingly facing absorption. This does not mean putting on faculty the onus of fixing things that should be a university priority, but it does require that faculty play an active role in building a curriculum capable of withstanding and exposing these marginalizing policies.

Our student-centered approach to curriculum revisions began with the questions "Who are our students?," "How do they find us?," and "What do they value?" We then decided to define our threshold concepts and redesign writing assignments to reinforce them at different levels. The underpinnings of our student-centered revisions are rooted in a decade of teaching experience that allows us to engage in two activities at once: thinking about what distinguishes LAS from other majors at Miami University and enacting a pedagogy that pushes historic, political, and empathic learning.

EMPATHY AND ETHOS IN THE CURRICULUM: ENCOUNTERING LATIN AMERICAN STUDIES IN COLLEGE

> *LAS teaches us to put ourselves in one another's shoes, which is always a useful skill.*
>
> —Anonymous student evaluation

Meet Alex, a typical Miami University of Ohio incoming undergraduate student. They are a bright, midwestern student from an upper-middle-class background. They chose Miami for its reputation as a public university with a liberal arts college feel and the comfortable social safety (for some) that the bucolic small college town of Oxford offers. Alex came to Miami with a plan to major in marketing or communications, degree programs with a guaranteed "return on investment," as per university publicity. But to fill out their Miami Plan for Liberal Education, Alex picked up an upper-level Spanish class to continue the momentum from their AP credit earned in high school and to add a language credential to their CV for the job market. A classmate recommended a history class that nuanced the context of the Perón-era Argentine essay they were reading. That history class was fascinating, and Alex took the next course offered by the same professor: this one had a cultural studies approach to the intersections of race, class, and gender in Latin America. It interrogated the core principles of global capitalism as a historical process that intensified the varied expressions of identity, social relations, and market behavior. It cast a new, critical light on the material Alex was studying in their primary major. During the spring break of junior year, Alex opted for a service learning trip to the US-Mexico border instead of the cruise the rest of their Greek community had planned. Before long, Alex had unintentionally completed the requirements for a minor in Latin American, Latino/a, and Caribbean studies and found themselves well on the way to completing a major in a program that was not even on their radar when they matriculated at Miami University.

Alex's academic trajectory, while a fictionalized composite, captures the experience of many of our LAS majors. As the core faculty designing and teaching in this degree program for the past decade, in this chapter, we aim to outline the way we have intentionally designed our interdisciplinary curriculum to meet the unique profile and experience of the students who find their way to our program. We intend to manifest intentionality in our curriculum design and writing assignments so our students can glean the best LAS can offer them: a set of tools that empower students as *engaged citizens* immediately upon embarking on their postgraduate careers.

What distinguishes LAS from other majors at Miami University? Depending on faculty composition and areas of expertise, an LAS course list can be quite capacious in its scope, or it can nearly mirror a bounded disciplinary tradition. In our case, our program tends heavily toward history, with most faculty members trained as historians or in cognate fields and with many course syllabi organized to deliver historical narratives. And yet, LAS contains a particular *ethos* that, while certainly present in many other majors, is uniquely situated at the core of intellectual inquiry for faculty and students alike. While we see substantial overlap with historical disciplinary practices as fundamental to an understanding of the Latin/o American context, the realities of the region's historical subjectivity bring a degree of political urgency to the program.

As with Alex, most students stumble fortuitously upon LAS, adding it as a second (or third) major later in their college career, inspired by language, a meaningful study abroad experience, or a case study learned in a specific class. In short, curiosity and engagement are at the core of what initially brings students to the major. A fundamental challenge is for the LAS curriculum to rise to the occasion and create learning environments and projects that match student passion and enthusiasm. Typical LAS student traits include a sense of empathy, a concern for social justice, and a desire to address systems of structural inequality. Given those imperatives, the LAS curriculum has the opportunity to galvanize student energy and create learning opportunities, and academic products, that can serve them in their postgraduate activities. The rise of public humanities has given us fodder for thoughtful curriculum redesign since not all learning is conducted or assessed through formal writing (Jay 2010). As we demonstrate below, we worked toward an engaged pedagogy in which students expand their worldview through experiential and cultural learning in the introductory-level courses and then work to imagine more egalitarian and just futures in the upper-level courses (Ochoa and Ochoa 2004).

TOWARD AN ENGAGED PEDAGOGY: ADDING INTENTIONALITY TO INTERDISCIPLINARITY

Scholarship has shown that the "integration of multiple disciplines provides a key indicator of interdisciplinary work, to the extent that the disciplines are changed or used in novel ways" (Holley 2018). We focus on the distinct and convergent genealogies of Latin American Studies and Latino/a studies because they point to a spectrum of values and practices that, in our view, inform the Latin American, Latino/a, and Caribbean (LAS) studies program at Miami University even though it has been subsumed into the Department of Global and Intercultural Studies. We revised the course offerings of LAS around a series of critical threshold concepts that have defined all fields from their origins and to design writing assignments that foster the development of students capable of seeing the world from a standpoint other than their own. We then developed a scaffolded, recursive approach to writing that guides students across a range of disciplines and provides them with skills to engage with new media platforms of delivering information. These principles provided the basis for our work as Fellows, helping us make our curriculum reflect our commitment to building more just and inclusive societies.

Understanding and moving beyond the bias for discipline-based knowledge has made us retrace our steps and take a new approach to how we teach our fields. Being committed to multidisciplinary scholarship should also require thoughtfulness about the limits and opportunities that shape its course. As a pioneer in theorizing interdisciplinary studies, Julie Thompson Klein (1990), in *Interdisciplinarity, History, Theory, and Practice,* acknowledges that interdisciplinary work offers unparalleled opportunities to advance knowledge but can never be separated from the political forces that define (and often constrain) the overlapping academic fields that characterize this effort. To this end, we looked closely at all required courses to identify what key themes and concepts ran across the curriculum. We were especially attentive to classes taught more frequently—every semester or academic year—to gain an accurate idea of how they work at every level and to avoid sending a misleading message to our students. After taking inventory, we realized the courses that fit these parameters could be divided into gateway surveys, broad-themed entry-level courses, specialized upper-level courses, and capstone courses (figure 11.1). Later in the chapter we will discuss what role each category plays in the LAS curriculum and what kind of writing skills we expect students to develop in those courses, but for now, we can say this was an important first step for determining what students should know at each level and in revising our writing assignments based on these goals.

Perhaps more important, we affirmed that our course offerings build on values that have centrally constituted Latin American and Latino/a studies for decades but that there was also a good deal of thematic cross-fertilization across the curriculum. These were reflected as we listed threshold concepts we recognized as central to our curriculum. To different degrees, the following concepts recurred at every level:

- imperialism, nationalism, and regionalism;
- migrations, displacements, and transnationalisms;
- identities, inequalities, and intersectionalities;
- culture-, power-, knowledge production;
- collective action, social movements, and social change; and
- engaged citizenship and community empowerment.

Scholarship has shown that disciplinary threshold concepts should not be seen as a checklist but that we must consider the complex relationship

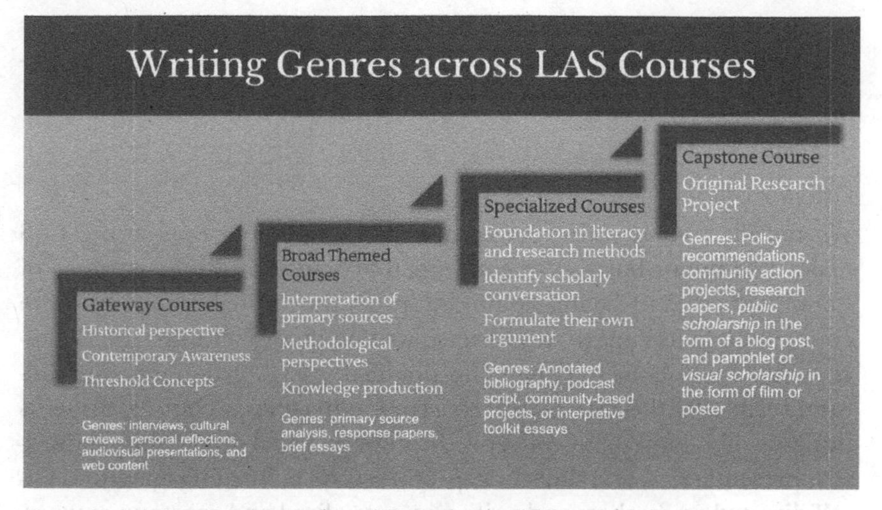

Figure 11.1. LAS assignment goals at different levels of the curriculum.

among multiple ideas and the challenging cognitive landscape of any academic discipline (Holley 2018). While we are not claiming these concepts are exclusive to our field, understanding their interrelatedness in the particular context of Latin American and Latinx communities is crucial to transforming how students think about the region, its diaspora, and its relation to the United States and consequently change their way of thinking about the broader world.

Since our work had less to do with building a consensus about the threshold concepts and more about how to make these concepts relevant for our students, the question that informed our work was, "Given the particular profile of our majors and the multidisciplinary and interdisciplinary nature of the field, how do we strike a balance between depth and coverage, on the one hand, and designing writing assignments that make these concepts valuable to our majors on the other?" Like scholars interested in teaching and learning have suggested, we took a "less is more" approach to curriculum revision (Cousin 2006). Rather than radically revamping our curriculum, we maintained what worked in terms of content and structure and focused our attention on understanding the difference between introducing threshold concepts in lower-division courses and historicizing and critiquing the same concepts in our upper-division specialized and culminating courses. Ultimately, we opted to meet students where they were as we thought about our revisions.

The sections that follow outline the assignment structures we have designed for each level of the LAS curriculum to optimize student engagement at different levels, whether they only take one introductory class as a diversity requirement or are an LAS major committed to lifelong study of the region and its diaspora.

Gateway Courses

We consider our introductory courses as gateways not only to the LAS major and minor but also to concepts that transform students' views of Latin America and Latinx communities in the United States. In these courses, students engage with diverse writing genres and threshold concepts to learn about the changing political, social, economic, and cultural realities of the region and its diaspora. In gateway courses, students think deeply about these concepts through personal reflections, audiovisual presentations, and short interpretive essays before engaging them as self-directed researchers and writers in specialized and capstone courses.

Introduction to LAS: Teaching Self-Reflection and Cultural Appreciation

> *I used to think most Latin American cultures were almost the same and now I realize that there is tremendous diversity in culture in each different part of South America.*
>
> —Anonymous student evaluation

The course Introduction to Latin America, a broad survey of the region since its independence era at the beginning of the 1800s, is taught each semester to about forty students per class. As one of the university's liberal education distribution requirements for diversity, it attracts students from across university majors, colleges, and programs. For many, this course is their only experience taking college-level content in the subject, and often it is their first exposure to issues of racial, ethnic, socioeconomic, and geographic diversity at the curricular level. While we always implicitly understood this to be the demographic of our intro courses, the identification of LAS threshold concepts—imperialism, nationalism, transnationalism, citizenship, race, and identity, among others—in the Fellows Program made us realize we needed to better scaffold our expectations for student engagement starting with this level of the curriculum.

Given the transitory nature of students through this intro class, we now see it as a space to spark and retain interest in a region and its people and to make students reflect on their own positionality in light of their exposure to Latin America. Rather than assign students a piece of writing for an unknown external audience, we now emphasize assignments that are self-reflective in nature: the course now serves to encourage students to see Latino/Hispanic contributions and imprint in their daily lives through interpersonal connections, cultural experiences, visual cultural literacy, and awareness of knowledge production. As a result, the writing assignments now emphasize summary and reflection and ask students to begin to see the contexts in which these experiences/artifacts are produced. By helping students expand their lens, it is our hope they now see more interconnectedness among global spheres of influence, even encompassing their own career aspirations and personal backgrounds.

Our goal in this introductory class is to counteract the conventional narrative that has defined the region for decades (Holloway 2011).[2] How do we do this? The first thing is change the students' preconceived notions of the region. We create activities that help students understand how dominant (media, pop-culture, and official history) narratives about the region have become our prime vehicle in defining what we know about Latin America. In its first phase, the introductory course combats this passive knowledge by deconstructing stereotypes.

One of our first activities is to create a mental map of the region students know as Latin America. Our goals are for the students to draw from memory a map that includes as many details as they can conjure of the region they know as Latin America: countries, capitals, cities, and geographical features. The results of this exercise have been consistent through the years. Central American countries prove very confusing; sometimes Costa Rica or Panama get guessed, rarely are other countries correctly identified. No knowledge or inclusion of the Caribbean countries is evident; many are not aware Haiti and the Dominican Republic share a political border. Of the South American countries, only Argentina, Brazil, and Chile are identified, and never their capitals. Many times, Spain is included in the mental maps (because the language of Spain is Spanish). The only consistency is that the students always demonstrate a keen awareness of where (they believe) Latin America begins: at the southern border of the United States. This activity consistently proves to faculty and students alike how little we know about Latin America outside what the media emphasizes and provides an immediate justification to embark on a semester-long study of the region to fill the gaps in our mental maps. We introduced ideas about imperialism and nationalism to address the issue of why Latin America looms so heavily in current political discourse while we know so little about the region and its people.

Introduction to Latino/a Studies: Towards a Transnational Frame

> *My LAS major definitely helped me with my critical thinking skills and perspectives on diversity. Growing up in a Latin American family, I already had my own opinions on many different issues in Latin America, but the LAS major challenged me to view those issues in different perspectives and develop my stance on different issues.*
>
> —Anonymous student evaluation

Like our introductory course to the region, our Introduction to Latino/a Studies forms part of the Global Miami Plan requirements (which students must fulfill to satisfy liberal arts requirements) and is one of three entry-level survey courses required for all LAS majors. In other words, the vast majority of students take it to satisfy a liberal arts requirement, but for those who end up declaring an LAS major, it serves as a foundation for specialty upper-division courses and the culminating course; hence, it falls under the category of gateway course. The usual class enrollment is forty students, about 85 percent white and about 10 percent Latina/o, the remaining 5 percent divided between Asian and African American. Although in the past the classroom reflected Miami University's uneven ethnic diversity, in the last years we have seen the enrollment of Latino/a students and students of color surpass their percentage at Miami.

Thematically the course offers content largely absent from other Global Miami Plan courses, as well as from US- and world-history courses. An important exception to this is a Latina/o literature course taught on our regional campus by the English department. The course is organized chronologically to emphasize connection and causation, with four interconnected themes recurring throughout the term: (1) the relation among nation, empire, and diaspora; (2) the geopolitical and cultural forces that shape what it means to be Latina/o in the United States; (3) the interethnic and cross-racial struggles for social and economic justice; (4) the erasure of Latino/a stories from historical narratives of the United States and the fight for the right to tell them. As students move through these topics, they are introduced to threshold concepts that challenge commonly held assumptions that depict Latinas/os as a people who arrived the day before yesterday and that complicate constructions of citizenship and race in the United States. An example of the former is when students learn how, in the early twentieth century, the arrival of Mexican immigrants to New Orleans and the Mississippi Delta shaped the racial ideologies of the US South. An example of the latter is when they learn how Black Panther and Young Lords militants not only established strategic alliances to fight discrimination but were also inspired by Third World anticolonial struggles in Latin America. In both cases, transnationalism becomes the thread that allows students to understand how immigration and race and Latin America and the United States are interconnected.

Besides providing historical perspective through a transnational frame, the Introduction to Latino/a Studies course also fosters contemporary awareness of pressing social concerns by dividing students into small research teams that undertake research based on a podcast that discusses a current issue that affects the Latino/a community. Students are asked to produce a short script and oral presentation that applies some of the threshold concepts and to generate a collective explanation of a particular topic. Since introducing this assignment two years ago, students have produced more impassioned writing and imaginative presentations than in previous iterations of the course.

Empowerment, or the Power of Representation

> *This class played a huge role in my decision to stay at Miami my first year. It made me believe that I could succeed at school and do everything that anyone else could do. It is incredibly valuable to have professors with a similar background and I would not be graduating without this influence.*
>
> —Anonymous student evaluation

A threshold concept that forms a core part of the LAS mission is to break down the self/other binaries that, in a homogeneous environment like a predominantly white institution, could (and often do) easily go uninterrogated. Therefore, an important component of the introductory course assignment portfolio is to expand students' worldviews outside the confines of the classroom, with the explicit goal of making Latino/a presence more visible in their lives. We are located in a part of the country that, at first glance, appears to lack diversity. For the majority of intro-level students, the local Mexican restaurant is perhaps the only fleeting awareness they have of Latin American presence at all, and Cinco de Mayo cardboard cutouts readily become a stand-in for the entire region's culture and history. Assignments at the introductory level therefore require a meaningful personal engagement that raises the visibility of Latin/o Americans in the fabric of American society. They strive to combat the hidden biases formed by the "bits of knowledge," or lacunae that can inform behaviors toward certain social groups (Banaji and Greenwald 2016; Cousin 2006). Assignments that encourage meaningful intercultural engagement include:

- attending and reviewing cultural and intellectual events that bring diverse perspectives and stories. They then reflect: What was new, unexpected, unknown, exciting, or uncomfortable? What was enjoyable, and what would I like to learn more about?
- interviewing someone from a Latin/o American background to learn more about how that person's life story has been informed by larger forces being studied in class. As they summarize what they learn, they reflect: How does this person's story tell something about a Latin American society, cultural reality, or historical episode? How does their experience convey something about the United States? How does their story enhance or change my understanding of the Latino/x presence in the United States?

Though the vast majority of our students come from Anglo-American backgrounds, a small but growing demographic in the LAS student population claims Latino/a heritage. Many find their way to LAS classes as described in the opening vignette of our fictionalized student Alex. But others appear in our classrooms with a more intentional goal to ground their identity and heritage in critically informed, historically attuned, culturally rich narratives in which they can see themselves. LAS classes offer them the opportunity to expand on the narratives inherited from their families, just as their presence and interventions in the classroom can help nuance the content LAS faculty have prepared to deliver. As this population of our student body grows, we are increasingly attuned to their unique needs, the value of their contributions, and the challenges they confront as minorities in predominantly white academic climates.

The interview assignment that encourages writing as a reflective practice in the process of identity formation can be particularly transformative for heritage students. In many cases, the formalized nature of the assignment allows a student to see their family's trajectory in a hemispheric context for the first time. They interview a parent, grandparent, or godparent with an eye to the material they are reading on the printed page for class and gain a new appreciation of their own place in larger historical processes. For example, a student interviewed her Guatemalan mother about the labels and categories she used to define herself and reflected, "I have always thought of myself as a Latina that lives in the United States, but after hearing my mom's response, [it] reminded me that I was born in the United States and am as much of an American as my peers." Such a powerful testimony of identity transformation puts in evidence the power of reflective assignments and should not be relegated to an emotional byproduct of the liberal arts curriculum but rather should be galvanized for future empowerment of the generation of students we have the privilege to teach (Fernández 2002; Ochoa and Ochoa 2004). This is not a traditional discipline-based approach to teaching because it connects what students are learning to their lives in the present moment.

Specialized Courses: Becoming Engaged Citizens

> *Living here [Dominican Republic] has been the hardest and most beautiful thing I have ever experienced but I know that having a background in Latin American and Caribbean Studies has made the process so much less painful than it could have been. . . . I hosted a group of Social Work students from the University of Iowa this week and a group was studying the same topic and their professor actually asked me to share my Independent Study paper with him so he could better understand the context of their research!*
>
> —Anonymous student correspondence

Taking an interdisciplinary approach to a thematic upper-level course can provide students with a sense of confidence in their well-rounded, informed authority on the subject at hand and equip them to confront instances of injustice as engaged citizens. Students graduating from our program have found fulfilment in the following careers: nonprofit agencies providing social services, speech pathology, policy analysis, immigration law, public health, and secondary education. Given the career trajectories taken by our majors, we want to send them off with critical thinking tools, a framework of thinking about the world, and the confidence that empathy constitutes a desirable—even marketable?—skill.

For example, in our upper-level course Cuba: Past, Present, and the Quest for Identity, students learn about the island's complex history and culture, drawing on US, Cuban, and international perspectives. They engage with historical, journalistic, literary, political science, oral history, and anthropological narratives. As a final written product, students are tasked with communicating *as constituents* with a public official regarding US policy toward Cuba. Many students choose to write to their elected district representative, mapping out their recently learned appreciation for Cuban cultural and economic contributions to the hemisphere the United States should welcome rather than alienate.

The most effective communications come when students draw from their other disciplinary backgrounds and project their own hoped-for professional and personal futures in their letters. For example, a student double majoring in teacher education and LAS combined her expertise in this upper-level course as a student of Cuban history with her concern for social studies curriculum development and demonstrated visual sophistication and intellectual acumen in the presentation of her class project in the form of a letter addressed and sent to Secretary of Education Betsy DeVos: "I am writing to you as a future educator and distressed citizen of these United States of America," the student urged. After outlining the inconsistencies she observed between secondary-school textbook portrayals of Cuban-US diplomatic history and the nuanced history she had recently learned, she argued for a more responsible portrayal in curricular revisions: "If it is truly your mission as the Department of Education to 'promote student achievement and preparation for global competitiveness by fostering educational excellence and ensuring equal access,' then it is crucial to actively and enthusiastically advocate for a curriculum that properly illuminates the complex relationship that the United States and Cuba share." She concluded by suggesting such reevaluations should extend to other non-Western countries' appearance in the curriculum as well. This assignment, and the civic engagement it promotes, allows students to see themselves as not just students in training for deferred political action but also as intellectual agents of change in the present.

This practice of writing for the public not only allows students to process the systemic injustices faced by Latin American and Caribbean people but also fosters a critical consciousness of our own positionalities within these structures of power. We hope that by recognizing that their own narratives are emerging within the context of the United States, students are able to develop a sense of social responsibility and compassion for others, leading them to direct action and engagement with advocacy, policy, or activist efforts across a range of civil, human, and environmental-rights issues.

Capstone Course: Culminating Projects: Making Meaning out of Schoolwork

> *After a very interesting semester with many ups and downs, I'm happy to finally see the culmination of all of my hard work start to show. I am now a published author!*
>
> —Anonymous student evaluation

A defining feature of the LAS major is a culminating research-based project conducted either in a small capstone setting or a one-on-one independent study with a faculty mentor. These intimate scholarly microcommunities respect diverse perspectives and value the disciplinary contributions of the students' other major areas of study. In our program, we encourage students at this stage of their degree to use those fields within which they have a solid grounding—whether that be finance or anthropology—and put their knowledge to work at the service of an LAS-related question or problem. But in the process, we also ask them to engage with other disciplines' methods, theories, frameworks, and writing genres as part of decentering knowledge around a topic that can be bounded by disciplinary traditions. We strive to make interdisciplinarity intentional, rather than happenstance, and to raise the visibility of the cultural and political work each discipline brings to bear on an issue.

Given that most, if not all, of our students have another major aside from LAS, they often are engaged in two or more culminating academic experiences to fulfill degree requirements. With that in mind, we have come to think of the LAS capstone project as a place for students to build productive supplements to their primary major program, one that draws on and builds upon each students' disciplinary training. Capstone topics revolve around a broad topic relevant to the region, with applicability across time and space. Semester topics might be Afro-Latin America; child and nation in Latin America; NAFTA; or Latin American music, culture, and identity, among others. Independent-study projects have covered themes of transnational adoption, the politics of corn in art across the Americas, race and public-health discourse, disability representations and neoliberalism, and other engaging projects. In an ideal world, after leaving Miami, students will engage meaningfully with the real-world structures, social groups, organizations, and individuals they studied in our classrooms.

After several years of building our capstone experiences around traditional (for humanities cognate fields) academic research papers, we began to observe (1) fatigue, both in students engaged in writing and in faculty having to read through a stack of lit-review-style reports with mediocre "original" arguments, and (2) waning relevance of long-form academic writing for postgraduate career prospects. With an eye to the epistemological conditions informing the creation of our field, and the transforming career landscape available to our students, we carefully rethought the assignment structure and written products around which our capstone is built. On one hand, we aim to validate the multiple ways of thinking about and acting on an issue (allowing us to be surprised by our students' respective talents cultivated in their other major fields). On the other hand, we hope to use our interdisciplinarity to raise the visibility of a wider array of career opportunities that meaningfully engage with the Latin/o American world.

One concrete way our curriculum can serve our students is by cultivating practices of public scholarship. In short, we see the capstone experience as a space to translate the academic rigor of the classroom to a broader audience in an accessible forum. In keeping with the LAS *ethos*, as engaged scholars, LAS capstone students should be able to "link . . . production of knowledge to community cultural, social, and/or economic development and the advancement of social justice" (Jay 2010, 59). To this end, we have designed a culminating project assignment with multiple components:

- **An academic component.** This takes the form of a very truncated formal written piece in which the student demonstrates their acquired expertise in the subject to the professor through a brief literature review, identification of historical structures framing the subject of inquiry, and demonstration of application of critical theories.
- **A public-facing scholarly contribution.** This takes the form of a well-documented (through good hyperlinks) blog post or digital article, written in an accessible, jargon-free style, that introduces the historical structures and critical theories to a general audience. It should adopt an engaging writing style, clearly situate the problem or subject in a specific time and place, and be visually appealing.
- **A meaningful action component.** Here the student helps channel the reader's response—whether it be rage, empathy, concern, or enthusiasm—into a socially productive activity by identifying organizations, lifestyle choices, political interventions, and volunteer opportunities that can help ameliorate the structural injustices they identify in their public-facing piece.

Through this multifaceted assignment, students learn to become particularly attuned to the different writing genres—and audiences—different disciplines and professions employ to address an issue or problem and begin to imagine alternative futures. Students demonstrate awareness of the ways different genres reach different audiences and learn to master conveying an idea across a range of registers. When they finish the course, they leave with a completed product that is already engaged with the community.

An example of the publicly engaged scholar model we newly seek to emphasize among our students can be seen in the class blog published by students of our LAS capstone course Child and Nation in Latin America. Students spent the first half of the semester viewing the region through the lens of childhood studies, with exposure to a broad range of disciplinary approaches that problematized children's relationship to the nation-state, international organizations, and processes of global capitalism. Students then chose individual issues to research in depth: child panhandlers in Mexico City, the Cuban Revolution's revised curriculum, Peru's neoliberal approach to education spending, child labor on Guatemalan coffee farms, and children and climate-change narratives in southern Mexico, to name a few. For the second half of the semester, they worked in several peer-to-peer configurations, in consultation with the professor, to translate their critically informed explorations of Western versus local constructions of childhood into a format readily accessible to a general public. The final product, a visually engaging website featuring blog posts that had hyperlinks to their primary source material (statistics, policy briefs, international human-rights documents, national constitutions, legal scholarship, oral histories, archival documents, etc.), had a professional sheen and drew in a broader public audience to the students' semester-long efforts.

In class conversations, the consensus was that many of the issues addressed contemporary, emerging, or ongoing issues of systemic injustice and would cause sensations of unease, guilt, concern, or anxiety in their readers. As a result, we added a page to the website that directs readers to channel their visceral responses into meaningful actions by listing and linking the organizations and behaviors endorsed by students as a result of their expertise gained through research. Students come away from the semester with a living document, readily accessible by future employers and family members alike, that makes a contribution to the existing body of knowledge about the issues of childhood in Latin America. Immediately upon publishing their website, students were gratified to see their public scholarship pieces picked up by a variety of popular and academic networks through social media, professional newsletters, and scholarly circuits, gaining accolades for the visual sophistication and intellectual acumen of their presentation.

CONCLUDING THOUGHTS

Beyond the rewards of learning about teaching and writing by participating in the Howe Faculty Writing Fellows Program, the three of us were struck by the intellectual rewards of collaborating and thinking about the past and future of LAS at Miami University. After weeks of learning about threshold concepts, troublesome knowledge, disciplinary value, and curriculum alignment, we realized how much work remains to be done to bridge the gap between undergraduate expectations about LAS and what the LAS faculty understand the field to be. More to the point, it drove home both the challenges and the indispensability of integrating these concepts and tools into the gateway and lower-level courses rather than just highlighting them in the upper-level and capstone courses. If the value of our curriculum is hard for students to grasp immediately, it is because they are accustomed to the idea that knowledge about Latin America and Latinx communities fits into neat disciplinary packages, rather than thinking of knowledge production through interdisciplinary and multidisciplinary models that move us beyond the paradigm of Latin American Studies and Latino/a studies as discrete fields.

Of course, we also learned a great deal by interacting both with other faculty groups as they focused on their unique goals and with each other as we revised the LAS curriculum. As engaged teachers, we found it extremely helpful to watch faculty in other disciplines tackle similar problems differently, which enlarged our pedagogical repertoire. But our greatest reward was that once we began taking stock of our curriculum, the task of making revisions seemed much less daunting and even an enjoyable exercise because it reinforced our values. It turned out we share a commitment to social justice and are equally dedicated to seeing our students mature into critically informed individuals with the skills to succeed professionally and positively influence society. Strictly speaking, just identifying these values and goals allowed us to accept resilience as a model for driving curricular revision. From this perspective, resilience is not a form of reactionary, functionalist risk management. Instead, it is opening a space for adaptation and innovation derived from the emancipatory politics that have animated Latin American Studies and Latino/a studies. We hope to show how bottom-up, participatory approaches for curriculum development start with identifying not the hazards but the strengths, and that determining the value of the curriculum for students, faculty, university, and the community is one of the best ways to safeguard its future. The political realities that disproportionately impact Latin American and Latinx communities today cannot be separated from issues of immigration, healthcare, racial justice, police violence, education, gender and LGBTQ rights, and climate change. These intersections remind us it is critically urgent for students to develop an understanding of the diverse histories and the interconnectedness of Latin America and Latinx communities.

This task is particularly significant as the university looks to the future, given that about 18.3 percent of the population of the United States is Latinx, and of that population, about 25 percent are under eighteen years old. Over the last decade, many US colleges have seen—and will continue seeing—a sharp rise in Latinx students, but the academy is ill equipped to recruit, teach, and prepare future populations. As we have seen, Latin American and Latino/a studies programs are often absorbed, underfunded, and understaffed, but the university continues to struggle to see this as the result of structural racism. It is time for it to consider other ways of facing changing demographics, budget constraints, and limited resources. At the micro-institutional level, we at LAS have accepted the challenge of transforming institutions of knowledge in which both faculty and students work, learn, and live. Through our conversations in the Fellows Program, we affirmed that our courses change lives. They give this growing population of students the tools necessary to challenge falsehoods and reinscribe themselves into narratives that have excluded them. We are doing our part by reinvigorating our values while revising the LAS curriculum. Is the university rising to the challenge?

CODA

At the time of the writing of this essay, racial tensions were unfolding close to home in Minneapolis after the brutal murder of George Floyd. A first-year student who had just completed our upper-level course Revolutions and Social Movements in Latin America wrote to reflect on having witnessed firsthand the burning down of Minneapolis Police Precinct 3. His LAS coursework, he said, "challenged my preconceptions more so than any other courses I have taken thus far. . . . Today, I'm seeing civil unrest with my own eyes at home in Minneapolis. . . . I'm very fortunate to have some historical knowledge and theoretical framework for understanding events like this. Otherwise I would be totally at a loss." This testimony encourages us that we are on the right path in providing students with the tools they need to interpret the history unfolding in the present and to respond in the most socially constructive way.

NOTES

1. A definitional clarification is in order at this point. We use Latino/a studies both to refer to a field that examines the diverse experiences of people of Latin American descent in the United States and to the academic units at university settings that focus on those populations. Moreover, we use the term Latinx to recognize queer, nonbinary gender identifications in these diverse communities.
2. Conventional survey courses on Latin America are problematic by definition, as the region is hazily defined at best. Most surveys ignore the relationships in the region connected to cultural influences that include English- and French-speaking Caribbean countries. For instance, should we ignore the region's influence of reggae music or Rastafarian lifestyle in Jamaica, or the carnival influences of Trinidad and Tobago (all former British colonies)? Upper-level courses can interrogate more meaningfully a revisionist approach that attempts to look at the region as more

inclusive and diverse. At the introductory level, the best we can do is to draw attention to the multiple ways the region gets defined by external forces (see Holloway [2011]).

REFERENCES

Alvarez, Sonia E., Arturo Arias, and Charles R. Hale. 2011. "Re-visioning Latin American Studies." *Cultural Anthropology* 26 (2): 225–46.

Banaji, Mahzarin R., and Anthony G. Greenwald. 2016. *Blindspot: Hidden Biases of Good People.* New York: Bantam.

Cabán, Pedro A. 2003a. "From Challenge to Absorption: The Changing Face of Latina and Latino Studies." *Centro Journal* 15 (2): 126–45.

Cabán, Pedro A. 2003b. "Moving from the Margins to Where? Three Decades of Latino/a Studies." *Latino Studies* 1 (1): 5–35.

Cousin, Glynis. 2006. "An Introduction to Threshold Concepts." *Planet* 17 (1): 4–5. https://www.tandfonline.com/doi/full/10.11120/plan.2006.00170004.

Fernández, Lilia. 2002. "Telling Stories about School: Using Critical Race and Latino Critical Theories to Document Latina/Latino Education and Resistance." *Qualitative Inquiry* 8 (1): 45–65.

Flores, Juan, and Renato Rosaldo, eds. 2009. *A Companion to Latina/o Studies.* Malden, MA: Wiley-Blackwell.

Hale, Charles. 2014. "The Future of Latin American Studies." *Americas Quarterly* 8 (3): 80.

Holley, Karri A. 2018. "The Role of Threshold Concepts in an Interdisciplinary Curriculum: A Case Study in Neuroscience." *Innovative Higher Education* 43 (1): 17–30.

Holloway, Thomas H. 2011. *A Companion to Latin American History.* Chichester: Wiley & Sons.

Jay, Gregory. 2010. "The Engaged Humanities: Principles and Practices of Public Scholarship and Teaching." *Journal of Community Engagement and Scholarship* 3 (1): 51–63.

Klein, Julie Thompson. 1990. *Interdisciplinarity: History, Theory, and Practice.* Detroit: Wayne State Press.

Mignolo, Walter. 2003. "Capitalism and Geopolitics of Knowledge: Latin American Social Thought and Latino/a American Studies." In *Critical Latin American and Latino Studies,* edited by Juan Poblete, 32–75. Minneapolis: University of Minnesota Press.

Muñoz, Carlos Jr. 1997. "The Quest for Paradigm: The Development of Chicano Studies and Intellectuals." In *Latinos and Education: A Critical Reader,* edited by Rodolfo D. Torres and Antonia Darder, 439–53. New York: Routledge.

Ochoa, Gilda Laura, and Enrique C. Ochoa. 2004. "Education for Social Transformation: Chicana/o and Latin American Studies and Community Struggles." *Latin American Perspectives* 31 (1): 59–80.

Rodriguez, Roberto. 2000. "Chicano Studies." *Diverse Issues in Higher Education* 17 (16): 26.

Salvatore, Ricardo Donato. 2016. *Disciplinary Conquest: U.S. Scholars in South America, 1900–1945.* American Encounters/Global Interactions series. Durham, NC: Duke University Press.

Swanson, Philip, ed. 2014. *The Companion to Latin American Studies.* Oxon: Routledge.

12

GATEKEEPERS OF KNOWLEDGE IN PSYCHOLOGY

Threshold Concepts as Guardians of the Gate?

Vrinda Kalia
Psychology

Imagine the first week of the fall semester on a college campus in a midwestern state in the United States. It is a beautiful day in August, and a new class of first-year students have descended onto the campus grounds. They are all excited and nervous at the same time. Amongst the thousands is one female student who identifies as a minority on more than one level. Her name is Mikala. She is a first-generation college student who also happens to be one of the few hundred students of color on a campus that is home to more than twenty thousand. None of the rules of life that have worked for her so far will apply anymore. Because she is smart, motivated, and ambitious, she instinctively knows this. But this knowledge doesn't help right now. As she looks around at other students cheerfully settling into their new lives, she is struck by how lost she feels in comparison. What are the new rules? And who is going to show her what she needs to know to thrive in this new world?

CRISIS OF FAITH IN PSYCHOLOGY

I am beginning this chapter with a narrative, rather than statistics or a theoretical perspective, in order to mindfully transgress the rules of writing in psychology. In traditional psychology journal articles, the introduction begins with a discussion of relevant prior research and the ways the author's presented work will further extend it (Hartley 2012). In effect, the construction of knowledge in psychology is steeped in a culture that values what is *known* and has been *acknowledged as known* by those who are in positions of power (i.e., editors and reviewers). Although psychology is not the only discipline that has a problem with hegemonic practices around knowledge production, it is important to

https://doi.org/10.7330/9781646423040.c012

pause for a moment to consider what this means for a science that has been roiled by accusations of a replication crisis (Shrout and Rodgers 2018). In the last decade psychology has been beset by high-profile instances of fraudulent data collection and questionable research practices that have raised serious questions about the way researchers in the field do science. As a result, psychology currently identifies itself as a discipline trying to find its way back to the security of scientific "truth" and away from the fact that only about one-third of its research findings can be replicated (Shrout and Rodgers 2018).

However, as Stuart Hall (1996) reminds us, identity work is inherently political and psychology's response to this replication crisis has been tellingly muscular. Suggestions to counter the problems plaguing psychological science have included increasing the sample sizes for presented studies to ensure greater power or conducting multiple studies on the same question to demonstrate veracity of the findings (Shrout and Rodgers 2018). This proposal may be logical, but it reflects a chilling disregard for the human-labor processes that provide the foundation for any research effort in psychology. Large teams of students, undergraduate and graduate alike, work many hours to produce data for a single study. Increasing the number of participants or the number of studies needed for publication will inevitably mean students work more hours or a larger number of students are engaged in the process of data collection. Yet there is no discussion of increasing rewards or compensation for the most vulnerable citizens of the discipline (Everett and Earp 2015). An unintended consequence of the adoption of these proposals is that research productivity has become even more challenging for those with less power and privilege. In effect, by proposing more stringent rules for acceptable sample sizes, psychology has also ensured graduate students, postdocs, and untenured junior faculty can spend years collecting data and writing manuscripts without being published (Everett and Earp 2015).

In addition, researchers in psychology have been asked to adopt increasingly sophisticated study designs (e.g., incorporating both physiological and behavioral measures) and advanced statistical tools to capture effects (Shrout and Rodgers 2018). Since human behavior is the product of both biological and sociological processes coming together in complex and nuanced ways, this suggestion also appears to be logical. However, it ignores the financial and pragmatic costs associated with doing research that combines physiological and behavioral measurements. For instance, learning to incorporate physiological measures programmatically requires intensive training in the measurements along with access to expensive equipment. Academic institutions without access to federal grant funding or adequate financial resources are unable to support their faculty and students in getting trained or acquiring expensive equipment that would make this type of research possible. This, in turn, prevents these faculty and students from doing research recognized as cutting edge, which also prevents these individuals from making any meaningful moves toward upward social mobility. In contrast to researchers from less privileged institutions who struggle to put together research labs and research programs in the absence of structural support, researchers in privileged and resource-rich institutions have access to a wide range of facilities (e.g., instruments that can costs upwards of hundreds of thousands of dollars) and funds that can support their training in the latest physiological and statistical techniques. In essence, by highlighting the need for more complex methods and techniques, psychology is reinforcing hegemonic structures of class inequalities and disadvantages that already exist in society.

Resonating with this muscular response, journals in psychology have increasingly encouraged the use of surveillance methods to ensure the data researchers present are accurate. Whereas some of these methods of surveillance have increased transparency (e.g., openly sharing decisions regarding data procurement with the reader, explicitly detailing methods used to conduct studies), which is good for the scientific discipline, others have resulted in bullying, vilifying, and pushing out female researchers from the discipline (Dominus, *New York Times*, October 18, 2017). Susan T. Fiske, Eugene Higgins Professor of Psychology and professor of Public Affairs at Princeton University, called this "methodological intimidation" (Fiske 2016). She wrote on the Association for Psychological Science website in 2016, "Our colleagues at all career stages are leaving the field because of the sheer adversarial viciousness. I have heard from graduate students opting out of academia, assistant professors afraid to come up for tenure, mid-career people wondering how to protect their labs, and senior faculty retiring early, all because of methodological intimidation." Academic bullying is not a new phenomenon (Frazier 2011), and it can take many forms, including ridicule, public humiliation, and discrediting the work of another person (Misawa and Rowland 2015). Past research has consistently shown such bullying has an adverse impact on the bullied individual as well as the organization (Misawa and Rowland 2015). For example, faculty who report being bullied experience feelings of anger, frustration, and increased stress and anxiety, which influence both the quality and the quantity of the work they are able to do (Johnson-Bailey 2015).

Even more problematic, research on academic bullying has indicated it has grave consequences for faculty of color. In addition to dealing with the emotional and psychological consequences of bullying (Johnson-Bailey 2015), faculty of color find it difficult to get tenure and are less likely to be promoted at their institution if they have experienced academic bullying (Frazier 2011). This latter outcome is particularly troubling for psychology as a field since it is a majority white male with a dominant European American perspective (Roberts et al. 2020). Indeed, Steven Roberts, Carmelle Bareket-Shavit, Forrest Dollins, Peter Goldie, and Elizabeth Mortenson (2020) note in their article on racial equality in psychological science, "Our research suggests that the psychological publication process is, understandably, subject to the same structural inequities that stratify the rest of society. Psychological research is mostly edited by White editors, under whom there have been fewer publications that highlight the important role of race in psychology. The few studies that did highlight race were written mostly by White authors, under whom there have been fewer participants of color" ("Moving Forward"). Whether intended or not, the message of noninclusion is transmitted clearly to both female faculty and female faculty of color within the discipline, as well as female graduate students of color who have previously reported feeling like "uninvited guests" in psychology classrooms (Vasquez et al. 2006). Because racial and ethnic minority females are dually burdened with Otherness due to their race/ethnicity and gender (Chang et al. 2013), being additionally bullied for their research can have a profoundly silencing effect on them.

The tragedy of replication in psychology is that somewhat akin to the myth of voter fraud (Minnite 2011), a few prominent examples of fraudulent studies have propped up the idea that researchers in psychology labs are ignoring established scientific standards in favor of quick and easy publications. I am not denying there are problems with replication in psychology, only suggesting that lack of replication does not negate the findings of a study or devalue the work the researcher has done (Stanley and Spence 2014). However, I do think there is a problem with generalization in psychological research that must be addressed. For instance, psychology's dependence on participants from Western, educated, industrialized, rich, democratic (WEIRD) countries has sustained the illusion that there are fundamental ways of thinking and seeing (i.e., perception) shared by people across the world (Henrich, Heine, and Norenzayan 2010).

I also believe the endeavor to improve methods and practices around the scientific process in the discipline is worthwhile. But I am concerned that without an explicit acknowledgment of existing power structures—and the ways they influence the scientific endeavor in psychology—any changes made will inevitably mean hegemonic structures of race, gender, and social inequity are reinforced. Ultimately, the attempt to improve methods could have a negative impact on diversifying psychology. As Hall (1996) has stated, "Every identity has at its 'margin,' an excess, something more" (5). Any changes should include the perspective from the margins; otherwise they will have the effect of constricting the margins of the discipline and further burdening those who must fight against oppression to make their voice available to the center (hooks 1989).

Framed within this overview, I am proposing that faculty in psychology explicitly commit to efforts to enhance diversity and inclusion and reduce inequity associated with minority identities. My suggestion is consistent with the recommendations made by Roberts et al. (2020), except I believe that if we do not prioritize diversity and inclusion *over* methodological issues, we will continue to re-create power structures that have fueled inequity in our society. Adopting Tony Becher and Paul Trowler's (2001) metaphor of disciplines acting as "tribes" allows us to see psychology is engaging in disciplinary self-defense to maintain relevance in an ongoing dialogue about our understanding of the human condition. The repercussions of this self-defensive engagement can be felt throughout the disciplinary realm. Within the territory of the classroom environment, I focus on the emphasis placed on ensuring undergraduate students learn APA-style writing, particularly in introductory psychology courses. My claim is that this focus on APA style creates yet another barrier for minority students to overcome in order to add their voice to the ongoing dialogue in psychology. Below, I outline how I came to this conclusion, highlight some of the ways teaching writing in psychology can reinforce inequity, and provide suggestions for those teaching psychology to counter this inequity with a focus on diversity and inclusion.

APA RULES OF WRITING AS THRESHOLD CONCEPTS IN PSYCHOLOGY

> *I am an untenured junior faculty member who struggles, like most others, to balance the demands of teaching and research. I am also passionate about teaching psychology and always looking for ways to improve my skills in the classroom. So when I was asked by my colleague to join her for the HCWE Faculty Writing Fellows Program, I said*

> *yes immediately. I was naïve to the literature on threshold concepts, but I was very motivated to learn about methods that would help me teach students about writing in psychology. I distinctly recall being very uncomfortable when we are asked to identify threshold concepts within our discipline. Having read the material we had been assigned, I knew the goal was to arrive at a consensus on foundational pieces of knowledge within our discipline.*
>
> *My faculty colleagues and I identify as developmental psychologists and teach courses within the same domain of expertise in psychology. So arriving at a consensus on conceptual ideas should have been fairly easy. Yet we struggled to find common threshold concepts we could all agree were fundamental to our students' learning. We bounced around some ideas, discussing a few and rejecting others. All the while we watched in dismay as our colleagues in other groups were efficiently creating lists of threshold concepts. I had a very uncomfortable feeling we were missing something.*
>
> *Then one of us, I don't recall who, mentioned methods of doing scientific research and APA-style writing. Suddenly, we weren't struggling anymore. In contrast to our stilted discussions about concepts, we had little trouble identifying and agreeing upon the discursive rules that govern writing in psychology. Despite the fact that we were a diverse group of female faculty (two women of color, one full professor, one associate teaching professor, and one untenured assistant professor), we had reinforced and reproduced the power structures of our discipline. We had defined the boundaries of the discipline around the methods.*

"How did we get here?" This was the first question I asked myself after we had established threshold concepts for our group in the Fellows Program. "*And why was I so uncomfortable with the outcome?"* I did not have answers for either question at that time. In the discussion that followed after we had finished identifying and listing our threshold concepts, I recall raising the problem of power and privilege in relation to the threshold concepts we had discussed in our group. The fact that as a woman of color and as a nontenured faculty member, I had parroted the privileged perspective in our group discussion was shocking to me. I had mistakenly assumed my intersecting minoritized identities would protect me from ventriloquizing the privileged perspective. But I was wrong, and I knew I had to spend time self-reflecting before I could understand how this had come about.

In my naiveté I had assumed we would travel out of our liminal space into threshold concepts that would be about, for the lack of a better word, *concepts.* Instead, we had disagreed on concepts fundamental to our work and agreed on practices that define our discipline. To be clear, I am not suggesting this is a problem inherent to threshold concepts (although I do raise this issue in the conclusion section later in the chapter) or the process by which we arrived at our threshold concepts. Others have previously indicated that this type of "troublesome" knowledge can emerge out of the endeavor to identify threshold concepts (Land et al. 2005), even though the focus is primarily on concepts students find troublesome to grapple with and learn. Threshold concepts are described as portals to new ways of learning and understanding ideas in a discipline (Meyer and Land 2005). Because portals are doorways, the implication is that a person going through the portal experiences a change in location. The only problem was, just like Dorothy in the Wizard of Oz, I was extremely uncomfortable with where I had ended up.

According to the literature on threshold concepts, by engaging with these concepts, the learner moves from a place of "innocence," where the meanings of concepts are unknown, to a location where the conceptual ideas fundamental to their discipline are assimilated into their psyche (Cousin 2006). This idea sounds good on the surface because it suggests a change in the student's worldview. But if we take a critical stance here, this transformative shift in thinking also implies the individual must *assimilate* into their disciplinary tribe. Davies has described it as *surrendering one's passport or "going native"* (Davies 2016, 6, 7, italics added). I use the literature on the psychology of immigration to show why the goal of assimilating the student's thinking into disciplinary boundaries is problematic, particularly for a discipline like psychology that is plagued with bias (Roberts et al. 2020).

In his seminal work, John Berry (1992) characterized acculturation as a process through which two cultures come in contact and adapt around one another. He focused primarily on the immigrant's experience and identified four acculturative strategies that enable this process of adaptation of the immigrant to the host culture. According to Berry's research, the most psychologically successful strategy is integration, which is characterized by a willingness exhibited by the immigrants and individuals from the host country to mutually accommodate each other. In effect, the immigrant changes in response to the host culture, but the host culture also adjusts to accommodate the immigrant. One example of the change that frequently occurs in a host culture due to immigrants is that the cuisine of the host culture/country changes. For instance, the popularity of Chinese food in the United States can be viewed as an indicator of the impact immigrants from China have had in the country. Amongst the other three less successful strategies identified by Berry is *assimilation*. In contrast to integration, assimilation is the result of the immigrant shedding, *not always voluntarily*, parts of their own culture in order to fit with their host culture. Assimilation, unlike integration, is a one-way process by which the immigrant is forced to silence parts of their identity to find a place in their host culture. Even if the immigrant *willingly* submerges parts of themselves in order to assimilate into their host culture, it is important to remember assimilation comes at a cost to the immigrant.

In applying Berry's theoretical ideas to my own experience with the Howe Faculty Writing Fellows Program and its discussion of threshold concepts, it becomes clear why I was mirroring the biased perspective within my field of study. I had assimilated the disciplinary rules into my psyche, *as one must*, in order to become a *native* in my discipline. In doing so, I had surrendered the parts of my identity marginalized by the discipline. Although the process of self-reflection was uncomfortable and difficult, it did clarify I had abandoned my position of resistance in order to feel *worthy* of being part of academe. In my pursuit of tenure, I had uncritically absorbed the rigid prescriptions about the standards of scientific work that characterize my discipline. In doing so, I also had to mute my identities as a woman of color and an immigrant. This experience, unfortunately, is shared by many female faculty of color (Chang et al. 2013). My experience—and those of too many other female faculty of color—suggests merely increasing diversity in the faculty ranks will not solve the problem of diversity and inclusion in psychology. The bias in psychology exists at the core of the knowledge-production process (Roberts et al. 2020) and can only be removed by employing strategies explicitly counter to this bias.

RULES THAT SILENCE DIVERSE STORIES

> *Inspired by bell hooks (1989), I am using the narrative of marginalized identities to move the struggle of the margins to the center of the dialogue. In order to give voice to those too often silenced in the average psychology classroom, I first attempt to define the space and location from which I speak. I am a woman of color and an immigrant. I came to the United States in my late twenties to pursue a graduate degree in psychology. All I had with me when I arrived in Boston, Massachusetts, was a suitcase full of clothes, $1,000 I had saved after years of hard work, and a promissory note from the university that had admitted me that my fellowship would pay my school fees and provide me with a small stipend to cover living expenses. All I have accrued after coming to the United States, both helpful (a PhD, faculty job in psychology) and hurtful (the realization that I speak English with a distinct accent, the knowledge that I am one among too few women of color in my discipline), and my experiences before my life in the United States inflect my voice.*

Proficiency in formal writing is critical to an undergraduate degree in psychology (Jorgensen and Marek 2013). In particular, students in psychology are taught a formal system of writing known as APA style. APA style is a formal writing system with prescribed rules detailed in a manual produced by the American Psychological Association. As of the writing of this chapter, the manual is currently in its seventh edition of publication. Amongst other things, APA-style writing provides guidance on ways to organize a manuscript, rules about citation, and presenting information in tables. In essence, reading the manual can be useful to a researcher when they are preparing a manuscript for publication.

However, over time, the rules of APA-style writing have become ossified into the epistemological process in psychology (Madigan, Johnson, and Linton 1995). As a result, APA no longer serves merely as a specialized writing system intended for publication. Instead, APA-style writing has taken on the role of an acculturative process by becoming enmeshed in the undergraduate curriculum in psychology. An example of this entanglement is that undergraduate psychology majors are exposed to elements of APA-style writing at all levels of the curriculum. As such, competency in APA-style writing has become an indicator of psychological literacy (Landrum 2013).

The adoption of APA-style writing as an integral aspect of psychological literacy has had the effect of creating a self-governing system that tightly regulates discursive moves made by the constituents of the discipline. In *Discipline and Punish,* Michel Foucault (2012) describes how the mere presence of a surveillance system restricts an individual's actions and agency. In psychology, not only are rules of formal writing at the core of the discipline, they are also being policed by a system of reward and punishment that extends all the way into the classroom. The inevitable effect of this self-governing system is that it constrains discursive practices within boundaries created by those with power and privilege. A byproduct of this, also, is that stories that don't align with the experience or expectations of those with power and privilege are silenced.

Below, I critically examine two of the rules of APA-style routinely taught in undergraduate classrooms and show how they may contribute to perpetuating bias in psychology. I do not intend for this to be an exhaustive list of issues with APA-style writing; for details about this topic, please see the work of G. Scott Budge and Bernard Katz (1995) and Robert Madigan, Susan Johnson, and Patricia Linton (1995). I am presenting these as examples to help me make a point.

The Use of Frequent Citations in Journal Articles

All undergraduate students in psychology courses are taught to cite sources to support their arguments. In teaching students to cite, faculty often highlight that citations should be a frequent occurrence in their writing. In my own teaching, I have noticed this instruction inevitably leads to a discussion on how many times one should cite in a paper (e.g., "*Is once per paragraph enough?*"). This focus on frequency of citation in student writing is reflective of the value system of the discipline, which uses the number of times a researcher has been cited to identify their eminence in the field (Haggbloom et al. 2002).

However, the focus on citation indices ignores the fact that journal editors, who are mostly white, act as powerful gatekeepers to determine the research that gets published. Additionally, racial/ethnic minority researchers often publish in specialty journals with low impact factors, which means they get cited less often than their white colleagues (Roberts et al. 2020). Essentially, by narrowly fixating on frequency of citations as an indicator of a researcher's success, psychology as a discipline reinforces the inequities that exist between faculty of color and their white colleagues. Similarly, when we specify the frequency with which students must cite or how many citations the research papers must have, we are reinforcing frequency of citations as a marker of quality. In effect, we are normalizing the inequity that already exists in the discipline.

Language as a Medium of Information and Not as a Product

In addition to citation, undergraduate students are taught that language is simply a medium through which information about the data and research findings is communicated. Consequently, students are encouraged to use impersonal language and discouraged from using linguistic flourishes or personalized language in their writing. This type of writing provides the veneer of objectivity by shifting the focus away from the authors/researchers to the data being presented (Madigan, Johnson, and Linton 1995). In my own teaching, I remind students to remove words that allude to feelings about the data (e.g., *interestingly, surprisingly, shockingly, happily*) when describing their findings.

However, this focus on objectivity in writing overlooks two important realities of racial/ethnic minority researchers in psychology. First, because psychological science is predominantly white and male, identities of female and racial/ethnic minority researchers are *necessarily* visible and marked in their manuscripts through their names. As a result, the objectivity supposedly achieved by abandoning one's space and location in society is a privilege rarely, if ever, made available to minority researchers.

Second, racial/ethnic minority researchers are more likely to be interrogated about their bias in comparison to their white colleagues, particularly if they propose to study minority populations that most closely represent them (Nzinga et al. 2018). As a result, these researchers have already lost the battle for objectivity even before the writing process has begun. When we uncritically insist our students write objectively or present the findings with objectivity, we are reinforcing a privileged majority white perspective. And, in doing so, we are also silencing the voices and experiences of minority students in the classroom.

Not only is APA writing style riddled with bias, it is also notoriously difficult for students to learn (Mandernach, Zafonte, and Taylor 2016). Because students struggle to learn the rules of writing per APA style, and psychology undergraduate programs value formal writing competence in their students, a veritable cottage industry on teaching APA style to students has emerged (Landrum 2013). Within this volume, my colleagues provide an excellent overview of some of the problems students encounter when learning to formally write in psychology (see chapter 7). In particular they highlight that students are frequently engaged in inauthentic writing practices (e.g., working alone) that do not reflect the ways professionals in psychology practice writing. These inauthentic experiences can push students who lack background knowledge or skills pertinent to formal writing into disengaging from psychology as a discipline. Often minority students attend underresourced high schools (Warburton, Bugarin, and Nunez 2001) and/or have learned English as a second language, so their skills in writing and discoursing need additional scaffolding to develop. These students may find the rigid rules prescribed by APA style even more challenging than students who have graduated from well-resourced schools and are monolingual English speakers. As a result, psychology may be losing the very students it desperately needs to add to its ranks.

If we are going to create any transformative learning experiences in the classrooms that allow our students to become contributing members of our disciplinary culture, we must first understand and empathize with their current space and location.

Now, imagine a student like Mikala, who is already asking herself what the rules of success are in this new culture, sitting in an introductory psychology classroom. Past research has shown that students with marginalized identities (e.g., first-generation students, ethnic/racial/linguistic minorities) are often uncertain about their place on college campuses. Much like Mikala, they worry about finding the right way to act so they can be successful in college (Stephens et al. 2012). In effect, minority students are like immigrants, seeking to make their place in a culture unfamiliar to them.

Without a critical understanding of the bias inherent in formalized writing systems like APA, psychology instructors might mistakenly believe they are helping minority students in their classroom find their voice by explicitly teaching them the rules of APA-style writing. But without an acknowledgment of the ways power and location create subjective truths, efforts to teach students discursive rules of formal writing could end up codifying these rules. Then, instead of affirming a space for minority students to resist academic socialization, instructors would be asking them to choose between their identities (i.e., minority versus student).

Teachers in the classroom have the power to create a culture that, at the very least, accommodates the minority student so they don't have to assimilate into the majority culture. However, if psychology is to move toward reducing the bias inherent to its knowledge production, we must foster a classroom environment that celebrates and amplifies the margins of the discipline. In order to do so, diversity, inclusivity, and equity must be at the heart of our teaching agenda when teaching writing in psychology.

SUGGESTIONS FOR ANTIBIAS TEACHING OF WRITING IN PSYCHOLOGY

As I argue above, the APA style of writing is biased against racial/ethnic minority students and researchers. If you are convinced by my argument and interested in employing antiracist strategies in teaching writing in psychology, I provide some suggestions below. I use ideas from Ibram Kendi's (2019) book *How to Be an Antiracist* as my inspiration. According to Kendi, "Racist ideas have defined our society since its beginning and can feel so natural and obvious as to be banal, but antiracist ideas remain difficult to comprehend, in part because they go against the flow of this country's history" (23). For some, implementing these strategies may feel like an unfamiliar yoga stretch in the beginning, but if we hold in place and tremble our way through the first uncomfortable days, we will be amazed at how far we can stretch outside our comfort zone:

1. **Acknowledge your own privilege and bias.** Similar to my own uncomfortable journey, you may have to spend time acknowledging and confronting your own biases and privilege. Without acknowledging our

own role in maintaining structures of inequity, we will fail in our effort to teach our students to critically engage with the disciplinary work in psychology.

2. **Explicitly acknowledge that the APA style of writing is biased.** One easy way to do this in the classroom is to acknowledge that APA is a specialized form of writing that is informative about the scientific practices in psychology but that it does not reflect how writing is done in other disciplines or in everyday life. Another way to do this is to contextualize the rules for your students. Show them how journals expect authors to know the rules of APA-style writing, but also show them journals that do not adhere to APA-style writing.
3. **Encourage messy conversations about race and power by making explicit the politics of authorship.** Instructors are often taken aback when conversations about racial inequity or social justice arise in classroom discussions about content. In the moment, it can be hard to come up with well-thought-out responses. Instead of waiting for students to bring up these topics of discussion, use the authorship system in APA writing style to make explicit the politics of power and authorship.
4. **Decouple the rules of APA-style writing from the reward system of grading.** Instead of assigning grades for writing in APA style, consider assigning completion points. Additionally, instead of spending time in class showing students how to cite in APA style, show your students how to use endnote or Mendeley or Google Scholar to format references in their papers.
5. **Amplify minority voices and perspectives.** This can be done in a couple of different ways. First, if you are planning to use journal articles in psychology for your course, please consider assigning articles written by minority researchers. Second, highlight the experience of minority populations in your teaching.

CONCLUSION

In this chapter, I provide an overview of the replication crisis in psychology in order to highlight the power wielded by gatekeepers of knowledge who have limited the ideas, identities, voices, and experiences of minorities in the discipline. I focus on the rules of APA-style writing as a system of self-governance that closely regulates the way knowledge in psychology is presented, read, and understood. My analysis also suggests threshold concepts can provide a framework for understanding the biases inherent in a discipline. As a result, they may need to be critically interrogated for their ability to reinforce and recreate dominant perspectives in a discipline. Whether this reinforcing is the result of the essentialist way threshold concepts are defined (i.e., transformative, irreversible, bounded) or the fact that they emerge as a consensus among authority figures in the discipline needs further examination. As the editors discuss in chapter 3 of this volume, making deep meaningful change at the curriculum level is hard. Professional development programs such as the Howe Faculty Writing Fellows Program can provide the spark for this work to begin but only if they also serve to provide *all* faculty the space to speak their truth. I believe making meaningful change begins with acknowledging that experiences of power and privilege differ across faculty and disciplines and encouraging meaningful conversation about these differences as part of the process of identifying threshold concepts.

REFERENCES

Berry, John W. 1992. "Acculturation and Adaptation in a New Society." *International Migration* 30 (s1): 69–85.

Becher, Tony, and Paul R. Trowler. 2001. *Academic Tribes and Territories: Intellectual Enquiry and the Culture of Disciplines.* 2nd ed. Buckingham: Open University Press.

Budge, G. Scott, and Bernard Katz. 1995. "Constructing Psychological Knowledge: Reflections on Science, Scientists and Epistemology in the APA Publication Manual." *Theory & Psychology* 5 (2): 217–31.

Chang, Aurora, Anjale D. Welton, Melissa A. Martinez, and Laura Cortez. 2013. "Becoming Academicians: An Ethnographic Analysis of the Figured Worlds of Racially Underrepresented Female Faculty." *Negro Educational Review* 64 (1–4): 97–118.

Cousin, Glynis. 2006. "An Introduction to Threshold concepts." *Planet* 17 (1): 4–5. https://www.tandfonline.com/doi/full/10.11120/plan.2006.00170004.

Davies, Jason. 2016. "'Threshold Guardians': Threshold Concepts as Guardians of the Discipline." In *Threshold Concepts in Practice,* edited by Ray Land, Jan H. F. Meyer, and Michael T. Flanagan, 121–34. Rotterdam: Sense.

Everett, Jim Albert Charlton, and Brian D. Earp. 2015. "A Tragedy of the (Academic) Commons: Interpreting the Replication Crisis in Psychology as a Social Dilemma for Early-Career Researchers." *Frontiers in Psychology* 6 (August): 1152. https://psycnet.apa.org/doi/10.3389/fpsyg.2015.01152.

Fiske, Susan T. 2016. "A Call to Change Science's Culture of Shaming." *APS Observer* 29 (9). https://www.psychologicalscience.org/observer/a-call-to-change-sciences-culture-of-shaming.

Foucault, Michel. 2012. *Discipline and Punish: The Birth of the Prison.* Translated by Alan Sheridan. New York: Vintage.

Frazier, Kimberly N. 2011. "Academic Bullying: A Barrier to Tenure and Promotion for African-American Faculty." *Florida Journal of Educational Administration & Policy* 5 (1): 1–13.

Haggbloom, Steven J., Renee Warnick, Jason E. Warnick, Vinessa K. Jones, Gary L. Yarbrough, Tenea M. Russell, Chris M. Borecky, Reagan McGahhey, John L. Powell III, Jamie Beavers, and Emmanuelle Monty. 2002. "The 100 Most Eminent Psychologists of the Twentieth Century." *Review of General Psychology* 6 (2): 139–52.

Hall, Stuart. 1996. "Who Needs 'Identity'?" In *Questions of Cultural Identity,* edited by Stuart Hall and Paul du Gay, 1–17. Thousand Oaks, CA: SAGE.

Hartley, James. 2012. "New Ways of Making Academic Articles Easier to Read." *International Journal of Clinical and Health Psychology* 12 (1): 143–60.

Henrich, Joseph, Steven J. Heine, and Ara Norenzayan. 2010. "Most People Are Not WEIRD." *Nature* 466 (July): 29.

hooks, bell. 1989. "Choosing the Margin as a Space of Radical Openness." *Framework: The Journal of Cinema and Media* 36: 15–23.

Johnson-Bailey, Juanita. 2015. "Academic Incivility and Bullying as a Gendered and Racialized Phenomena." *Adult Learning* 26 (1): 42–47. https://doi.org/10.1177%2F1045159514558414.

Jorgensen, Terrence D., and Pam Marek. 2013. "Workshops Increase Students' Proficiency at Identifying General and APA-Style Writing Errors." *Teaching of Psychology* 40 (4): 294–99.

Kendi, Ibram X. 2019. *How to Be an Antiracist*. New York: One World.

Land, Ray, Glynis Cousin, Jan H. F. Meyer, and Peter Davies. 2005. "Threshold Concepts and Troublesome Knowledge (3): Implications for Course Design and Evaluation." *Improving Student Learning: Diversity and Inclusivity*, edited by Chris Rust, 53–64. Oxford: Oxford Centre for Staff and Learning Development.

Landrum, R. Eric. 2013. "Writing in APA Style: Faculty Perspectives of Competence and Importance." *Psychology Learning & Teaching* 12 (3): 259–65.

Madigan, Robert, Susan Johnson, and Patricia Linton. 1995. "The Language of Psychology: APA Style as Epistemology." *American Psychologist* 50 (6): 428–36.

Mandernach, B. Jean, Maria Zafonte, and Caroline Taylor. 2016. "Instructional Strategies to Improve College Students' APA Style Writing." *International Journal of Teaching and Learning in Higher Education* 27 (3): 407–12.

Meyer, Jan H. F., and Ray Land. 2005. "Threshold Concepts and Troublesome Knowledge (2): Epistemological Considerations and a Conceptual Framework for Teaching and Learning." *Higher Education* 49 (3): 373–88.

Minnite, Lorraine C. 2011. *The Myth of Voter Fraud*. Ithaca, NY: Cornell University Press.

Misawa, Mitsunori, and Michael L. Rowland. 2015. "Academic Bullying and Incivility in Adult, Higher, Continuing, and Professional Education." *Adult Learning* 26 (1): 3–5. https://doi.org/10.1177%2F1045159514558415.

Nzinga, Kalonji, David N. Rapp, Christopher Leatherwood, Matthew Easterday, Leoandra Onnie Rogers, Natalie Gallagher, and Douglas L. Medin. 2018. "Should Social Scientists Be Distanced from or Engaged with the People They Study?" *Proceedings of the National Academy of Sciences* 115 (45): 11435–441.

Roberts, Steven O., Carmelle Bareket-Shavit, Forrest A. Dollins, Peter D. Goldie, and Elizabeth Mortenson. 2020. "Racial Inequality in Psychological Research: Trends of the Past and Recommendations for the Future." *Perspectives on Psychological Science*, June 24. https://doi.org/10.1177%2F1745691620927709.

Shrout, Patrick E., and Joseph L. Rodgers. 2018. "Psychology, Science, and Knowledge Construction: Broadening Perspectives from the Replication Crisis." *Annual Review of Psychology* 69: 487–510.

Stanley, David J., and Jeffrey R. Spence. 2014. "Expectations for Replications: Are Yours Realistic?" *Perspectives on Psychological Science* 9 (3): 305–18.

Stephens, Nicole M., Stephanie A. Fryberg, Hazel Rose Markus, Camille S. Johnson, and Rebecca Covarrubias. 2012. "Unseen Disadvantage: How American Universities' Focus on Independence Undermines the Academic Performance of First-generation College Students." *Journal of Personality and Social Psychology* 102 (6): 1178–97.

Vasquez, Melba J. T., Bernice Lott, Enedina García-Vázquez, Sheila K. Grant, Gayle Y. Iwamasa, Ludwin E. Molina, Brian L. Ragsdale, and Elise Vestal-Dowdy. 2006. "Personal Reflections: Barriers and Strategies in Increasing Diversity in Psychology." *American Psychologist* 61 (2): 157–72.

Warburton, Edward C., Rosio Bugarin, and Anne-Marie Nunez. 2001. *Bridging the Gap: Academic Preparation and Postsecondary Success of First-generation Students*. Washington, DC: National Center for Education Statistics. https://nces.ed.gov/pubsearch/pubsinfo.asp?pubid=2001153.

13

GETTING MESSY

Talking and Walking Threshold Concepts to Advance Social Justice Learning in Teacher Education and Beyond

Scott Sander, Brian D. Schultz, Sheri Leafgren, and Barbara J. Rose

Teacher Education

*I can't breathe. I have my ID right here. My name is Elijah McClain. That's my house. I was just going home. I'm an introvert. I'm just different. That's all. I'm so sorry. I have no gun. I don't do that stuff. I don't do any fighting. Why are you attacking me? I don't even kill flies! I don't eat meat! But I don't judge people, I don't judge people who do eat meat. Forgive me. All I was trying to do was become better. I will do it. I will do anything. Sacrifice my identity, I'll do it. You all are phenomenal. You are beautiful and I love you. Try to forgive me. I'm a mood Gemini. I'm sorry. I'm so sorry. Ow, that really hurt. You are all very strong. Teamwork makes the dream work. (*crying*) Oh, I'm sorry I wasn't trying to do that. I just can't breathe correctly.*

—Elijah McClain, August 24, 2019

AMY COOPER: Sir, I'm asking you to stop.

CHRISTIAN COOPER: Please don't come close to me.

A COOPER: Sir, I'm asking you to stop recording me.

C COOPER: Please don't come close to me.

A COOPER: Please take your phone off.

C COOPER: Please don't come close to me.

A COOPER: Then I'm taking pictures and calling the cops.

C COOPER: Please call the cops. Please call the cops.

A COOPER: I'm going to tell them there's an African American man threatening my life.

C COOPER: Please tell them whatever you like.

A COOPER: There's an African American Man. I'm in Central Park . . . he is threatening myself and my dog. I am being threatened by a man in the Ramble. Please send the cops immediately.

—May 26, 2020

https://doi.org/10.7330/9781646423040.c013

> *After a review of the charge and work underway by the President's Diversity, Equity and Inclusion (DEI) Task Force, the students of this committee have decided to cease further engagement. In joining the task force, our hope was built upon the respect and priority for the lived experiences of marginalized students at Miami. We expected to have a high degree of trust in this committee's desire to hear the needs and demands of its students. We hoped for a clear path from brainstorming to proposal-making . . . working to manage the process of implementing real solutions. Furthermore, we anticipated the members of the task force already having competent knowledge of DEI, instead of meetings becoming an impromptu training session on basic terminology like implicit bias, microaggressions, etc. . . . there is an overwhelming presence of condescending behavior by some members of the committee, especially in regards to Miami's history of racist professors and the realities that many of our students are facing. . . . Therefore, we will not involve ourselves with the DEI Task Force any longer.*
>
> —Kamara and Small 2020

> *Today at a Black Lives Matter rally in Oxford, a man drove up and began yelling at us, referring to our group as a bunch of "monkeys." That man is . . . current faculty [the faculty member was retired but was teaching during retirement] in the Department of Teacher Education . . . I can personally verify that he used that term and he did so intentionally as a racial epithet.*
>
> —Jason Bracken, protester

These vignettes all highlight injustices around the country and on our campus: the power of white supremacy contributed to the killing of Elijah McClain; the criminalization of Christian Cooper; the resignations of fifteen student members of Miami University president's Diversity, Equity, and Inclusion taskforce at our university; and the very public reveal of a (retired) professor in the Department of Teacher Education at our university as virulently racist. In the current moment of a long-overdue international awakening on systemic racism, we frame this chapter as a reflection on the collaborative, justice-oriented work over the past several years by the faculty of our Department of Teacher Education.

This chapter narrates a series of collaborations, most occurring between 2017 and the summer of 2020, whose goal has been to shift the collective consciousness and mindsets of a faculty of thirty toward justice, with the idea that this paradigm shift will also impact how (we) faculty think about preparing future teachers. The use of threshold concepts (TCs) have caused us all to confront personal identities long afforded the privilege of staying silent around issues of white supremacy and remaining ignorant about its ever-present and far-reaching influence.

The story begins in 2017 with a small group of faculty wrestling with the internal self-work reflected in one of the goals named in our unanimously agreed upon Department of Teacher Education (EDT) Strategic Plan: critical introspection. Critical introspection, as described in our strategic plan, requires that we "examine, confront, and expand [our] own beliefs and understandings about issues of diversity and social justice while infusing discourses around anti-oppression into curricula." Animating the efforts of these faculty were questions: "How can a department of teacher education develop and actualize a strategic plan and curricula with social justice as a core principle?" "How can the learnings from the process (talking) and products (walking) be used by others?" "How do educators shift deeply flawed assumptions about education given their own experiences/practices and systemic challenges?" "How do teacher educators co-construct understandings with students that change rather than reinforce the system and promote students as knowledge producers so they can promote their future students to do the same?"

Serendipitously, as we continued to grapple with these questions after forming the strategic plan, five of us found our way to an opportunity to participate together as Howe Faculty Writing Fellows. Although we did not enter the Fellows Program to explicitly wrestle with questions and concepts set forth in our strategic plan, the Fellows Program may have given us a way to do just that: operationalize and work towards the goals we had set for ourselves. The semester-long program—in which we met for one hour a week over fourteen weeks—was, according to the seminar description given to participants at the time, "designed to support faculty members and their departments/programs in their efforts to teach their students to write more effectively in their professions/disciplines and to use writing in ways that support deep learning of disciplinary material . . . [with an expectation that] departmental cohorts [would] create an implementation and delivery plan for their larger departments/programs regarding how to enhance writing instruction and student writing abilities and/or assessments of them." In the rest of this chapter, we reflect on our work in the Fellows Program and the ways we have continued these conversations as a full department in a local and national culture at odds with our social justice goals.

MESSING ABOUT IN THE FELLOWS PROGRAM

We entered the program without clear expectations. We did not know what would happen during those fourteen meetings, nor did we know what was likely to result from a "writing program" when it seemed what we needed was a straight-up revolution. We did know a few things. We knew we wanted to continue to engage with our animating inquiries and so many more. We knew we wanted to collaborate with one another. We knew we needed compulsory meeting times to *make* the space to come together to contemplate the ideas that drive each of us. We knew the ten goals of the department strategic plan were not magic or instant or possibly even achievable. We knew the work we do with and for young people compels us to radically (re)conceptualize schooling toward a more authentic and disruptive relationship with curriculum. We knew we were *hungry* to find ways to advance our mutual efforts to challenge "conventional thinking around what we currently know as 'school' . . . [embracing the] radical imaginary in that it seeks to understand the world in its current state while vehemently working with others to change the current condition" (Stovall 2018, 51). This radical imaginary challenges simplistic visions of school improvement by forcing us to view them as sites based on rigid compliance and dehumanization where our actions must break down these structural inequalities.

We also knew that whatever we did, we would ultimately bring our work to a faculty that included those who—in spite of a unanimously approved mission statement and strategic plan—are deeply enamored with schooling, our department, and the field of teacher education just as it is. In earlier conversations with faculty about goals for the department and how to plan for change, many in positions of power—through membership in dominant groups in terms of status, race, gender, and experience—proposed that we should "just keep the ship on the course" and that we should invest our efforts in "celebrating [and continuing] our 200 years of excellence." Some noted that they did not come to Miami University for social justice work and that our students did not either—they just came to learn to "be good teachers." Others, who ostensibly were on board with our goals of an anti-oppressive curriculum, claimed they were and had been doing justice work all along. We knew that among our faculty were those who held beliefs profoundly antithetical to this work:

> A man drove up and began yelling at us, referring to our group as a bunch of "monkeys" . . . that man [was] . . . [retired] faculty in the Department of Teacher Education. (Bammerlin, *Miami Student*, June 7, 2020)

Knowing that amongst our faculty, albeit retired (but still teaching while in retirement), was an alleged racist teaching *our* students created an overriding sense of urgency. We knew from the beginning that creating an "implementation and delivery plan for [our] larger department/program" in the Fellows Program must include careful and consistent consideration of ways that would somehow entice at least *most* of the faculty to be a part of the change.

Our first meeting at the Howe Center for Writing Excellence offered a way of entering this critical task. Plans for change that focus on merely changing faculty practices without deep intellectual investments in the underlying principles that drive the change risk implementation of changes in routinized and inflexible ways . . . a disconnect that can actually result in harmful outcomes. We learned that framing our work's threshold concepts could serve as a mechanism for processing and articulating critical principles.

We began with a careful analysis of our department mission statement:

> We prepare future and current teachers who design and implement culturally and contextually relevant curriculum and pedagogy. Empowered by a critical and substantive understanding of research, these teachers are positioned to confront social injustices, apply global perspectives, and actively participate in democratic society.

In essence, we pulled it off the wall in order to *use it* to guide, influence, and shape our shared path. Over the following weeks, we generated lists of words, concepts, and deeply considered articulations that revealed our personal and collaborative ideas. Discussing these ideas shifted the ways we each thought about various aspects of our work in teacher education, curriculum, and pedagogy. We considered how TCs might help shift the departmental climate and culture steeped in disciplinarity or technical aspects of teaching and learning towards humanistic and culturally responsive pedagogy in the name of using education for social justice ends. We also considered the imperative that faculty engage personally with threshold concepts and the ways TCs can inherently alter how as faculty we engage with our students in more authentic and justice-oriented ways.

At each weekly meeting, we shared our personal writings on the work—and collaborated in composing representations of highly complicated and critical constructs fundamental to our field. The shared process of writing together made visible our thinking; it emerged as unique and generative, creating knowledge together—a synthesis of ideas as opposed to a summary of words.

As faculty with a multiplicity of educational perspectives from science, preschool, elementary, and TESOL teachers to a plurality of ways we socially locate ourselves, we brought to the table a wealth of diverse experiences and a willingness to question what we thought we knew. Some of our conversations later played into the composition of our "implementation and delivery plan" as we came to realize there exists a departmental division in what it means to prepare teachers. This rift in beliefs regarding how teachers should be prepared led one of our former students, Alli, to describe her experience in one of our programs as "whiplash," the forceful, rapid back-and-forth movement between opposing views on education as she moved from classroom to classroom and professor to professor.

While we seemed united on items on the strategic plan and unanimously approved a beautiful mission statement, it's clearly easier to talk about social justice than to live it with no shared understanding of what it means to be a socially just educator on a day-to-day basis. We are surrounded by a language used in education and across the university that represents an unexamined adherence to the banking model. This simple transactional model drives university structures for course construction and approval, which continue to reflect the power of the antiquated Ralph Tyler (1949) view of curriculum as "setting objectives, selecting learning experiences, organizing instruction, and evaluating progress" and the power of the ever-popular and oppressive requirement of Benjamin Bloom's taxonomy for learning (1956). It is also a model that informs many of our faculty, so the challenges and barriers exist within the department as much as outside it.

The Fellows Program allowed us to consider how writing generatively and toward the yet unknown might be used across the program to confront these barriers so we could move toward a shared understanding of social justice and the EDT mission/vision. We concluded that the writing/thinking of our graduates should be influenced by TCs and pathbreaking, critical, and important scholars in the field of education. We most frequently included Paulo Freire, followed by Howard Zinn, Kevin Kumashiro, William Ayers, Gloria Boutte, and Vivian Paley in this list, as illustrated in the following word count.

We felt it was important to adopt a mirrors-and-windows approach to our collaborative efforts so we would be living the TCs, not just teaching about them. If we are able to look inward to (potentially) see for ourselves what needs to be changed versus merely focusing on outward practices (tips and tricks), there exists a greater potential to effect systemic change in a significant way. Examining these concepts within

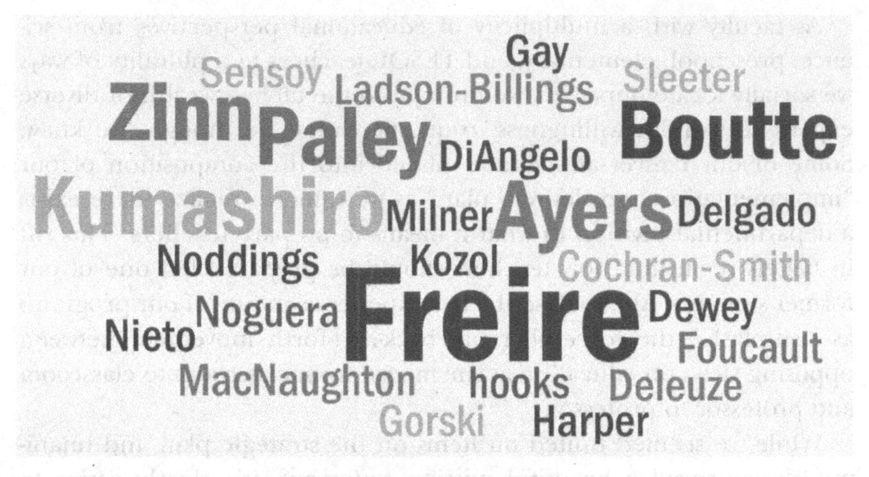

Figure 13.1. Word cloud of path-breaking, critical, and important education scholars as identified by Miami University's Department of Teacher Education faculty.

ourselves would inherently change how we engage with students and content (curriculum). Understanding the challenges and barriers of systemic change would allow us to strategically plan for and navigate them (they would not be easier, just expected and anticipated). Frederick Douglass (1886) was right about justice, and through supporting our own growth and our students' growth in understanding and living these threshold concepts in our programs, partnerships, and scholarship, we aim to disrupt schooling as it acts as an arm of the state that, paraphrasing Douglass, denies justice, enforces poverty, is built on prevailed ignorance, and is organized toward oppression.

The process of tackling such questions and complex issues was (and continues to be) exhilarating, messy, and urgently necessary. Threshold concepts scaffold our department-level work and give us sanctuary to explore deeply our intellectual journey toward educational transformation. Our process, challenges, learnings, and products so far are shared in this chapter, with emphasis on what is transferable to other disciplines that aim to advance social justice learning.

TALKING THE THRESHOLD CONCEPTS: THE FIRST RETREAT

Engaging in the Fellows Program as an experienced but new-to-Miami department chair provided a way for coauthor Brian Schultz to lead the department in actualizing the strategic plan the faculty had recently, unanimously approved. But when a colleague invited him to join the professional development group, he was hesitant about the time commitment and did not know what to expect. Not too far into the weekly sessions, it became clear the notion of TCs could anchor our collective strategic-planning work. The ideas we as a small group of colleagues thought of as cornerstones to the ways we lived and envisioned teacher education had deep potential. After naming these ideas, it become clear how the TC efforts could transform the work already occurring within the department. The department was going through transition: Brian was the sixth chair in ten years, and the roller coaster and instability of leadership had proved frustrating to the faculty. Whereas the critical mass of faculty was pivoting toward the ideas inherent in the department's mission statement, there was significant work to do, and we needed an organizing center for it. The strategic plan was one such step, but a collective set of values that would be our TCs would prove to be a next step.

After two groups of faculty members engaged in the Fellows Program, we invited Liz (Elizabeth Wardle) and HCWE graduate assistant Caitlin Martin to facilitate our department's opening retreat for the academic year. Having Liz as an outsider with insider information proved to be invaluable—she witnessed the Fellows contemplating and deliberating the very ideas that would become our threshold concepts. Having someone with deep knowledge of TCs and limited knowledge of teacher education positioned her as a process expert willing to listen to and document the rich conversation of a large faculty. This framing and the ensuing discussion provided the faculty with a collective and shared experience. It also raised awareness within some individual faculty as the collective was prompted to see how the TCs were (or were not) present in each program and each course. It also begged questions of why and how the TCs could be a part of every course in each program. TCs, it became clear, were not add-ons or topics with which only certain professors in certain classes engaged. Rather, TCs were the guidepost ideas that would drive the work of the department from its very first engagement with our students to the time our students were engaging with students of their own during a student-teaching experience.

Although the retreat aspired to larger goals than were possible to accomplish in the several hours dedicated to the retreat, it quickly and emphatically allowed an awareness of the possibilities of taking up unifying principles. A document emerged by the end of the retreat detailing the big ideas connected to TCs that the faculty could stand behind. This document, along with the work from our time in the Fellows Program, proved to be great fodder for contemplation for the department leadership team.

The departmental leadership team, made up of faculty and staff, determined that the generative ideas from the retreat and those earlier Fellows documents could be the nexus for a one-page document that could anchor conversations and decisions and curriculum work with the department. If we all agreed on these concepts as the guiding ideas that framed our collective work, why would we not rely on these very ideas in making decisions, prioritizing labor, and challenging our students as they matriculated through our programs?

With the faculty in the department seemingly on board with organizing ideas to guide the department, and the department leaders in agreement, Brian approached a critical, well-liked junior faculty member with a challenge: Could she, or would she, synthesize the ideas into a single-page document for debate and deliberation among the rest of the faculty? Was it possible to distill complex ideas into that single page? Would that be worthwhile?

It was possible. It is proving its worth.

With the insightful and compelling synthesis of the faculty member charged with distilling the notes, the aggregated work of two Fellows groups, and the ideas generated from the retreat, she, along with the leadership team's editing, composed, in part, the following:

> What we aim to foster in our teaching candidates:
>
> - Becoming critically conscious curriculum makers for social justice
> - Working in solidarity within community contexts
> - Developing a critical lens to see power and privilege and the consequences within and beyond educational contexts
> - Building intellectual framing/lenses toward various ways of being (knowing, learning, reflecting, and acting) as pedagogues
>
> Based on our commitments, the following threshold concepts [must] be directly addressed through the experiences we offer at EDT. This will help students shift their thinking about teaching, learning, and education.
>
> - Education is not neutral/teaching is political.
> - Curriculum is more than standards, textbooks, or courses of study.
> - Curriculum is coconstructed.
> - Both teachers and students have empowerment/agency.
> - Teaching is/as intellectual engagement.
> - Teachers and students engage in critical consciousness.
> - Teaching and learning honor people's full humanity.
>
> These threshold concepts help define social justice in education and foster this orientation in our students:
>
> - Social justice requires awareness, action, activism, and practice.
> - Social justice questions power and how institutionalized powers are enacted in specific instances that privilege some and marginalize others.

The power of a one-page document provided the department with a simple go-to place where the multiple teacher-education disciplines could all latch on. The initial steps of this process (from Fellows to faculty retreat) pull from chapter 3 of this book regarding how existing cultures and long-standing systems continue to operate, even thrive, alongside the messy, challenging work required for second-order, deep change. Our ongoing work involves changing underlying belief systems about what it means to be a teacher and how teachers should be prepared. We've seen that this is not a linear process and can actually go against common-sense notions of teaching and learning. As a department we've been continually asked to critically reflect on our own identities, as well as our work with students, in an attempt to create a consistent narrative—avoiding "whiplash"—that requires challenging and navigating history and tradition within our department.

WALKING THE THRESHOLD CONCEPTS: THE SECOND RETREAT

If we really believed curriculum change was to happen alongside students and in solidarity with the community, how could we make that change a reality? Rather than the usual faculty meetings where we do a lot of talking about what we will or want to do, we needed to immerse ourselves within the community. Therefore, Brian proposed locating the next year's opening retreat in one of the communities served by our Urban Cohort.[1] If faculty could literally walk the community, they might well see some of the TCs in place and in action. This experience created a greater potential for influencing change among faculty who had yet to see how TCs are part of their work.

Tapping into the insights of those outside the field of education who have shared goals in mind helped Brian and a small team of faculty who helped plan the second retreat to navigate how to approach this work with the department. We arranged neighborhood walking tours with community-based organizations and invited our colleague from the Department of Architecture, John Blake, to introduce us to the space known as Buddy's Place, the home of Miami University's Center for Community Engagement, and to share his perspectives as the center's director. Our department thus shared an experience in a long-standing space of community partnership—a space a large majority of the faculty did not know existed and so had never visited. Partners from the Peaslee Neighborhood Center, an old schoolhouse that now anchors the community in justice work and provides a multitude of place-based experiences for our Urban Cohort students, joined us to take small groups of faculty members on walking tours of the neighborhood surrounding Buddy's Place. Walking in the community with our community partners as our leaders positioned these partners as experts to shine light on issues, topics, and concerns that must be embedded within the coursework of teacher candidates. They taught us. As we know and articulate in our TCs, the teacher education curriculum goes well beyond the content of how to teach math or reading or science. These subjects are in relation to all the contextual factors present (and hidden) where students teach and learn.

While walking—with mindful attention to the aesthetics of the place and the people, and adopting a sort of critical lens—we interpreted the text of the neighborhood. This interpretation was unique to each of us according to what we were internalizing apropos the TCs. When one faculty member spoke of his memory of "the riots" in the community nearly twenty years earlier, Jen, the community-based guide in that group, gently corrected: "protests." When another faculty member responded to the evidence and explanation of the impact of gentrification on the community, especially on specific individuals and families, with worry about whether or not she was part of the problem because she had begun "coming down here to shop and eat once it got better," others in the group responded with concerns of their own about ways they were perhaps complicit in contributing to the pain of others. Both these anecdotes are powerful. Powerful in terms of cognitive dissonance. Powerful in how change is both perceived and received. Seemingly innocent on the surface, they are situated within deficit perspectives of the very communities we claim to prepare teachers to enter. They speak to the self-work and critical introspection TCs position faculty to do. Only with this kind of introspection will change occur within the classrooms and with the students we teach.

That day, in our own form of "walking meditation," we walked with no destination other than coming to understand that TCs might serve as a critical lens through which to read the texts of people, histories, and places. We walked together not toward a destination but toward a *beginning* of troubling our own apathy, disconnectedness, and assumptions—apathy, disconnectedness, and assumptions that have manifested in our department for years as dismissive glances and condescending head shakes at the very mention of social justice in the context of teacher education. We walked for ourselves and we walked for everyone toward recognition of the ways privilege had led us to believe we are and *should be* sheltered, protected, actively kept apart/distanced from the lived realities of Others/those Othered. Privilege that held us together, warm and secure in our ignorance of "it's always been this way" and "what does justice have to do with teaching?" Safe. We walked together into unknown spaces and unexplored ideas; we walked together across the threshold.

THRESHOLD CONCEPTS IN PLAY: MESSING ABOUT WITH MANDATES AND MYOPISTS

> *In the port is safety, comfort, hearthstone, supper, warm blankets, friends, all that's kind to our mortalities. But in that gale, the port, the land, is that ship's direst jeopardy.*
>
> —Herman Melville

Like New Bedford in *Moby Dick*, schools are both secure and oppressive. Often those who choose to teach—in pre-K–12 and in higher education—have sought and found safe harbor: comfortable, secure, and nurturing of their schooled identities as conforming, obedient, and complicit actors in their storied journeys that arc toward the safely familiar. "Safe harbors are places where people anchor themselves in what is comfortable and secure, in a fixed sense of who they are" (Carlson 2002, 2); this fixed sense of self morphs into myopia and gridlock.

When considering the work we do in our department of teacher education, we labor under the watchful eyes of many entities: accreditation, state, university, federal, tenure, college, and even department mandates and expectations. These structures of control—constructed on white supremacy and designed to maintain and defend systems of wealth, power, and privilege—manifest in our very own department as schooled faculty willingly—even eagerly—aspire to achieve goodness in exemplary mandate-meeting. This is safe.

Challenging the romanticized image of safe harbors, toward living "landless and shoreless" (Carlson 2002, 2), the department took on a strategic plan in 2017. Faculty collaborated to develop the plan over six months, resulting in ten goals, including a goal for curriculum:

> Challenge candidates to become critically conscious curriculum makers for social justice, in solidarity with communities, within diverse contexts.

We also included a goal for critical introspection:

> Examine, confront, and expand faculty's own beliefs and understandings about issues of diversity and social justice while infusing discourses around anti-oppression into curricula.

While no one objected to the plan and its goals—it was approved by the faculty unanimously—there was little in the day-to-day life in the department for students and faculty that suggested any significant venture into the discomfort of the unknown such efforts require. Expressions of seeking safety, narrowing interpretations of possibilities, and resisting outright included statements such as "I'll get bad evaluations," "We have to do it this way or we'll lose accreditation," "This could get me fired," "You won't be happy unless all of our students are fired from their first teaching job," "You're going to the wrong schools," and "Who am I to tell them what to think?" Whether due to the security of successful adherence to the system of mandates or the comfort of myopic views of roles and expectations, the strategic plan existed as words on a page yet lacked shared understanding and therefore was not enough to move us offshore.

Enter the threshold concepts. As noted earlier in this chapter, our TCs provide a quality, a narrative, that insists that faculty engage in the study and practice of education as politically, socially, economically, or culturally charged. We were forced to look in the mirror as individuals with the responsibility to make decisions that radically reimagine education (and schooling) and actively combat structural inequities. David Stovall (2018) names the radical imaginary as imperative to interrogating School "as a US institution [that] primarily rewards students [and faculty] for order and compliance, which should also be considered part and parcel of the larger projects of settler colonialism and white supremacy/racism . . . the call . . . is for radical educators to challenge themselves . . . to eliminate the order, compliance and dehumanization that happens in [in school] while allowing for the capacity to imagine and enact a radical imaginary" (51).

The threshold concepts serve as a compass—a kind of moral compass—to guide us into spaces of work that, in a small way, allow us to negotiate the morass of mandates and narrow myopic interpretations, and even myopic colleagues. Dennis Carlson (2002) writes, "A storm is brewing on the national horizon, yet the good citizens of New Bedford, in their safe harbor, cling to a false sense of security" (2). As the epigraphs that begin this chapter make clear, we are in the midst of a devastating storm of the consequences of whiteness and white supremacy. But we aren't the citizens of New Bedford.

The following anecdotes illustrate a few ways TCs are impacting the day-to-day life in the department for faculty and students—moving us all away from safe harbor.

Pre-K–5 Redesign and Those Who Are Our Bosses: CAEP, State, and Other Assholes

In 2018, the State of Ohio passed SB 216, the Public School Deregulation Act, which included a licensure grade band change, eliminating the

Early Childhood Education (prekindergarten through grade three) license and replacing it with a PK–5 Primary license (prekindergarten through grade five). Every university in the state was required to change what had been their early childhood education programs to accommodate new licensure requirements. We saw this mandated change as an opportunity to create something new, different, *radical.*

During the eighteen-month-long process of program (re)visioning—again laboring under those watchful eyes (state, university, accreditor, and so on) surveilling through procedurals, submissions of forms, layers and layers of standards, mandates, house bills, senate bills, and the seven circles of approval (analogous to Dante's nine circles of hell)—we dreamed that with fidelity to the threshold concepts, we could somehow overcome the panoptical power of that omnipresent scrutiny and make something new. We imagined ways the TCs would/could compel us to generate new ways of being and acting as educators and learners.

We gathered over the course of those months—a process tasked to the same people running the old/current program. Early on, it became apparent that engaging in the sort of thinking, conceiving, writing necessary to bring about the change we sought was not everyone's cup of tea. Without change in the individuals in the room, how could we expect a new/different product/outcome? Recall that one of the goals in the now two-year-old strategic plan included critical introspection, an element we very clearly needed. Critical introspection requires a willingness to peer inside, to query one's motivations, and to question long-held beliefs. This is not safe.

Progressing into the work, one could imagine the faculty positioning themselves on a first- to second-order change continuum of willingness and ability. First-order changers wondered with annoyance why we didn't just add the standards for the two new grade levels to what we already offered in our program; some suggested "better" ways to teach X, Y, and Z; some thought adding a detached unit on social justice would do the trick; and one objected to the thought of conceiving anew the state mandate requiring phonics (Ohio Laws) through a framing in constructs of critical literacies, stating dismissively and with certitude: "Phonics is phonics." This resistance was another small but powerful reminder that without change within the individuals in the room, how could we expect a new/different product/outcome?

Those in the working group approaching second-order change wanted to approach the program revisions not only in ways that would involve changing underlying belief systems and practices within themselves but also in ways that would impact our teacher candidates. It was clear the TCs must play an integral role in reconsidering how we critically read the myriad mandates and reconsidered what the required contents could be, recognizing the social-political nature of critical scientific, mathematical, social science, and language literacies. Phonics isn't merely fonix. It has a historical, cultural, and political context even if we choose to not see it or are privileged to ignore it. Fundamental to living the TCs required *everyone* to be willing to resee their relationship with their respective content specialties as something more complicated and contextual. Moving from reading and reciting the department's TCs to embodying them toward changing our institutions and hegemonic practices can feel like a Sisyphean task.

But we can share here one example of how the TCs came to be represented in the documented program changes, approved by all seven layers of Dante's inferno of university politics and surveillance. Our university's Course Inventory Management System (CIM) requires statements of rationale in its "approval process in order to assist the University in utilizing the structure and options of all functional capabilities to the fullest" (Miami University n.d.). Our overseers demanded that we present for approval a rationale for the new program and rationale for each course in the program. The TCs directly influenced the language of these rationales, concurrently and reluctantly abiding by the mandates foisted upon us. Below are the texts of our Program Rationale and the Course Rationale for one of the courses in the new program.

> Program Rationale: The Primary PK–5 program serves to position teacher candidates as intellectuals who co-create new knowledge and who come to take responsibility for their professional learning. Engagement in the Primary PK–5 will contribute to the critical consciousness of teacher candidates as they work to negotiate the chasm between critical curriculum/pedagogy and what is perceived as narrowly mandated (often scripted) curriculum. The Primary PK–5 will support teacher candidates' abilities toward realizing a critical, social justice pedagogy based on the assumptions that teaching is political and curriculum is more than standards, textbooks, or courses of study.

> Course Rationale, Social Studies PK–5: Child and Curriculum Integration: This course aims to empower pre-service teachers to co-construct a socially- and culturally-relevant social studies curriculum within diverse PK–5 classroom settings serving diverse communities. The rationale derives from a concern that political animosity, polarization, and inability to work together to solve national problems is in some ways linked to the marginalization of history, government, economics, and other social studies courses in the national curriculum. In this course, teacher candidates—many of whom did not have consistent access to the social sciences in their own schooling—will engage with the fullness of the social studies toward

> an appreciation and commitment to providing rich and challenging social studies instruction to their own PK–5 pupils.

It remains to be seen if the rationale emerging from interpretations of mission, vision, and TCs, and approved at all levels of oversight, will themselves lead to the kind of mandates faculty fearful of leaving safe harbor will find comfort in adhering to. The alternative is to see these words as just words on a new document that doesn't spark any awareness of uncertainty, leading to a business-as-usual approach. But perhaps the goodness-through-compliance-seeking that holds such power for evil over thought and action will now apply to thought and action for good.

A FEW WORDS ABOUT TC PLAY IN OTHER SPACES

Change occurs slowly and is most often a result of top-down demands, which often originate with the university's capitalistic opportunism. The words of Audre Lorde (2007) run with excruciating persistence through our heads:

> For the master's tools will never dismantle the master's house. They may allow us to temporarily beat him at his own game, but they will never enable us to bring about genuine change. Racism and homophobia are real conditions of all our lives in this place and time. I urge each one of us here to reach down into that deep place of knowledge inside herself and touch that terror and loathing of any difference that lives here. See whose face it wears. Then the personal as the political can begin to illuminate all our choices. (112)

Nonetheless, we are steeling ourselves to respond to every required change and shift in programming by surreptitiously leading each scheme of change with the power of TCs. We outline four examples that contextualize how we've been able to leverage threshold concepts.

Dual Licensure: Emerging most predominantly as a means to increase enrollment and increase our graduates' marketability, dual licensure became another top-down expectation for change to the early childhood program at precisely the time the grade-band changes were occurring. The process of engaging in this change required that faculty from the Department of Teacher Education collaborate with faculty from Department of Educational Psychology, school-district personnel, and university student-teacher supervisors (generally, retired school administrators), who quite naturally knew nothing of our commitment to the TCs and the role these ideas must play in every aspect of our department's work. First steps in the work, then, included presenting the TCs and explaining the history, social-political context, and expectations inherent in the application of TCs. Watching the faces of former principals and some faculty immersed in positivism as we used quotes from Frederick Douglass, James Baldwin, David Stovall, and (strategically) our dean, Michael Dantley, to introduce them to the landless and shoreless spaces required by TCs was simultaneously comical and concerning. But those expressions reminded us that our TCs emerged from our experiences and professional orientations, and these people were hearing about them for the first time. We invested much time and intellectual effort in developing and enacting TCs, which further impacted our beliefs and priorities in ways, perhaps, we did not even recognize, so this audience's lack of connection should have been expected. Those blank, confused, and sometimes terrified faces jolted us into the realization that our intimate relationship with the TCs could contribute to possibly discouraging or even excluding others in taking the leap into the threshold. It was an important lesson.

Transformative Education: A co-listed (with educational leadership) graduate program, transformative education, was prompted to redesign itself in order to apply for a significant university grant. The second-order changers who are involved in this project are bringing the language and constructs of TCs to the table, informed by stories of student and faculty experience in the program as it stands. One such graduate student, Alli, cried foul when her first few courses in the current program consisted of faculty engaging in status quo practices that represent their power and powerlessness to resist the comfort of safe harbors. She shared with us her frustrations at pervasive use of deficit language by faculty and fellow students, and she especially challenged the use of course texts authored by Robert Marzano (e.g., Marzano 2009), whose methods are commonly employed by local school districts to narrow, and so simplify, the choices and experiences of teachers and students. While we appreciated the pain of Alli's experience, we were more concerned about the other graduate students—many of whom were practicing classroom teachers—who would nod their heads in agreement as the professor was actually confirming what so many teachers and preservice teachers believe they need—classroom management techniques or fun and easy lesson plans (likely pulled from Pinterest! or Teachers Pay Teachers)—while drifting—no, *bolting!*—away from the stated mission/vision . . . further away from the liminal space. Alli and students like her are powerful drivers in our commitment to TCs and their potential to confront the too-often unexamined status quo.

Bookends, part 1: Introduction to Education: Even prior to the development of a strategic plan and creation of threshold concepts, efforts had been made by a critical mass of faculty to reimagine the initial step in teacher education, our Introduction to Education course. Much time and energy was spent considering the types of experiences and ideas our students should be exposed to from day one of the program. Realizing this course would only be the beginning of a four-year program, we knew it also had to do some heavy lifting to redirect the students' thinking about what is possible to imagine as teachers.

This introductory course explores the purposes, organizations, and outcomes of schooling from the perspectives of the field of social foundations of education, primarily historical and cultural disciplines. Now framed around the teacher education mission and vision statements as well as the TCs, candidates undertake critical inquiry into teaching as a profession. We explore historical, philosophical, and contemporary purposes of schooling in order to open up new possibilities for students and teachers in a complex, multicultural, and democratic society situated within an interdependent world.

The Introduction to Education course at Miami University is designed to scaffold students into professional conversations about diversity and inclusion. We look to challenge deficit thinking about aspects of diversity like race, class, and gender in order to prepare teachers with cultural consciousness and competence. The course is intended to help undergraduate students examine their identity and positionality, grapple with issues of power and privilege, and consider *what needs to be learned, unlearned, and relearned* to become a transformative teacher.

During the process, conversations about this course have also opened up conversations within our faculty about TCs. How do educators shift deeply flawed assumptions about education given their own practices and systemic challenges? How do teacher educators co-construct knowledge with students that changes rather than reinforces the system and promote students as knowledge producers so they can promote their future students to be the same? We know the experiences and ideas that happen in the course, but how do conversations continue and build afterwards across the program? What are topics or concepts we feel uncomfortable or unprepared to teach and how do we still move forward? If the current moment has revealed anything it's the need for critical conversations about diversity and difference along with an increased sense of urgency. The TCs have been an invaluable resource to shape, guide, and make these conversations internal for faculty, which then opens the potential for engaging students in more critical questions and discussions.

Bookends, part 2: The AR/WT: The Antineoliberal TPA: A delightful side effect of the TC-driven shift in writing—for both faculty and for students—is that engaging in a process informed by TCs leads to products that are generative, emergent, surprising, and painfully authentic rather than transcriptive, underanalyzed, depersonalized, and formulaic. An example of this side effect emerged from a project in the department to honor the college and department missions and visions. Several years ago, faculty who would later be a part of the Fellows Program determined that the commercial edTPA—a gatekeeping exit exam that determines if teacher candidates are eligible for licensure that is administered by the publishing behemoth Pearson Education—used by our university to determine the "success" of the student teaching experience for each of our teacher candidates was a straight-up distraction from what we valued in teacher preparation, especially as the culminating (bookend) experience. In order to intentionally confront the power of whiteness and to encourage curricular understandings as social and political, we decided to upend the teacher-performance assessment process administered by the monolith that is Pearson Education through its ubiquitous edTPA.

The instrument we devised in its place is called the Assessment of Readiness/Willingness to Teach (AR/WT), and over the years of its development, it has been impacted not only by the input of students who took part in the process of the AR/WT in its early iterations but also by the emergence of our department's threshold concepts. While the AR/WT is composed of nine prompts and has a rubric of expectations, we make clear to our teacher candidates that they may interpret this instrument in ways that enhance their student-teaching experience and advance their own forays across the threshold concepts vital to *them.* Not nine algorithmic responses to nine schooled prompts, not written as a sense of writing to expectations for a reader looking for what is already predetermined as right and correct, but rather responses that emerge from experiences in schools and communities that are authentically unique, deeply personalized, and clearly shoreless and brave. In our radical reimagining of curriculum, we prefer that our students produce writings impossible to fit into any formal rubric because we can experience these writings as realizing thresholds *with* or *alongside* our students. As an example of the impact of threshold concepts on students' culminating experience in our program, we include here a too-brief excerpt from one student teacher's response to the AR/WT—a beautifully written, poignant, powerful, and singular essay. Here is Maggie:

> I am Bad at Using the Copier and Should be Dead: A Gay Vermin Story
>
> "Are they good people?" We are doing worksheets on handwriting. We are on day one "A." I tried to make it a little less soul crushing. More mean-

> ingful. I told them "We all write our letters different ways, but today we're going to practice them the way the people who made this worksheet want us to write them." Jazmin asks a very good question. Are the people that make these worksheets good people? My soul screams "NO! They are bad! Let's stop doing this!" but what I say is "I don't know these people, so I don't know if they are good or bad. Mrs. Winthorpe found this page on the internet, and we'll use it today, just to practice."

And here is a little more of it . . . just a taste . . .

> School makes me feel like Gregor from Metamorphosis. Vermin that got into the building somehow. I am always hiding and trying not to let anyone in the building know that I'm a filthy deviant insect. We have two pet rats in the apartment. Taylor once looked at them sleeping and yawning and remarked that it was such a good feeling to see a prey animal that was relaxed. There are really four rats in the apartment.
>
> I feel an upsetting dissonance when I am trying to help a kid work and he is pretending to know what is going on, putting on an act for me like I put on an act for people that I perceive to be watching and assessing me. I want to tell him that I am not his factory foreman, I just want to get him through this, I would never yell at him, poke him, I would never expose him as a fellow animal of prey. I'd like to see him relaxed, yawning, smiling. I'm thinking of a specific kid, never saw him smile, never spoke unless spoken to. He was in the "LOW" math group. What a perfectly delicious descriptor for what it feels like to be in that group: low, lowly, scampering, sweating. I hope perhaps when he gets older he'll be able to enjoy the camaraderie of being with the kids in the low group, the rat cage. We all know we are dim and we love the joke of it. There is no need to deny it when surrounded by nothing but your own kind. There is such uncomplicated love in that den of vermin. When I was in stupid math in high school I knew a boy who broke into cars to steal things from them. I asked him to skip over my grandma's if he was ever in her neighborhood and he kept his promise. (Petroski 2020, 1, 2–3)

What score would Pearson have assigned to this? Moot point. Maggie would have never written this for a score.

RESPONDING TO RACISM IN OUR RANKS

The TCs position the department to take action and take a collective stand beyond the curriculum endeavors. Since TCs were first introduced to the department as a whole two years ago, they have become part and parcel of the work we do as a department. This was particularly apparent when a retired colleague allegedly made racist remarks at a community protest in response to the murder of George Floyd.

The current moment of a long-overdue racial awakening has challenged all groups and organizations from educational institutions to corporations to respond to the racial injustice and structural racism inherent to our country. What to do about the retired colleague's actions? Do we add to the cacophony and make a statement? Will that statement have meaning? Or simply add more noise? The department chose to take a stand in words, but also with actions.

As chair, Brian called an emergency department meeting with less than a day's notice. Almost all faculty who received the message while being off contract showed up. As we discussed the fallout of our former colleague's alleged reprehensible behavior, we also were purposeful that we wanted and needed to take action. With the encouragement of the entire department, a group of half the faculty sprang into action to construct a statement that would be sent to colleagues, recent alumni, current students, and incoming students. TCs set the department up to be positioned in such a way as to take action and do something. Important, this letter went beyond the rhetoric, acknowledging what many colleagues felt had been both complicity and complacency about matters of racial justice for far too long. With the statement was a consciousness to take action. In the letter that follows is the invitation to attend the Black Lives Matter: Racial Justice and Education Panel presented by Black faculty, Black recent grads, and current Black students as an initial platform for their voices to be heard. This letter and the panel were simply first steps.

June 16, 2020

> We, the Department of Teacher Education (EDT) faculty, and many of our students, alumni, staff, community members and partners recently witnessed clear evidence of blatant racism. This racist incident is inflammatory and contemptible and, as EDT faculty, we are ashamed. During this moment of collective global grieving and outrage at the ongoing violence toward Black Americans and the reprehensible murder of George Floyd, Breonna Taylor, Ahmaud Arbery, and countless other Black Americans, we acknowledge the legacy of slavery, and how white supremacy, and antiblackness leads to countless deaths of fellow Black citizens in our country, now and for the past 400 years.
>
> We are writing this letter to you to acknowledge our complicity, to express our pain, and to convey EDT's stance and action in response to this moment and our country's ignominious history. We commit to make more concerted efforts toward racial justice and equality in the EDT department, the local community, and society.
>
> Our Vision Statement is that we, the Department of Teacher Education (EDT), are people dedicated to the improvement of the common good through teaching and learning. Our Mission Statement is designed to prepare future and current teachers who create and implement culturally and contextually relevant curriculum and pedagogy, and who are empowered by a critical and substantive understanding of research, are

positioned to confront social injustices, apply global perspectives, and actively participate in democratic society. We commit to all of you that we will engage in the hard work necessary to live our mission and vision that we claim as our collective identity as teacher educators.

These statements guide the experiences of EDT students and faculty, toward shifting our thinking about teaching, learning, and education:

- Education is not neutral and teaching is political.
- Curriculum is co-constructed and more than standards, textbooks, or courses of study.
- Both teachers and students have empowerment/agency.
- Teaching is intellectual engagement.
- Teachers and students engage in critical-consciousness.
- Teaching and learning honors people's full humanity.

Part of our commitment in fulfilling this vision and mission is through our Threshold Concepts (9/2018). The threshold concepts help define social justice in education and foster this orientation in our students:

- Social justice requires awareness, action, activism, and practice.
- Social justice questions power and how institutionalized powers are enacted in specific instances that privilege some and marginalize others.
- EDT is committed to ongoing development of a socially just curriculum pedagogy.
- EDT is committed to active engagement in practices inside and outside the classroom that fosters social justice for all. Practicing racism is never part of our curriculum nor will evidence of it be tolerated, whether it comes from faculty, staff, or students.

However, in response to the incident, we build on this framework to explicitly practice anti-racism and confront the ongoing consequences of white supremacy in the field of education. In collaboration with students, alumni, and community, we will develop plans of action to ensure that no student, faculty member, community/school partner, or alumni has cause to feel unsafe, unheard, or damaged while engaged with the EDT department in any context, through actions that will include the following:

- Preparing our teacher candidates to be agents of change in their schools, in the profession, and in society so as to confront injustice, prejudice and racism.
- Collaborating with students, alumni, and community to create a truly brave space for learning and living: being safe in a physically, psychologically, emotionally, and intellectually protected environment where prejudice and racism are not given quarter or ignored.
- The development of a widely accessible detailed procedure and policy for students to protect themselves from racism, sexism, homophobia, ableism, ageism, and classism, co-authored by faculty, students, and alumni.
- Consultation with students and alumni on further developing this list of actions to better honor our mission and vision and our students.

- One such event featuring African American professors/alumni/current students from EDT is a virtual panel—Black Lives Matter: Racial Justice and Education—tentatively planned for July 9 at 3:30–5:00pm. Please save the date; more information will be forthcoming.

We are actively involved in seeking out and co-constructing with students and community educational pedagogies for social justice. We will no longer stay silent on any issues of racism, sexism, homophobia, transphobia, ableism, classism, ageism, nativism, now or in the future. We are eager to have your active participation in critical discussions, decisions, and actions which will ultimately advance social justice.

We deeply apologize for the vicious, and incendiary comments that were reportedly made by a retired faculty member, and the complicity of the Teacher Education Department in any and all incidences of bigotry inside and outside of our classrooms. Please know that we intend to ensure that the reported actions and voice of one individual will not represent the voice of our department.

We look forward to seeing you this fall,
Sincerely,

The Faculty & Staff of the Department of Teacher Education

POSTSCRIPT

The TCs continue to have a lasting and ongoing effect on the department. As the fallout from the despicable racist incident of early summer continues, recent graduates are calling for more changes within the department. In a recent letter to the editor (July 27, 2020) in the student newspaper, the *Miami Student*, a cohort of students called out the department and prepared a list of recommendations. The initial response from within the university was to engage with university marketing to respond to the students and hopefully make the "problem" go away. But within the department we had a different response: we were proud of the students, but we also knew we needed to continue doing the work in which we have been engaging over the last three years related to TCs. Rather than silencing or dismissing the critique, we invited the students *in*, into our most recent department retreat. Their words in the newspaper were prereading for the retreat, and their presence, albeit virtually because of the pandemic, was a prompt for us to learn from them. As the students reiterated their recommendations, they challenged us as faculty to do better. In their articulation, though, it was clear the ideas inherent in their critique were there because we had (in part) instilled the values of our TCs during a portion of their programs. It was not by accident or chance that they were pushing back on how things were; instead, they were living the TCs in their new roles as novice teachers. Their insights and perspectives continue to propel our work to make good on mission statements and in realizing the vision we embrace, yet we acknowledge there is much more work to do. Echoing the words of Maxine Greene (1998), we as a department have an end in mind but *we are what we are, not yet.*

NOTE

1. The Urban Cohort is a community-based approach to teacher education. Miami faculty and Urban Cohort students collaborate with high-need schools and community-based organizations in Cincinnati, Ohio, to prepare teachers who are grounded in the life of the community. See https://miamioh.edu/ehs/academics/departments/edt/academics/urban-teaching-cohort/index.html.

REFERENCES

Bloom, Benjamin S. 1956. *Taxonomy of Educational Objectives, Handbook I: The Cognitive Domain.* New York: David McKay.

Carlson, Dennis. 2002. *Leaving Safe Harbors: Toward a New Progressivism in American Education and Public Life.* New York: Taylor and Francis.

Douglass, Frederick. 1886. Speech on the 24th Anniversary of the Emancipation Proclamation. History. https://www.history.com/topics/black-history/frederick-douglass.

Evon, Dan. 2020. "Are These Elijah McClain's Last Words on Police Video?" Snopes, June 26, 2020.

Greene, Maxine. 1998. "Towards Beginnings." In *The Passionate Mind of Maxine Greene: "I am . . . not yet,"* edited by William F. Pinar, 256–57. Bristol, PA: Falmer.

Kamara, Jannie and Brandon Small, et al. (@miamiasg). 2020. "We Will Not Work for Free: Another Committee, Another Facade." Instagram story, July 13, 2020. Associated Student Government Miami University (miamisag) Instagram Account.

Lorde, Audre. 2007. *Sister Outsider: Essays and Speeches.* Trumansburg, NY: Crossing.

Marzano, Robert J. 2009. *Designing and Teaching Learning Goals and Objectives: Classroom Strategies That Work* [*sic*]. Centennial, CO: Marzano Research Laboratory.

Melville, Herman. 1992. *Moby Dick; or, The Whale.* New York: Penguin. First published 1851.

Miami University Office of the Registrar. n.d. "Curriculum Management." https://miamioh.edu/emss/offices/registrar/curriculum-management/index.html.

Ohio Laws and Administrative Rules. Rule 3301-35-06-A: Educational Programs and Support. http://codes.ohio.gov/oac/3301-35-06.

Petroski, Maggie. 2020. "Maggie's AR/WT." Submitted to Miami University to meet student teaching Teacher Performance Assessment requirements, May.

Stovall, David. 2018. "Are We Ready for 'School' Abolition?: Thoughts and Practices of Radical Imaginary in Education." *Taboo: The Journal of Culture and Education* 17 (1). https://doi.org/10.31390/taboo.17.1.06.

Tyler, Ralph W. 1949. *Basic Principles of Curriculum and Instruction.* Chicago: University of Chicago Press.

Vera, Amir, and Laura Ly. 2020. "White Woman Who Called Police on a Black Man Bird-Watching in Central Park Has Been Fired." CNN, May 26, 2020. https://www.cnn.com/2020/05/26/us/central-park-video-dog-video-african-american-trnd/index.html.

PART 3

Taking Stock and Moving Forward

Part 3 takes a look back at the major themes in this collection, synthesizing key points from across chapters and from across our reflections on facilitating the program, and looks forward to the larger implications.

Chapter 14 reflects on the major lessons learned from facilitating the Fellows Program, pointing to what research and experience have demonstrated about the complications and intense challenges of trying to effect deep change through writing-related faculty development. The chapter also provides suggestions for those who wish to design similar initiatives in varied institutional contexts.

The afterword takes a look at some of the underlying causes of the current disintegrative view of education. If the project outlined in this book has been about changing conceptions—often *mis*conceptions—about what writing is and how it works, the afterword asks why such misconceptions exist in the first place.

14

PRINCIPLES FOR ENACTING AN INTEGRATED VISION OF TEACHING AND LEARNING

Angela Glotfelter, Caitlin Martin, Mandy Olejnik, Ann Updike, and Elizabeth Wardle

We began this collection by examining the messy and recursive nature of student learning and writing, as well as how difficult it can be for faculty to engage students in such deep learning due to the often isolated nature of faculty working alone across and through curricula. Faculty need, as we argue throughout the first three chapters, educational development opportunities to come together and understand how writing and learning operate in their disciplines and across their courses. Such discussion and collaboration can lead to faculty examining and expanding their *own* conceptions of writing that can, in turn, inform their practices in their courses and in their programs in meaningful and generative ways.

The Howe Faculty Writing Fellows Program is one approach toward such educational development. In our work and throughout this collection, we ask how teams of faculty can lead from the bottom up to reimagine learning environments that enact integrative, research-based ideas about learning, especially with writing. The chapters in this collection illustrate the complexities of this work. Yet, the contributors to this volume demonstrate it *is* possible for faculty to engage in sensemaking practices together to design curricula, courses, and assessments that put student learning first. Their efforts to learn in teams *about* learning and writing (through the lens of the threshold concepts framework) resulted in many cases in changed conceptions (about teaching, learning, writing, and curriculum) and then efforts to change practices. This approach to educational development reflects the sort of grassroots change that happens from the bottom up when faculty are given the opportunity to innovate and work from research-based best practices. This type of WAC and educational development is possible and rewarding work, but always challenging.

https://doi.org/10.7330/9781646423040.c014

In concluding, we do two things: first, we underscore a few key themes and points from across the chapters in this collection, as well as our overall experience facilitating the program, that might be of interest to other WAC and educational development leaders. Second, we address more practical matters: How might faculty developers create similar types of initiatives at their own institutions?

IMPLICATIONS FROM THE WORK OF THE FACULTY FELLOWS

The successes and difficulties of implementing change, as expressed in the faculty narratives of this collection, as well as from our experience working with Faculty Fellows across the disciplines for the last four years, suggest a number of implications about how to effectively support faculty members in deep change efforts.

Changing Curriculum Requires Leading with Disciplinary Expertise

A number of these narratives suggest faculty members and educational developers, including WAC program directors, who want to institute new university-wide writing requirements around writing and learning might best do so by beginning not with writing or learning in general but with disciplinary perspectives on writing and learning. As economics and philosophy faculty illustrate in chapters 4 and 5, faculty members in the disciplines bring expertise in particular communities of practice to bear in their classrooms, and those practices are an important part of a meaningful approach to reimagining teaching and learning in their fields. This is an important illustration of Elaine Maimon's (2018) principle that "curricular change depends on scholarly exchange among faculty members" (45) and Linda Adler-Kassner's (2017) assertion that "writing is never just writing" (317). Helping faculty members (re)develop curricula or support new writing requirements benefits from opportunities to explore writing, teaching, and learning conceptually and in relation to their own disciplinary expertise. This process is more time intensive than top-down, mandated changes but will also lead to more lasting change (Kezar 2018). The chapters in this collection share the innovative teaching of writing faculty can design when given the space, time, and opportunity to work from their own disciplinary expertise coupled with an understanding of how writing and learning work.

Programmatic Change Is Multilayered and Time Intensive

Designing courses and programs for deep learning and from disciplinary expertise is an activity with many tentacles often unseen by changemakers when they begin particular initiatives: coming to bear on nearly every effort are the nature of the educational system overall and of the local college or university and division; the labor practices of a particular institution and program; bureaucracies and procedures around curriculum approval; the prior knowledge and experiences of both students and faculty; and even, as we see in several examples in this collection, institutional biases. Working through all these challenges to effect deep change takes a considerable amount of time and also often requires efforts far beyond the level of one course or program, even if such far-reaching efforts were not initially planned or anticipated by the change agents. In other words, a group may set out to revise one course and end by recognizing that the placement of their entire program is problematic (as described in chapter 11) or that their courses as a whole may be giving students "whiplash" (as discussed in chapter 13) and must be reconsidered collectively and conceptually. Recognizing the complexities of the larger task at hand is not easy nor speedy, yet it is crucial for deep and meaningful change efforts to succeed.

This work calls the scope and scale of writing-focused faculty development initiatives into question: If faculty teams design innovative curricular changes that are impeded by current policy and practice, what is the role of the educational development center or program in helping to clear the way? What additional training and support do faculty need in order to make meaningful systemic changes? We discuss in chapter 3 the need for leadership training, but the narratives in these chapters suggest there are other layers of changemaking that must be addressed, such as the institution's processes for approving new programs or setting course caps—and the unnamed values that underlie these. The educational developer is in a role to see where bottlenecks and impediments might be, but are they in a role to help remove those? How might they be?

Faculty Positionality Impacts Change Efforts

In addition, not all changemakers have the same resources and affordances at their disposal. Positionality and labor come up implicitly and explicitly across a number of these chapters. For example, at Miami, full-time non-tenure-track faculty are rewarded for engaging in service around curriculum, and often the work of changemaking falls to them (in this collection, both authors of chapter 4, and one author of chapters 5, 7, and 13, hold such lines). Yet sometimes having department chairs involved in the working teams can help move the conversation forward in the larger department or program in ways faculty on non-tenure-track lines (or even untenured faculty on tenure-track lines) may not be able to do. The importance of chair participation is implicit in chapters 5 and 13, in which one of the authors of each chapter is a department chair who helped clear the way for meaningful conversations at the department level.

Even more instructive may be what—and who—is missing from this collection. Several teams of untenured Fellows alumni who did not write for this collection are encountering deep resistance to change within their programs and departments and are unable to move forward with innovations until, as one of them said to us recently, "some people die." Other Fellows alumni who had been on visiting lines left Miami for more secure positions elsewhere, some left academia altogether, and several left due to concerns about bias, racism, and sexism. And as the authors of chapter 11 point out, sometimes the challenge is not the positionality of a person but of an entire program; as the authors of that chapter illustrate, they lost some control of their own narrative when they were put into a new department with other area studies who did not share their values and goals.

Programmatic Change Requires Group Leadership

When we first designed the Fellows seminar model, we assumed the sorts of deep change we wanted to help facilitate required teams of faculty, and the experiences of Fellows alumni so far support this assumption. As Adrianna Kezar (2018) points out, making changes within the larger more complex system from the bottom up requires groups of faculty from the same program to engage in sensemaking together as they talk with groups from other programs; they need space and time to think not as individuals but as (and across) communities of practice. And what Kezar does not say, but the previous point brings into focus, is that having teams of faculty at the table also ensures people from multiple positions and with access to multiple resources and affordances are pooling their resources, abilities, experiences, and social and cultural capital. Changemaking is not a solitary activity, and meaningful facilitation of change by groups of faculty requires trust and goodwill among people bringing different resources to the project who all respect and listen to each other.

Fellows Teams Should Be Sustained as a Larger Community of Practice

Given the importance of group leadership in enacting meaningful change, another charge of such team-based change initiatives should include sustaining the faculty teams as a larger community of practice *after* leaving Fellows. We often tell Fellows upon their graduation from the program that they are "with us for life." They may finish the semester-long program with us, but their work across their disciplines and their departments is only just beginning. In fact, Fellows' work arguably is the most difficult *after* completing the program due to the real roadblocks and resistance they may face from disciplinary colleagues who haven't undergone the same type of conceptual shifts in their thinking (as we discuss above). Thus, an important role of our programming is not only to *start* such conversations around meaningful change but also to support faculty in sustaining those conversations and the changes they seek.

To do so, it's important to design and implement follow-up programming specifically for faculty who have undergone such sensemaking and changemaking initiatives. At our center we've offered Fellows-only workshops and opportunities for Fellows alumni to come together and support one another in their work across their departments. We've offered working lunches where Fellows alumni could come together and share useful tactics and approaches they've taken to work with their broader department, we held a Leadership Reading Group where Fellows alumni who were department chairs or program coordinators could read scholarship on how to lead change, and we've encouraged our graduated Fellows to participate in other longer-term programming, such as a year-long leadership seminar and a year-long faculty learning community dedicated to supporting graduate writers. The exact configurations can vary, but what's important is providing faculty with space and support *after* experiencing their important conceptual shifts so they can continue to learn and reflect on ideas and attempt to make change in their programs and across their larger departments. In this way, they become part of a larger community of practice that consists of other faculty dedicated to making deep change around learning and writing across the university.

Underlying Conceptions and Biases Must Be Made Explicit

Organizational learning is messy and recursive, as Janice Kinghorn and Ling Shao note in chapter 4. As we outline in chapters 1 and 2, and as chapters 11, 12, and 13 powerfully illustrate, institutions have many reasons for holding on to more problematic and top-down models of learning. Some seemingly easy curricular changes can fail because of a lack of shared underlying conceptions/values. Collective sensemaking can uncover, name, and address underlying conceptions and biases to facilitate this process. This is especially true when it comes to inherent but usually unrecognized institutional racism. This unacknowledged racism disenfranchises programs like Latin American, Latino/a, and Caribbean studies (chapter 11) and individuals of color (chapter 12) while couching that racism in the language of neoliberalism. Neoliberalism, as we discuss further in the afterword, *sounds* like it is concerned with student learning but does not actually support that learning except in the cases of the most privileged students.

Reexamining biased or problematic conceptions is yet another place where the threshold concepts framework can serve as a useful tool. Threshold concepts ask experts and insiders to examine unstated beliefs and assumptions so they can be made visible and teachable. Not only that, but naming the implicit also requires coming to terms with those underlying biases and conceptions; after all, the implicit and hegemonic practices of any discipline, as well as higher ed overall, represent the views of those who are (or have been) in power. This collection includes an example of what it means to name and then call into question the dominant threshold concepts of a field as exclusionary (chapter 12). It also includes an example of what it can look like to use the framework to collectively decide on a different set of guiding threshold concepts (what Wardle, Adler-Kassner, Alexander, Elliot, Hammond, Poe, Rhodes, and Womack call "aspirational threshold concepts" [2019, 31]) to bring about large-scale change within a department and confront long-standing inequities in the larger discipline (chapter 13). And it includes examples of how particular threshold concepts can help open students to new perspectives and understanding of the world around them, such as Otherness, discussed in chapter 9, and multiple, related concepts, discussed in chapters 8 and 10.

It is important to recognize the tension of working with the TC framework. While the threshold concepts framework can bring values and practices to conscious awareness, when those are brought to conscious awareness, practitioners might recognize they are exclusionary. If what we learn by naming our threshold concepts is that they are either exclusionary or incomplete, we must be willing to expand and/or revise our ways of thinking and practicing.

WAC and Other Educational Development Leaders are Boundary Brokers

Finally, we want to return to the role of WAC leaders and other educational developers. This is, in part, a book about how people in those roles can help empower faculty members to take control of the narrative about learning and revise their own pedagogical practices to support integrative learning and invite students into the ways of thinking and practicing of their fields. In other words, educational developers serve as what Etienne Wenger (1998) calls "boundary brokers," or those who can "make new connections across communities of practice, enabl[ing] coordination" across the siloed departments and disciplines of the university setting (38). Directors of WAC programs or centers for teaching and learning are not typically recognized as either administrators or leaders as institutions of higher education typically define those roles. But given the view of leadership and change we have outlined in this collection, it seems fair to recognize them as both of those. Because they work with faculty from across the disciplines and also because they typically have no formal part in assessing those faculty for promotion and tenure, they have a special role to play in helping activate faculty leadership around teaching and learning from the bottom up. They can help faculty change institutions of higher education for the better, working with teams and acknowledging disciplinary expertise and making theories of learning, leadership, and change accessible.

Overall, the work of this book takes up many highly nuanced challenges we currently face in higher education and offers examples of how to meet them. We and the Faculty Fellows' alumni have used the threshold concepts framework as a way to design assignments, courses, and programs to encourage students to deeply engage with the parts of learning that are messy, troublesome, and difficult to traverse. As WAC leaders, we have supported faculty in taking up this important and hard work and have worked with them to enact change. In the end, we offer hope in the ability of motivated faculty to draw from their disciplinary expertise and from theories of learning and writing to create integrative learning environments for their students. The next logical question, then, might be, How can other institutions and faculty development programs design and implement similar initiatives?

DESIGNING SIMILAR INITIATIVES IN VARIED CONTEXTS

At the Howe Center for Writing Excellence (HCWE) at Miami University, we are fortunate to have a large endowment dedicated to writing-related professional development on campus. This funding enables us to experiment and innovate programs and activities. In fact, it is part of our mission to pilot innovations and share our research about these pilots with those beyond our institution. We recognize our generous funding and resources may discourage others from attempting to recreate programs like the one we discuss in this collection, but we hope not because the program's principles can be implemented under various resource scenarios.[1] Below we provide some suggestions for how others can incentivize participation in similar programs. We encourage others to extrapolate and generalize from our experience and imagine strategies that can be usefully applied to their own contexts.

Proceeding from Theory and Conception and Working Interactively with Teams across Time

Regardless of the specifics of institutional context and seminar contents, our experience suggests a program designed to enact deep curricular change requires theory and research first, as well as an explanation of *why* the program is designed as it is; working within disciplinary teams while dialoguing with teams from other disciplines; and extended time for thinking and talking.

Leading with theory and research helps faculty engage around ideas, a strategy put to work in the very first WAC seminars facilitated by Harriet Sheridan and Elaine Maimon. However, a majority of the time should be spent engaging in interactive activities or reflection to apply the theory and research to participants' own experiences and practices.

Faculty will likely come with preconceptions about the nature of WAC workshops and may expect to discuss writing and to design assignments and activities from day one. We've found it's important to set their expectations early in the semester about the theory- and researched-based approach of the program that will engage them in discussion and activities for learning new concepts and uncovering implicit knowledge.

Faculty should work in disciplinary or programmatic teams who work together and interact with teams from other disciplines/programs. Enacting change requires pooling resources, and recognizing what we implicitly know requires talking with others who are both like us and unlike us. Teams are also more successful at long-term change if departmental leaders (like chairs) or "influencers" within the department are on the teams.

Time to reflect and talk with colleagues is essential. Enough time should be built in for reading, thinking, reflecting, and designing; thus, a single workshop is not sufficient. As we note earlier, we have witnessed that threshold concepts themselves can be a threshold concept, and faculty need time to process and pass through their own portals. In addition, faculty need time to really talk with their program colleagues and institutional peers within the seminar to more fully realize and understand their conceptual shifts, which makes providing discussion space during the weekly meetings crucial.

Length is important but also can be variable. One of us has replicated the Fellows process in shorter two-day or three-session workshops with faculty at other institutions. Even though the outcomes were not exactly the same as a full semester of work, these compressed workshops were still productive for faculty who attended. While we prefer to meet weekly for a full semester, we have also had strong success with daily meetings for two or three weeks during the summer because faculty are more fully immersed in the material as they give more undivided attention to it instead of juggling the seminar on top of their myriad other responsibilities during the regular semester. Whatever the configuration, providing longer-term opportunities that extend beyond a single, one-hour workshop are essential for educational development programming dedicated to deep change to be successful.

Recruiting and Compensating Participants

We strongly advise anyone seeking to recruit participants for a similar program to do so with carrots and not sticks (this is the common philosophy of most such programs, but in our experience, upper administrators often like to push the stick model instead, as it appears to garner speedier results). The goal of the program is to engage faculty in the intellectual enterprise of reconceptualizing their teaching and curricula in creative and innovative ways. This kind of change will *not* happen if participants are forced to attend by their deans or provost. Rather, we advise finding the campus influencers and innovators and inviting them to be a part of a pilot program dedicated to having long-term conversations around learning and writing. If the pilot goes well, those faculty members are the best recruiters and ambassadors for future seminars and variations. Allies on campus who can recommend your program's services or vouch for its engaging nature will also be excellent partners in this recruiting. Offering the first pilot during a down time such as the week after school ends in the spring could be helpful. If larger initiatives such as strategic plans, general education revision, new writing-intensive requirements, and QEP projects are underway, linking to them could also be a helpful way to recruit participants and provide them time, space, and resources for undertaking something they have to undertake anyway.

There are many ways to compensate participants for their time and energy. Money is good, of course—offering small or large stipends or professional development money lets participants know their time is valued. Course releases are even better but perhaps even harder to come by than stipends. Without such funding or release time, other forms of creative compensation are still possible. Faculty participate in things for which there is some reward and recognition; rewards might include recognition for promotion and tenure and in their annual reviews. Educational developers can find out if departmental promotion and tenure documents allow for professional development work and curriculum design to be officially recognized in either scholarship or teaching. If they are not, consider asking chairs, deans, and provosts whether they could be. Another option for reward is to frame participation as leading to publishing opportunities. If faculty members can follow up on their participation by researching their curricular designs and writing, and presenting and publishing about them, they will then have found another way to receive credit in annual reviews and promotion and tenure dossiers. They could, at minimum, be provided with lists of scholarship of teaching and learning (SOTL) journals in their fields and more generally, as well as be notified of upcoming conferences where they might share their work, and they could even be encouraged to submit to journals such as *Prompt*, where they could more quickly and easily publish about an innovative assignment. Awards could be given to participants, programs, and departments whose work in the seminar results in innovative curricular designs, and the institution's communication and marketing group could be asked to write features on the award winners. (At Miami, as two examples, we have created a Miami Writing Spotlight on our website where we write profiles of innovative writing practices, and we have created an annual award for individuals or teams who forward the work of writing in the disciplines. And, as this collection illustrates, we work to regularly provide publication opportunities for interested Fellows alumni.) Some institutions provide continuing-education credits for institution-approved minicourses; if educational development seminars such as this one could be added to that list, faculty would have something tangible to show for their work. The point is, there are many ways to reward participation, even if direct funding is hard to come by.

Staffing, Space, and Partnerships

In the HCWE, we have the luxury of assigning each team a staff liaison who works with them during breakout sessions and project design and stays in touch with them after the program is over to further support their work. This is, however, a luxury, not a necessity. What is necessary is a workshop leader who understands writing and learning theory and is adept at motivating faculty participants.

Having a space on campus to do such work can be important as well, although recent research (Martin 2021) suggests a dedicated space for WAC efforts may be hard to come by. We often invite faculty to use our writing center space to work and talk together before or after seminar meetings, as well as invite faculty to attend to work on their own writing during our weekly dedicated writing hours. Such initiatives help faculty feel more at home in our space and with our program and are further ways to build community and rapport that really play a central role in supporting them through their changemaking processes. If a program does not have its own dedicated space, hosting regular events in the library, teaching and learning center, or eLearning center could be helpful for encouraging ongoing conversations. (Advocating for some dedicated space, however small, seems important for visibility and creating community.)

Given the shoestring budget on which many WAC and other educational development centers (or individuals) operate and given the focus of the seminar on learning theories we describe in this collection, pooling resources from across units seems like the most realistic option for appropriately staffing similar seminars and compensating participants. Natural partnerships might be formed between WAC programs, writing centers, centers for teaching and learning, library staff, eLearning offices, and graduate schools. Other possible sponsors or partners might be the office of undergraduate studies or even the honors college, if one exists, where there might be a strong interest in innovating new curricular design. We hope this book might serve as a useful opening for conversation with these units since it provides an illustration of the kind of innovations that might occur if campus partnerships allowed for similar program design and implementation locally.

Sustaining Communities of Practice

Change does not happen overnight, and teams need support after the seminar ends as they try to put their ideas into action. All this support does not need to come from the seminar leader. In our experience,

Fellows alumni are the best resources for one another. Leaders could set up listservs for program alumni, regular working lunches, workshops limited only to alumni, and even reading groups. Fellows alumni like to brainstorm with others who share their language for talking about writing and learning. If the seminar leader plans to follow up with teams on a regular basis personally, this follow-up work should be built into the program budget so there is appropriate compensation for the person doing that consulting (if it is not their full-time job).

When it comes to matters of design and sustainability of the overall educational development structure, we recommend readers draw on Michelle Cox, Jeffrey Galin, and Dan Melzer's (2018) excellent guide, *Sustainable WAC: A Whole Systems Approach to Launching and Developing Writing Across the Curriculum Programs.*

IN CONCLUSION

Learning (and writing) is necessarily messy, nonlinear, context dependent, and hard. So too is the teaching of writing and the learning of faculty who engage in efforts to better support their students in systems of higher education that do not always or necessarily value the work they do or the models of learning they promote. In this book, we provide an overview of one program, the Howe Faculty Writing Fellows Program at Miami University, which takes student learning as its ultimate goal, in order to demonstrate how the principles for deep change and sensemaking can be enacted. We believe our research results and the faculty chapters in this collection indicate that bottom-up, transformative curricular change attending to deep learning is achievable.

As we have engaged in this work, we have come to more frequently question how the larger paradigms governing higher education color and constrain the innovative work of faculty members. In the afterword, we turn directly to this question, arguing that understanding how the current paradigm came to be, naming its values, and pointing to its consequences for students might be a useful affordance for faculty changemakers.

NOTE

1. The HCWE provides the following to faculty for completing the semester-long seminar: the title of Howe Faculty Writing Fellow; $2,000 in professional development funds; copies of the books used in the seminar; access to subsequent grant funding to support research, publications, and conference attendance related to their work from the Fellows Program.

REFERENCES

Adler-Kassner, Linda. 2017. 2017 "CCCC Chair's Address: Because Writing Is Never Just Writing." *College Composition and Communication* 26 (1): 317–40.

Cox, Michelle, Jeffrey Galin, and Dan Melzer. 2018. *Sustainable WAC: A Whole Systems Approach to Launching and Developing Writing Across the Curriculum Programs*. Champaign, IL: NCTE.

Kezar, Adrianna. 2018. *How Colleges Change: Understanding, Leading, and Enacting Change* 2nd ed. New York: Routledge.

Maimon, Elaine P. 2018. *Leading Academic Change: Vision, Strategy, Transformation*. Sterling, VA: Stylus.

Martin, Caitlin. 2021. "Facilitating Institutional Change through Writing-Related Faculty Development." PhD diss., Miami University.

Wardle, Elizabeth, Linda Adler-Kassner, Jonathan Alexander, Norbert Elliot, J. W. Hammond, Mya Poe, Jacqueline Rhodes, and Anne-Marie Womack. 2019. "Recognizing the Limits of the Threshold Concept Theory." In *(Re)Considering What We Know: Learning Thresholds in Writing, Composition, Rhetoric, and Literacy*, edited by Linda Adler-Kassner and Elizabeth Wardle, 15–35. Logan: Utah State University Press.

Wenger, Etienne. 1998. *Communities of Practice: Learning, Meaning, and Identity*. Cambridge: Cambridge University Press.

AFTERWORD

Tracing the Rise of the Disintegrated View of Education and Imagining Challenges Ahead

Angela Glotfelter, Caitlin Martin, Mandy Olejnik, Ann Updike, and Elizabeth Wardle

Over our years of facilitating the Howe Faculty Writing Fellows Program, we have been inspired by the radical ability of faculty across disciplines to come together, engage in collective sensemaking, and reform their conceptions about what learning and writing are and, consequently, how good teaching works. Targeting faculty conceptions as a site of change has helped us think deeply about conceptions, beliefs, and practices surrounding effective teaching and learning. However, as inspired as we have been by the dedicated faculty we have met, built relationships with, and continued to support in their efforts to innovate teaching after they leave the program, watching Faculty Fellows try to make broader change across the university and listening to their challenges has made us realize there are many impediments to making deep change beyond a single classroom. We continue to believe that changing conceptions is one important way to spark grassroots change, but we have also come to recognize how difficult such change can be. This collection deals with changing conceptions—many times misconceptions—about what writing and learning are and how they work. In the process of conducting this work and writing about it for this collection with the Fellows alumni, we increasingly came to ask why so many misconceptions about learning and writing still persist, especially when there is so much evidence-based research to combat them.

In chapter 4, economics Fellows Janice Kinghorn and Ling Shao describe how their conception of writing education before the Fellows Program was that teaching writing was "a distraction from the core mission of teaching economics." Furthermore, they had previously accepted other common misconceptions about writing, including that it could

https://doi.org/10.7330/9781646423040.c015

be taught in a single first-year course and that, by the time students entered into upper-level economics courses, they "[would] have already learned and know how to write papers." In chapter 12, psychology Fellow Vrinda Kalia describes how publishing practices in the field of psychology "[reflect] a chilling disregard for the human-labor processes that provide the foundation for any research effort in psychology." She argues that the demand for increased sample sizes and more studies on the same question may result in increased rigor but will also "inevitably mean students work more hours or a larger number of students are engaged in the process of data collection" and that, overall, "research productivity [will] become even more challenging for those with less power and privilege." Kalia's observations are reflective of broader trends within academia that expect teachers and researchers to be constantly even more productive—publishing more papers, teaching more students, doing more service—all while resources and funding are cut more and more, a trend that has ensured poor working conditions for many in academia.

We wondered how these problems and misconceptions about learning, ideal labor structures, and disciplinary knowledge arise in the first place? Why are misconceptions about how learning, teaching, and writing work seemingly so commonsense and foundational in education? How did we get to a place where deep student learning is often sacrificed in the name of things like efficiency or linear pathways to graduation? Our interest in these questions has led us to reexamine the foundational ideologies and beliefs often invisible in academia. These problems extend far beyond any one teacher, school, or state system and likely stem from historical trends in how the purpose and goals of education in the United States are imagined in the popular consciousness. In the United States, a college degree is seen increasingly as an investment for which students (and their parents) must individually bear the burden because a college degree is seen as a socioeconomic investment in the competitive earning potential of an individual, helping them develop a competitive and unique portfolio of skills that make them desirable on the free market. Thus, education is seen as a linear pathway through coursework where students encounter and acquire various skills and competencies that prepare them for a job. In other words, in the United States, education is seen as a personal, private investment that is exclusively economic in nature.

In response to this view and to the public's subsequent demand for how education should be and what it should do, higher education has also adapted its business model to more corporate structures. To compete for ever-decreasing state funding and ever-more-competitive sources of private funding, universities have adopted assessment and accountability metrics that do not actually measure deep learning. They have invested in models that allow students to gain skills and competencies quickly, with few delays and little struggle—which means investment in lower-cost methods of instruction, such as competency-based education or hiring low-paid adjuncts to teach hundreds of students in a given semester. Such methods also allow universities to gain revenue, even as revenues fall. As these changes have taken place, any focus on deep learning has often been sacrificed—and perhaps also the well-being of all stakeholders in the higher ed system, teachers and students included. Seeing education as an exclusively revenue-based enterprise (e.g., universities as businesses that make money from students and students as investors in an experience that grants them upward socioeconomic mobility) also sacrifices many of the other purposes of higher education, such as developing critical perspectives and empathy.

In other words, there is today in higher education a mismatch between what many educators feel the goals and purposes of higher education should be and what many upper administrators, government officials, and even the public think higher education should be and do. When it comes to what is important in education, most educators would argue "that what matters most is enabling students to make connections and integrate their knowledge, skills, and habits of mind into an adaptable and critical stance toward the world" (Bass 2017, 145). However, achieving the kind of learning offered in this view is not an efficient, linear, or lucrative process. Thus, many universities have adopted "granular and modular modes of learning, often targeted at specific skills, subjects, and elementary competency-based learning" (145) that allow for students to progress quickly and efficiently through curricula and for universities to invest fewer resources in learning experiences for students. As we note throughout this collection, Randy Bass (2017) describes this dichotomy as *integrative* versus *disintegrative* views of education, respectively, and he identifies this central tension as one of the main reasons so many educators feel they are working and teaching in systems that don't share their values.

An example of the disintegrative model in practice is competency-based education, or CBE, which is growing in popularity across both K–12 and higher education. The US Department of Education (n.d.) describes competency-based approaches as "transitioning away from seat time"; "[creating] flexibility, regardless of time, place, or pace of learning"; "[allowing] students to progress as they demonstrate mastery of academic content"; "[providing] flexibility in the way credit can be earned"; and "[providing] students with personalized learning opportunities." The Department of Education also argues that hyperpersonalization leads to "better engagement" and "better student outcomes" and that CBE can "save time and money" by letting students work on their own (US Department n.d.). Technology is often implicated in competency-based education, replacing faculty and peers in the learning environment. As an illustration, CBE might involve an individual student working through preprogrammed online content modules, where their work is automatically assessed, and analytics provide feedback on their progress and adjust content according to the student's pace of mastery (University of Wisconsin n.d.). Increasingly, data (and lots of it) has become the proxy for learning: whether machine-graded test scores improve, how much time is spent on a task, and even how frequently a student's eyes move from a screen. One remedial math program, for example, uses "mouse clicks, logon times, correct and incorrect answers, selected distractors, time spent logged in, etc." as measures of success (Lane and Finsel 2014, 12). In the learning scenario presented by competency-based education, teachers don't serve as content experts with pedagogical expertise but instead act more as coaches or tutors to students who are learning on their own.

C. W. Gallagher (2016) has written extensively about the pitfalls of CBE for writing studies. He argues that CBE entails distinct transformations of the meanings and roles of education, learning, writing, students, and teachers:

> [In competency-based education,] *writing* is understood as a discrete, commodified, vocational skill; *writing students* are understood as individual workers-in-training who need to "pick up" this skill for purely instrumental purposes; *writing teachers* are understood as success coaches to, or evaluators of, those individuals; and *writing classrooms* are quaint relics of a bygone era when we naively thought the best way to learn to write was to study and practice it with other writers under the guidance of a teacher who facilitated a set of coordinated learning activities. (22–23)

Although competency-based education is often framed as beneficial to students and student learning, the reality is that "no reliable data . . . have been proffered by advocates of CBE" to prove that CBE actually results in better learning experiences (Gallagher 2016, 29). While personalizing the learning experience to the student and allowing for different learning paces for students are arguably admirable goals, we question whether the downsides to CBE outweigh potential benefits if deep learning is the goal of higher education. The reason CBE is popular and gaining traction is *not* because it demonstrates greater student learning or aligns in any way with learning theories, but because it fits in with mainstream disintegrative views of education as a commodity.

Given the dominance of the disintegrative view that produces models like CBE, it can be difficult to know what educational developers can do to support faculty members in transforming our institutions of higher education so that they embody an integrative view of education. This book is about one such effort to empower faculty to change the understanding and enactment of what it means to learn in higher education today. While faculty members are caught up in a system that increasingly values commodification over learning, we are not powerless. We have the power to name and enact another set of values—at least (as a starting point) in our own courses, programs, and departments. For that to happen, however, faculty members from all disciplines benefit from educational development programs that provide them with a lens for naming another set of values and putting them into practice—and with opportunities to engage in distributed leadership in order to enact integrative views of learning from the ground up, beginning in their programs and departments.

Faculty members also benefit from being able to *name* the often invisible, commonsense nature of disintegrative approaches that have had a long history in our educational system. Although its consequences may feel recent, disintegration is not new. However, disintegration's unsustainable economic and human-labor practices have reached a critical tipping point in the post-COVID educational world. It is up to forward-looking teachers and researchers in education to take action to spark grassroots change.

As we end this collection, we thought it might be useful to some readers if we stopped to take a look back at how we arrived at the place where higher education is currently. In this history, educational developers and grassroots faculty leaders may find some explanations for what frustrates them, as well as a language for talking about the change they hope to effect.

THE ROOTS OF DISINTEGRATION IN K–12

What happens in K–12 often doesn't stay in K–12. In other words, educational policy for K–12 is often an instructive preview for what is to come for higher education. This was certainly true of the disintegrative view of learning and its policy consequences. The 1980s were a crucial time for the disintegrative view to take root in US educational policy, and disintegrative ideas have enjoyed bipartisan support from presidents Reagan onward. In the 1980s, failure to meet near-perfect assessment and accountability standards began to be punished with decreased state and federal funding nationwide for the first time in the United States' national educational policy. These accountability regimes in combination with decreased funding have resulted in a culture of austerity in education. Even as public funding for higher education has decreased year after year (Mitchell, Leachmann, and Saenz 2019), demands that institutions demonstrate return on investment for those shrinking funds have grown exponentially. Ultimately, Reagan-era educational reforms introduced assessments and accountability measures that moved the focus of teaching and learning from the messiness inherent in the learning of individual students and their expert teachers (and from equity for all students, as noted by Tyler Branson [2022]) to an interest in students' intellectual abilities as a commodity and in learning (and teachers) as measurable by simplistic scores on high-stakes tests.

In 1983, the US National Commission on Excellence in Education, led by Ronald Reagan's Secretary of Education Terrel Bell, published *A Nation at Risk* (National Commission 1983). This report reflected the bipartisan concern at the time that US schools were failing and other nations, most notably Japan and Germany, were surpassing us in "commerce, industry, science, and technological innovation" (National Commission 1983). The report argued that US education was "mediocre" and that other countries were "surpassing our educational attainments." The language of the report is similar to many such "crisis" documents that likely sound all too familiar to scholars of writing: we had lost sight of the "basic purposes of education" and the "disciplined efforts needed to attain them" (National Commission 1983). In other words, according to these crisis narratives, at some point in the past there existed the "good old days" when education in the United States was excellent and superior to every other country's system, and those days were gone.

Reflecting broader and growing concerns about global economic competition, *A Nation at Risk* ushered in an era of what would become the United States' continuing and increasing obsession with testing and accountability (and thus the disintegrative view of education) in public schools as a route to intellectual and ultimately economic supremacy. In 2002, the Bush administration extended the logics in *A Nation at Risk* with the No Child Left Behind (NCLB) Act, which cemented ideas previously introduced in the Reagan administration and "declared that all states must test every child annually in grades three through eight in reading and mathematics and report test scores by race, ethnicity, low-income status, disability status, and limited-English proficiency" (Ravitch 2013, 11). Important, NCLB also mandated all students must achieve proficiency on state tests by 2014, and schools and teachers who "failed" to meet these standards would be threatened by state action, including the possibility that the state would fire and replace school leadership and teachers, allow parents to move their children to other schools, or even close the school entirely.

These changes to state educational policy also opened up the enterprise of K–12 education to a whole host of entrepreneurs in the private sector (Ravitch 2013). The years following *A Nation at Risk* and NCLB saw the beginnings of what has now become an entire industry that developed around the assumptions that (1) public schools are failing and that (2) because they have been refined by the fire of the free market, private educational ventures are the best way to educate US children. Good examples of this are the contributions economist Milton Friedman imparted to the US educational system. A longtime advisor to world leaders like Reagan and Thatcher, Milton Friedman (1955) advocated for a number of free-market economic policies, notably the idea of school choice and a voucher system. He argued that trends toward collectivism had resulted in "indiscriminate extension of governmental responsibility" (1) and that schools should be opened up to the free-market logic by allowing parents to "express their views about schools directly, by withdrawing their children from one school and sending them to another, to a much greater extent than is now possible" (4). What's important about Friedman's ideas is that he successfully argued for the extension of free-market, capitalistic logics to the realm of public education. Trends like these have continued, with the increasing involvement of private companies in educational ventures and even forays of venture capitalists like Bill Gates into arenas like charter-school advocacy.

Putting the privatization of education aside, the educational reforms that began in the Reagan era also set an implicit standard for student achievement dependent on two faulty assumptions: (1) that standardized testing was an accurate and meaningful way of assessing achievement and (2) that 100 percent of students should be able to perform to a certain standard on such testing. The obsession with US superiority and the concern that US schools be the best in the world led easily to arguments that teachers and curricula and students should be tested and held accountable. Of course, accountability always hinges on the standards by which one is being measured. And in the case of US schools, accountability measures over time came to have less and less to do with learning and more and more to do with efficiency, control, and quantifiable change within short periods of time as related to a single, specified intervention.

SPREADING DISINTEGRATION TO HIGHER ED

While the educational reforms described here were largely focused on K–12, these ideas have taken root in how legislators and the US public view education and its purposes, and policymakers have increasingly turned their attention to higher education. The arguments made for bringing these logics to higher education are often framed in the language of achievement or equity or student success, but the policies and products at play have led higher education down the same road on which K–12 found itself after *A Nation at Risk*. For example, state lawmakers have increasingly withheld funding from public colleges and universities unless they can meet metrics that are approximations (or "proxies" as Cathy O'Neil [2016] calls them) for learning—and usually not very good ones (for example, average salary of new graduates one year after graduation, time to degree, retention rates for students moving from first-year to sophomore year). This model is called "performance funding" (see Dougherty et al. 2016) and has come to constrain and define how colleges and universities think and talk about what they do. In one study of this type of funding model, Kevin Dougherty, Sosanya Jones, Hana Lahr, Rebecca Natow, Lara Pheatt, and Vikash Reddy (2016) found it had many unintended (and negative) consequences: restriction of student admissions, weakening of academic standards, narrowing of institutional mission, high costs of compliance, low morale, and less faculty voice in academic governance, among others (173).

Underlying the austerity politics of these performance-linked cuts is the assumption that government involvement in education should be limited. Such ideas are largely intended to replace New Deal-era resolutions with free-market thinking. In fact, trends to decrease public funding for higher education began in the 1960s in California, where "Ronald Reagan's insistence on charging some tuition for UC students meant not only a doubling of overall student fees between 1970 and 1972, but also a new 'era of the politics of tuition' " (Newfield 2018, 169). As California Democratic state senator Al Rodda put it at the time, "We have abandoned a 101-year tradition which has been supported by fourteen Republican Governors and now seven Democratic Governors. The Regents no longer have a principle of no-tuition to stand on. They will have to bargain on the tuition question and tuition will now become a part of the budgetary debates and deliberations each year" (Newfield 2018, 169). And it did, in California and elsewhere. In the ten years prior to the 2008 economic crisis, "higher education budgets in California had grown more slowly than those of any program area other than job training. . . . The cuts to higher education were larger than those in any other sector" (167). And in 2008, of course, things went from bad to worse as "thirty-six states cut their public college funding more than 20 percent" (167).

California is just one example of the effects of cuts to public spending on higher education, but across the country, institutions of higher education have been required to spend more and more time accounting for their activities and providing "evidence" of their effectiveness even as the public funding they have received has plummeted (Mitchell, Leachman, and Saenz 2019; Newfield 2018). Policies focusing on austerity and accountability for higher education have enjoyed bipartisan support since the Reagan administration. In 2013, for instance, Obama continued the trend with the introduction of the College Scorecard, which extended the logic of NCLB to higher education, "[using] metrics like speed to degree completion, loan default rates, and post-graduation earnings" (Welch and Scott 2016, 4). What's notable about policies like NCLB and the College Scorecard is that, in contrast to New Deal-era reforms that entailed increased government spending for public education to motivate improvement, educational policy from Reagan onward has tended to cut funding and increase accountability measures to spur improvement.

THE CONSEQUENCES OF A DISINTEGRATIVE AUSTERITY APPROACH TO HIGHER ED

The effect of all these cuts to public education has been profound. Schools have hiked tuition rates in response to cuts and then had to find ways to convince students high tuition is warranted. They fight for student tuition dollars by investing in expensive student unions, dorms, and gyms in order to entice "consumers" whose dollars will keep them afloat. The result is an increase in costs to students, meaning many students either go into debt or can't attend college (Mitchell, Leachmann, and Saenz 2019). As the Center on Budget and Policy Priorities explains in a damning report about state defunding of higher education, "Higher tuition combined with weakly rising or stagnant incomes" is especially harmful to students and families with low incomes. Rising tuition costs "may harm students of color and reduce campus diversity" and deter "low-income students, in particular, from enrolling" (Mitchell, Leachmann, and Saenz 2019). Furthermore, a review conducted by POLITICO illustrates that *US News and World Report* rankings "create incentives for schools to favor wealthier students over less wealthy applicants" and, indeed, a 2017 report from the Equality of Opportunity Project found that "many top universities, including Princeton and Yale, admit more students from the top 1 percent of earners than the bottom 60 percent combined" while simultaneously vying annually for the top spots in *US News and World Report* rankings (Wermund 2017). Schools like Georgia State University, in contrast, dropped thirty spots in the rankings after purposefully working to become "a national model for graduating more low- and moderate-income students." The president of Louisiana State University has said *U.S. News and World Report* "has done more damage to the higher education marketplace than any single enterprise that's out there" (Wermund 2017). Value-added assessment approaches—borrowed from predictability measures used to increase revenue in the agricultural sector—have been applied to students and schools (Harris 2011). Overall, these accountability measures and the data on which they rely lend themselves easily to persuasive sound bites and policy arguments. But they have very little to do with what empirical research tells us about how learning works.

To survive in a climate for funding characterized by financial austerity and by the logics that drive such austerity, higher education institutions have adjusted their practices and structures to accommodate the disintegrative view of education. As we have mentioned already, the *U.S. News and World Report* rankings are a relevant example of how universities have shifted along with disintegrative logics. In an apparent coincidence, the infamous *U.S. News and World Report* rankings made their first appearance in 1983, the same year *A Nation at Risk* was published. These rankings are formulated by considering factors such as student performance on standardized tests (which research has shown correlates most with family income), having a lower acceptance rate (which often hinges on early-decision admissions, which hurts students who need to compare financial aid packages across schools), surveys of high-school guidance counselors from highly ranked high schools, and alumni giving (Wermund 2017). In order to improve their rankings on this list, schools enact all sorts of practices that have little if anything to do with learning—and which demonstrably harm low-income students and students of color.

The defunding of public education combined with narratives about higher education's failures have also spurred an entire arena of entrepreneurial activity around higher education, as was the case with K–12. For instance, for-profit educational-technology companies like Civitas, EAB, and Degree Analytics capitalize on performance-based accountability measures by marketing proprietary analytics solutions to address problems related to retention and the now ubiquitous "student success," which, according to Educause, has tended to mean "completion" (not "learning") (Pelletier 2019). These companies promise improved student retention and graduation rates by helping administrators do things like send out "nudges" to remind at-risk students to study, complete their enrollment process, or visit their advisor (see EAB's 2019 "Daily Briefing: Why Nudges Work" as an example). What these companies rarely if ever do is define success in relationship to deep learning. Tristan Denley, a mathematician and provost who developed a predictive analytics program called Degree Navigator, has described the goal of the software as helping students get down a "nice clean path" and reduce opportunities for failure and struggle—which is, in essence, exactly the opposite of what is required for deep learning. Big data uses like these unfortunately don't "spark insight about teaching and learning in classrooms. . . . They . . . report outputs and outcomes, not the impacts of learning on the lives and minds of learners" (Sahlberg and Hasak 2016). EAB, for example, cites Southern Methodist University's associate provost describing why and how they use EAB's predictive analytics: "It's a resource issue, it's a reputational issue, it does impact—I'll say it—the rankings." The first priority is not student learning at all but effective use of limited resources to improve school rankings on measures like the *U.S. News and World Report*.

The results of forty years of the educational reforms introduced by educational policy like *A Nation At Risk* are particularly ironic because the stated intention of these efforts was to improve education. Even the burgeoning educational-technology industry that has grown up around these reforms frames its efforts as an ethical enterprise (Mullen 2016) concerned with ensuring that all students "succeed" and that the most at-risk students find their way through college and to a degree as quickly as possible. Yet the consequence of disaggregating learning and defunding higher education while at the same time requiring more and more time-consuming accountability measures is that at-risk and low-income students actually suffer greatly—they go into debt or they can't attend college at all. Wealthy students, of course, pay whatever is needed to go to private schools. The gap between rich and poor students is greater than it ever has been, not only *while* entire sectors are created around "student success" and meeting metrics outlined by magazines and legislatures but also *because* these sectors exist and frame the narrative and, thus, direct teachers and administrators to attend to accountability over learning. It is difficult to object to the language used by many of these companies because they frame their products as putting student needs first and helping the most at-risk students.

Countering such arguments requires complex thinking rather than soundbites. The kinds of grassroots change the Faculty Fellows in this collection were able to make is a good example of what we can do to counter disintegrative views of education from the bottom up. At times it can be hard to recognize that the small local constraints we face to change—such as a desire to "streamline" or "scale down" curriculum or eliminate "curricular bloat"—are really the local enactment of these larger narratives about what an education is and how we measure its success. But that is exactly what these local constraints are, and the collective sensemaking and the resulting change Fellows in this collection were able to collectively accomplish demonstrates that we have power to shift the narrative of higher education away from disintegration.

FIGHTING THE COMMONSENSE LANGUAGE OF NEOLIBERALISM

The historical trends we have described here are consequences of the introduction of the disintegrative views into education. Within the disintegrative view, higher education is pulled away from a core mission of learning and toward revenue and efficiency. A disintegrated university looks like privileging privately funded research at the expense of teaching and learning, placing the full debt burden of a college degree on individuals and families, and viewing a college degree as a ticket to a job and nothing more.

The disintegrative approach as we have described it in this afterword is, of course, a consequence of neoliberalism as it has come to be enacted in education. Neoliberalism is a set of ideas associated with free-market capitalism that tends to encourage deregulation, free trade, austerity, and a reliance on private-sector funding at the expense of government spending. Neoliberal approaches rest on the assumption that "human well-being can best be advanced by liberating individual entrepreneurial freedoms and skills within an institutional framework characterized by strong private property rights, free markets, and free trade" (Harvey 2005, 2). In education, neoliberal policy manifests as "direct, government-facilitated, private sector intervention into public services and social domains" (Scott 2016, 13). We can see such interventions clearly today, as "state governments facilitate private market interventions through such means as mandating textbooks, assessments, and curricular technologies produced by the private sector; contracting with private entities to manage teacher training and certification; and channeling public money toward private schools through tax incentives, charters, and voucher systems" (13–14). At work here is the neoliberal philosophy that free-market solutions, privatization, competition, and austerity and accountability politics lead to the betterment of the human condition and decrease inequalities.

While this philosophy is currently so common as to be almost impossible to counter, even a cursory glance at education and the economy today shows its promises are unfulfilled. State legislatures, magazine rankings, and the metrics they value have led to a system of higher education that does not prioritize or invest in learning but instead invests in solutions and strategies built by private companies that help them achieve largely meaningless metrics that lead to a more unequal and less intellectually rigorous system of higher education.

How do we disentangle ourselves from a disintegrative view of learning in higher education? How do we embrace an integrative approach to education that proceeds from research-based ideas about learning and values students as learners, not commodities? How do we work to change the terms of the narrative about what higher education is and should be? In this book, we argue and illustrate through numerous examples that it is possible for faculty to reclaim the narrative about learning and to design curricula, courses, and assessments that put student learning first. We argue that one lens for looking at learning and learners, the threshold concepts framework, is particularly useful in this enterprise, as it helps us see learning as messy and recursive. Faculty can redesign teaching and learning from the ground up in their departments and disciplines and thus work from the grassroots to change the narrative about what higher education does and should be. Yet the task ahead of us all is greater than making change in one department or at one institution. If we truly care about deep learning and about ensuring the ability of all students to engage in meaningful learning experiences in higher education, our challenge is to collectively marshal our resources to fight back against the commonsense language and policies of neoliberalism and disintegrative learning.

REFERENCES

Bass, Randall. 2017. "Writing Transfer and the Future of the Integrated University." In *Understanding Writing Transfer: Implications for Transformative Student Learning in Higher Education*, edited by Jessie L. Moore and Randall Bass, 144–54. Sterling, VA: Stylus.

Branson, Tyler. 2022. *Policy Regimes: College Writing and Public Education Policy in the United States.* Carbondale: Southern Illinois University Press.

Dougherty, Kevin J., Sosanya M. Jones, Hana Lahr, Rebecca S. Natow, Lara Pheatt, and Vikash Reddy. 2016. *Performance Funding for Higher Education.* Baltimore: Johns Hopkins University Press.

EAB. 2019. "Daily Briefing: Why Nudges Work and How to Use Them to Keep Students On Track." EAB. https://eab.com/insights/daily-briefing/student-success/why-nudges-work-and-how-to-use-them-to-keep-students-on-track/.

EAB. 2020. "EAB Helps You Support and Graduate More Students." EAB. https://eab.com/colleges-and-universities/student-success/.

Friedman, Milton. 1955. "The Role of Government in Education." In *Economics and the Public Interest*, edited by Robert A. Solo, 123–44. New Brunswick, NJ: Rutgers University Press. Archived (PDF) from the original on May 10, 2017. http://la.utexas.edu/users/hcleaver/330T/350kPEEFriedmanRoleOfGovttable.pdf.

Gallagher, C. W. 2016. "Our Trojan Horse: Outcomes Assessment and the Resurrection of Competency-Based Education." In *Composition in the Age of Austerity*, edited by Nancy Welch and Tony Scott, 21–34. Logan: Utah State University Press.

Harris, Douglas N. 2011. *Value-Added Measures in Education: What Every Educator Needs to Know.* Cambridge, MA: Harvard Education Press.

Harvey, David. 2005. *A Brief History of Neoliberalism.* Oxford: Oxford University Press.

Lane, Jason, and Alex Finsel. 2014. "Fostering Smarter Colleges and Universities: Data, Big Data, and Analytics." *In Building a Smarter University: Data, Big Data, and Analytics*, edited by Jason Lane, 3–26. Albany: SUNY Press.

Mitchell, Michael, Michael Leachmann, and Matt Saenz. 2019. "State Higher Education Funding Cuts Have Pushed Costs to Students, Worsened Inequality." *Center on Budget and Policy Priorities.* https://www.cbpp.org/research/state-budget-and-tax/state-higher-education-funding-cuts-have-pushed-costs-to-students.

Mullen, Carol A. 2016. "Corporate Networks and Their Grip on the Public School Sector and Education Policy." *In Education Policy Perils: Tackling the Tough Issues*, edited by Christopher H. Tienken and Carol A. Mullen, 27–62. New York: Routledge.

National Commission on Excellence in Education. 1983. *A Nation at Risk: The Imperative for Educational Reform.* https://edreform.com/wp-content/uploads/2013/02/A_Nation_At_Risk_1983.pdf.

Newfield, Christopher. 2018. *The Great Mistake: How We Wrecked Public Universities and How We Can Fix Them.* Baltimore: Johns Hopkins University Press.

O'Neil, Cathy. 2016. *Weapons of Math Destruction: How Big Data Increases Inequality and Threatens Democracy.* New York: Crown.

Pelletier, Kathe. 2019. "Student Success: 3 Big Questions." Educause Review. https://er.educause.edu/articles/2019/10/student-success—3-big-questions.

Ravitch, Diane. 2013. *Reign of Error: The Hoax of the Privatization Movement and the Danger to America's Public Schools.* New York: Knopf.

Sahlberg, Pasi, and Jonathan Hasak. 2016. "Next Big Thing in Education: Small Data." pasisahlberg.com. https://pasisahlberg.com/next-big-thing-education-small-data/.

Scott, Tony. 2016. "Subverting Crisis in the Political Economy of Composition." *College Composition and Communication 68* (1): 10–37.

US Department of Higher Education, Office of Elementary and Secondary Education. (n.d.) "Competency-Based Learning or Personalized Learning." https://oese.ed.gov/archived/oii/competency-based-learning-or-personalized-learning/.

University of Wisconsin System, UW Flexible Option. 2021. "How UW Flexible Option Works." https://flex.wisconsin.edu/how-flex-works/.

Welch, Nancy, and Tony Scott, eds. 2016. *Composition in the Age of Austerity*. Logan: Utah State University Press.

Wermund, Benjamin. 2017. "How U.S. News College Rankings Promote Economic Inequality on Campus." *Politico*. https://www.politico.com/interactives/2017/top-college-rankings-list-2017-us-news-investigation/.

APPENDIX A

LIST OF PROJECTS COMPLETED BY HCWE FACULTY WRITING FELLOWS TEAMS

SPRING 2017

Anthropology: *James Bielo, Jeb Card, Yang Jiao, Leighton Peterson*

- Developed a disciplinary writing guide; modified courses based on concepts learned in Fellows. See disciplinary writing guide.

Economics: *Jacob Brindley, Janice Kinghorn, Ling Shao*

- Developed plans to design an advanced-writing course; surveyed the department to determine where writing was already happening; after Fellows, developed a curricular writing plan for multicourse Advanced Writing requirement; modified courses to align with learning from Fellows. See writing spotlight and writing assignments.

Interdisciplinary and Communication Studies: *Jeff Kuznekoff, Caryn Neumann, Leland Spencer*

- Developed a set of videos and guides for their online courses.

SUMMER 2017

FSB First-Year Integrated Core: *Julie Alexander, Rob Morris, Rebecca Morrison*

- Redesigned the curriculum of the integrated core.

Gerontology: *Kate de Medeiros, Jennifer Kinney, Suzanne Kunkel*

- Redesigned the graduate curriculum; began developing their gerontological-voice concept about which they later published an article. See disciplinary writing guide, writing spotlight, and writing assignments.

History: *Wieste de Boer, Erik Jensen, Lindsay Schakenbach Regele, Dan Prior*

- Presentation to the department about threshold concepts; updated their own courses to include more scaffolding, peer review, and

https://doi.org/10.7330/9781646423040.c016

instructor feedback earlier in the process; worked on being more explicit. See disciplinary writing guide, writing spotlight, and writing assignments.

FALL 2017

Family Science and Social Work: *Karleah Harris, Kate Kuvalanka, Anne Roma, Sherrill Sellers, Carolyn Slotten, Jon Trauth*

- Developed an advanced-writing course. See disciplinary writing guide and writing spotlight.

Political Science: *Erica Edwards, Youn Ki, Michael Marshall, Abby Matthews*

- Developed a repository of shared resources for faculty to include syllabi, assignments, etc. See disciplinary writing guide.

Project Dragonfly and Hefner Museum: *Jamie Anzano, Jill Korach, Kevin Matteson, Steve Sullivan (Hefner)*

- Developed a set of videos for their asynchronous online graduate program courses. See disciplinary writing guide.

SPRING 2018

ACE and ESL Composition: *Larysa Bobrova, Kyung Min Kim, Nugrahenny Zacharias*

- Revised an assignment to be more explicit and added scaffolding.

Psychology: *Brooke Spangler Cropenbaker, Yvette Harris, Vrinda Kalia*

- Developed a set of scaffolded assignments to help 300-level students improve their understanding of psychology journal article conventions, reading comprehension, and psychology disciplinary writing values. See writing spotlight.

Teacher Education: *Jeannie Ducher, Sheri Leafgren, Barbara Rose, Scott Sander, Brian Schultz*

- Addressed changes/integration in various areas to align with the EDT strategic plan (EDT 190 Intro to Education course, TESOL curriculum, and Assessment of Readiness to Teach). See disciplinary writing guide and writing spotlight.

SUMMER 2018

International Studies: *Dilchoda Berdieva, Carl Dahlman, Naaborle Sackeyfio, Charles Stevens*

- Revised advanced-writing course: redefined SLOs; added scaffolding to prepare students for the larger assignment; enhanced the persuasive public writing assignment to help students understand the genre.

Philosophy: *Keith Fennen, Elaine Miller, Gaile Pohlhaus*

- Developed a detailed *Writing in Philosophy Guide for Students* with annotated sample student writing assignments. See disciplinary writing guide and writing spotlight.

Teacher Ed and Educational Psychology: *Martha Castaneda, Darrel Davis, Xiang Shen*

- Created a Canvas module that situates various courses in the EDP discipline; created a *Writing in EDP* guide; created a semester-long writing experience focused on threshold concepts.

FALL 2018

Biology: *Joyce Fernandes, Kathleen Killian, Haifei Shi, Hank Stevens*

- Developed an advanced-writing proposal for the department that included writing across four required courses in the major; inventoried genres, purposes, amount of writing, and writing instruction across those courses.

GRAMELAC: *Mila Ganeva, Kazue Harada, Benjamin Sutcliffe*

- Developed an inventory of writing activities and assignments in the department (300–400 level); verified integration of threshold concepts into Student Learning Outcomes.

Project Dragonfly: *Karen Plucinski, Amy Sullivan, Rachel Yoho*

- Created videos for their online graduate program courses on topics such as writing about concepts and disciplinary citation practices. See disciplinary writing guide.

SPRING 2019

Art History: *Annie Dell'Aria, Jordan Fenton, Pepper Stetler*

- Wrote a disciplinary writing guide with annotated sample assignments for undergraduates. Updated assignments and teaching approaches to include threshold concepts. See disciplinary writing guide and writing spotlight.

Music: *Claire Boge, Elizabeth Hoover, Tammy Kernodle, Brenda Mitchell*

- Mapped the graduate writing curriculum to standardize guidelines for the graduate research project and developed a vision statement for the graduate academic curriculum. See writing spotlight.

FALL 2019

Geography: *Bruce D'Arcus, Roxanne Ornelas, David Prytherch, Damon Scott*

- Researched and developed plans to begin an ePortfolio program for their majors. See disciplinary writing guide.

Latin American Studies: *Jose Amador, Elena Jackson Albarran, Yuridia Ramirez, Juan Carlos Albarran*

- Redefined their program goals and values; identified the writing genres taught in courses; produced a student writing guide. See disciplinary writing guide.

Mechanical and Manufacturing Engineering:
Mark Sidebottom, Muhammad Jahan

- Surveyed department to see where and how faculty teach writing across their department; developed a detailed writing guide for engineering graduate students.

Political Science: *Ann Wainscott, Lisa Frazier, Benjamin Bartlett*

- Expanded a disciplinary writing guide on writing as a political scientist to be embedded in Canvas. See disciplinary writing guide.

Psychology: *Jay Smart, Jennifer Quinn, Carrie Hall*

- Developed a new assessment and rubric for teaching team writing in a psychology research methods course. Piloted the course after Fellows. See disciplinary writing guide.

SPRING 2020

We conducted a special seminar for graduate students who individually developed scaffolded assignments for a course based on learning theory and threshold concepts of their field.

FALL 2020

Havighurst Center: *Hannah Chapman, Scott Kenworthy, Neringa Klumbyte, Steve Norris, Zara Torlone*

- Began a *Faculty Teaching Guide* for their cross-listed 254 course that explains their threshold concept of interdisciplinarity that provides resources for nondisciplinary faculty to teach the course, including explanations of disciplinary approaches to the material and suggested readings and assignments from their respective fields.

Justice and Criminal Studies: *Theresa Conover, John Forren, Jessica Warner*

- Surveyed writing assigned and taught throughout their curriculum (in collaboration with department colleagues); plan to continue post-Fellows with student roundtables and writing awards.

SPRING 2021

Architecture and Interior Design: *Mary Rogero (Chair), Mary Ben Bonham, Gulen Cevik, Diane Fellows, Elizabeth Keslacy, Jeffrey Kruth*

- Surveyed department faculty to create a curriculum grid of writing taught in every course (from 100 level through graduate) by nineteen genres, categorized into formal academic writing, writing to learn, and professional writing; whether students received feedback and revised; and the amount of writing. Plan to engage entire department and evaluate the effectiveness of writing in their curriculum.

Commerce: *Mary Kovach, Patrick Lindsay, Tom Mays*

- Created an introductory module for specific commerce courses to help students learn core disciplinary skills (define situation, summarize, analyze, recommend).

Music: *Thomas Garcia, Wallis Vore, and Aaron Pergram*

- To teach two cultural-music threshold concepts identified in the seminar (cultural awareness/competency/sensitivity and affective experience), the music team is redesigning their three large introductory courses to incorporate more scaffolding; more interactive, low stakes writing; and projects rather than traditional term papers.

Teacher Education (Adolescent Young Adult [AYA] Program):
Kathy Batchelor, Nathaniel Bryan, Jeannie Ducher, Todd Edwards, Eva Howard, Ann Mackenzie, Tom Misco, Molly Sawyer, Robin Schell

- Developed a set of threshold concepts for their faculty to move them forward toward realizing/living their department's social justice mission statement; drafted a pilot plan to pair up AYA faculty as critical partners who will work together over the fall semester to set goals, engage throughout the semester, and reflect on their progress to be included in annual reporting; plan to extend to the whole program.

SUMMER 2021

History: *Kimberly Hamlin, Andrew Offenburger*

- Developed new scaffolded assignments to help honors, BA/MA, and MA students learn to incorporate and synthesize primary sources; began a list of primary-source repositories for assignments; will present to the department in fall semester to begin discussion of building an accessible primary-source list and how to best add this learning/skill building into the curriculum.

Spanish: *Tamise Ironstrack, Julie Szucs, Katie Fowler-Córdova, Tiffany Belka*

- Building on their SPN 101–102 pilot curriculum based on a language acquisition-driven model rather than grammar-driven, the team developed a curriculum map of linguistic functions at each level with specific goals; core target structures and vocabulary for those goals; high-frequency structures to spiral and revisit; and core cohesive devices. Plan to realign prompts and rubrics for the new model.

APPENDIX B

SAMPLE SCHEDULE FOR SEMESTER-LONG FELLOWS PROGRAM

Date	Topic	Activities During Seminar	Read Prior to Seminar	Complete Prior to Seminar
Week 1	Threshold concepts of your fields	Identify your field's threshold concepts (or TCs for a particular course or course sequence)	Meyer and Land "Threshold Concepts and Troublesome Knowledge" and "Threshold Concepts and Troublesome Knowledge: Issues of Liminality" Cousin, "An Introduction to Threshold Concepts"	
Week 2	Threshold concepts of your fields	Teach one of your threshold concepts to the other team		Finish your list of TCs and be ready to teach one to the other teams.
Week 3	How learning works		Ambrose et al, *How Learning Works*, chapters 1, 4, 5, and 7 *How People Learn*, chapter 2: "How Experts Differ From Novices"	Learning principles pledge
Week 4	Threshold concepts of writing	Engage in activities to examine the nature of writing (vs. common conceptions of writing)	*Naming What We Know*, Metaconcept and Concepts 1 and 2 (pages 15–47)	Writing log
Week 5	Threshold concepts of writing	Continue to engage in activities to examine the nature of writing (vs. common conceptions of writing)	*Naming What We Know*, Concepts 3 and 4 (pages 48–70)	

continued on next page

https://doi.org/10.7330/9781646423040.c017

APPENDIX B—*continued*

Date	*Topic*	*Activities During Seminar*	*Read Prior to Seminar*	*Complete Prior to Seminar*
Week 6	Nature of writing in particular disciplines/fields	Examine a piece of writing from someone in the other group	Hyland, *Disciplinary Discourses: Social Interactions in Academic Writing* • "Disciplinary Cultures, Texts, and Interactions" • "Academic Attribution: Interaction through Citation" John Swales, summary of CARS model of research introductions Optional: Swales, "Research Articles in English"	Each person in your group upload to this folder an electronic copy of one peer-reviewed research article from a journal in your field that you think exemplifies "good" or at least "typical" research writing in your field.
Week 7	Naming the conventions of writing for students	"Mad libs" Teach your "mad libs" to the other group	Look at disciplinary writing guides created by other Fellows, particularly the philosophy guide	Bring a short (2–3 paragraph) statement on **what it means to "write well" in your field** of study that is targeted toward students learning to write in your field. **What do people expect of writing there? What makes writing "good" for people in your field? What makes writing effective/persuasive to readers in your field?**
Week 8			Bean, chapters 4, 6, and 7	
Week 9	Using writing in classrooms		Read Miami Writing Spotlights for economics, gerontology, art history, philosophy, and history (all short) to see how they are helping students understand writing differently. Bean, skim chapters 10, 15, and 16	

continued on next page

APPENDIX B—*continued*

Date	*Topic*	*Activities During Seminar*	*Read Prior to Seminar*	*Complete Prior to Seminar*
Week 10	Discuss and plan for your group projects and begin working			
Week 11	Work on group projects			
Week 12	Work on group projects			
Week 13	Work on group projects			
Week 14	Work on group projects			
Week 15	Works in Progress Showcase			

INDEX

Page numbers followed by *f* indicate figures. Page numbers followed by *n* indicate endnotes.

ABOUT THE AUTHORS

Elena Jackson Albarrán is an associate professor of history and global and intercultural studies at Miami University. She teaches classes on modern Latin American history, popular culture, revolutions, and comparative childhood studies. Her monograph *Seen and Heard in Mexico: Children and Revolutionary Cultural Nationalism* (Nebraska 2015) won the María Elena Martínez Prize from the Conference on Latin American History for the best book on Mexican history.

Juan Carlos Albarrán is a senior lecturer in the department of global and intercultural studies and the Latin American, Latino/a, and Caribbean studies program at Miami University. Professor Albarrán teaches course topics on Latin America such as Introduction to Latin American Studies; Contemporary Latin American topic courses like: Cuba, Latin American Music and Dance, Sustainable Tourism, Refugee Migration, and NAFTA, among others. He has directed a social entrepreneurship program since 2018 in collaboration with Miami University colleagues, the University of Arizona, and the Institute for Training and Development (ITD) Amherst College in the Study of United States Institutions (SUSI) under the sponsorship of the Education and Cultural Affairs (ECA) in the US State Department.

José Amador is an associate professor of Latin American Studies in the Department of Global and Intercultural Studies. He is the author of *Medicine and Nation Building in the Americas, 1890–1940* (Vanderbilt 2015), recipient of the Norman L. and Roselea J. Goldberg Prize for best book in the area of medicine. He teaches courses on the history of public health and race, the African diaspora in the Americas, and gender and sexuality. He has been a National Humanities Center Fellow and has received awards from the National Endowment for the Humanities, the Ford Foundation, and the Rockefeller Foundation.

Annie Dell'Aria is an associate professor of art history at Miami University. Her research concerns the intersection of contemporary art, screen media, and public space. She is the author of *The Moving Image as Public Art: Sidewalk Spectators and Modes of Enchantment* (Palgrave Macmillan 2021), and her writing has also appeared in *Afterimage, Artforum, Millennium Film Journal, Moving Image Review and Art Journal (MIRAJ), Public Art Dialogue*, and other journals and edited volumes.

Kate de Medeiros, PhD, is the O'Toole Family Professor of Gerontology in the Department of Sociology and Gerontology at Miami University. Her research is broadly concerned with experiences of growing old, including the meaning of place and space, flourishing with dementia, and the limits of life stories. Her courses include global aging, issues and controversies in aging (which is a designated writing course), advanced qualitative research methods, and theories and the advanced construction of knowledge in gerontology. She has authored, coauthored, or edited four books and more than forty peer-reviewed journal articles and fifteen book chapters.

Keith Fennen is a teaching professor in the Philosophy Department at Miami University and received his PhD from Emory University. His philosophical interests are wide ranging, but he has particular interests in early modern philosophy (sixteenth and seventeenth centuries), philosophical writing, and the value of philosophical inquiry. Keith teaches courses ranging from the introductory level to the graduate level. In all of his courses, special attention is paid to the practice of philosophical writing and thinking, and guiding students through the disorientation they most often experience in these areas.

Jordan A. Fenton is an associate professor of art history in the Department of Art at Miami University. Fenton is a specialist of African Art and has been carrying out research in Nigeria since 2008. He received his PhD in the history of art from the University of Florida. Fenton offers his Art 162: Africa, Oceania, and Native America course every semester and teaches a writing and research practicum, as well as introductory and advanced courses exploring Africa and its Diaspora. Fenton is author of *Masquerade and Money in Urban Nigeria: The Case of Calabar* (University of Rochester Press).

Angela Glotfelter is an assistant professor of English at the University of Alabama in Huntsville, where she teaches graduate and undergraduate courses on professional and technical writing. She researches the impact of emerging technologies on writing education, and her work on algorithms and writing has appeared in *Computers and Composition.* Currently, she is studying the impact of analytics on writing.

Carrie E. Hall, PhD, is an associate teaching professor at Miami University. She has taught over twenty different courses across the past fifteen years. She is the course coordinator for the psychological statistics and research methods courses in the Psychology Department at Miami University. Related to this role, she studies the developmental alignment of writing assignments and works with a hub of faculty to design effective writing assignments. She also has a deep interest in effective sprint-course design, which was inspired by her undergraduate experience on the One Course At A Time (OCAAT) academic calendar at Cornell College.

Erik N. Jensen is an associate professor of history at Miami University, where he teaches courses on world history, as well as European and German history. His first book, *Body by Weimar: Athletes, Gender, and German Modernity,* explored the role of sports in shaping social and cultural ideals after the First World War. He is currently finishing a textbook on the Weimar Republic and working on a deep biography of the tennis player and pioneering journalist Paula von Reznicek, whose fraught identity and increasing marginalization reflected the twentieth-century Germany through which she lived.

Vrinda Kalia is an associate professor in the psychology department at Miami University. She studies how individuals achieve their goals. In particular, she is interested in the role of contextual forces (i.e., family, culture, language environment, stress) that shape the development of cognitive and emotional processes that enable or prevent goal achievement. Professor Kalia's work is interdisciplinary, intersecting with educational psychology, cultural psychology, health psychology, and cognitive psychology. She often combines the use of behavioral data with physiological measurements (i.e., EEG and fNIRS) in her published work.

Janice Kinghorn is a teaching professor in the Department of Economics at Miami University, where she teaches microeconomic theory, economic development, and poverty and economic inequality. Janice earned her PhD from Washington University in St. Louis. Janice is interested in how to use writing with quantitative data to encourage students to think critically about the economic environment. She is also the director of assessment for the Farmer School of Business.

Jennifer Kinney, PhD, is a professor of gerontology in the Department of Sociology and Gerontology and a research fellow with the Scripps Gerontology Center at Miami University. Her primary research interests are gerontological pedagogy and how to foster quality of life among people living with dementia. She has taught undergraduate and graduate gerontology courses for over thirty years. Recent course offerings include perspectives in gerontology and a course on gerontological writing for masters and doctoral students. She has authored or coauthored one text book, more than forty-five peer-reviewed journal articles, and ten book chapters.

Sheri Leafgren is a very recently retired associate professor of teacher education at Miami University. She builds her scholarship on experiences from her nineteen years as a K–3 classroom teacher in a large urban school district. Sheri is particularly interested in the spiritual and moral wisdom of young children and how children find space to enact their moral and spiritual selves while swaddled tightly by the rules, procedures and surveillance of the schoolroom. Of late, she is expanding this inquiry to examine the spiritual and moral wisdom of preservice and early-career teachers similarly constrained by State rules, procedures, and surveillance. She is the author of *Reuben's Fall: A Rhizomatic Analysis of Disobedience in Kindergarten* and has published in journals such as *Global Studies of Childhood, Cultural Studies of Science Education, the International Journal of Social Education, the Journal of Curriculum Theorizing,* and the *International Journal of Children's Spirituality.* Sheri can be reached at leafgrs@miamioh.edu.

Elaine Maimon, PhD, advisor at the American Council on Education, is considered to be one of the founders of Writing Across the Curriculum. Her coauthored book *Writing in the Arts and Sciences,* has been designated as a landmark text. She is a Distinguished Fellow of the Association for Writing Across the Curriculum. For twenty-four years she served as chief executive officer at three regional public universities: Arizona State University West, University of Alaska Anchorage, and Governors State University. She is the author of *Leading Academic Change: Vision, Strategy, Transformation.*

Caitlin Martin is an assistant professor of composition and director of the writing program at Embry-Riddle Aeronautical University in Daytona Beach, FL. She earned her PhD in composition and rhetoric at Miami University, where she also served as a graduate assistant director of writing across the curriculum in the Howe Center for Writing Excellence. Her research interests include transformative learning theories, writing across the curriculum, writing program leadership and administration, and institutional change. Her work has appeared in *Peitho* and the collection *Making Space: Writing Instruction, Infrastructures, and Multiliteracies.*

Elaine Miller is a professor of philosophy at Miami University. She researches and teaches nineteenth-century German philosophy and contemporary European feminist theory, particularly aesthetics and the philosophy of nature. Her books include *Head Cases: Julia Kristeva on Philosophy and Art in Depressed Times* (Columbia University Press 2014), *The Vegetative Soul: From Philosophy of Nature to Subjectivity in the Feminine* (SUNY Press 2002), and an edited collection, *Returning to Irigaray: Feminist Philosophy, Politics, and the Question of Unity* (SUNY 2006). She has also published articles in the *Hegel Bulletin,* the *Palgrave Handbook of German Romantic Philosophy, Idealistic Studies, the Journal of Nietzsche Studies,* and *Oxford Literary Review,* among others.

Mandy Olejnik is the assistant director of Writing Across the Curriculum at the Howe Center for Writing Excellence at Miami University, where she supports faculty and graduate students in their teaching of writing. Her work has appeared in *Composition Studies* and *Transformative Works and Cultures.*

Gaile Pohlhaus, Jr. is a professor of philosophy and affiliate of women's, gender, and sexuality studies at Miami University. Her research focuses on the politics of knowledge and draws upon feminist philosophy, critical race theory, queer theory, and disability studies. She has published in such journals as *Hypatia, Social Epistemology, Feminist Philosophical Quarterly*, and *Philosophical Papers*. She is also coeditor of *The Routledge Handbook of Epistemic Injustice*.

Jennifer J. Quinn, PhD, is an associate professor in the Department of Psychology at Miami University. Her research addresses the neurobiological mechanisms of memory formation, consolidation, and retrieval, with a particular interest in how early life stress alters future learning about both threat and safety. She teaches courses in research methods and design, writing, and neuroscience at the undergraduate and graduate levels. She has authored more than twenty-five peer-reviewed journal articles and book chapters.

Barbara J. Rose's academic work focuses on social justice and student writing. Publications in recent years include articles in *Educational Forum*, the *Currere Exchange Journal*, and the *Brock Education Journal* and chapters in *Why Kids Love (and Hate) School* (Meyers Education Press) and *Effective or Wise: Teaching and the Meaning of Professional Dispositions in Education* (Peter Lang Publishing). In 2018, she won the "Two-Minute Book Pitch" competition at the Tennessee Williams Literary Festival and is working on a book on student writing. She is an avid photographer and has restored an historic Lustron house that is a short-term rental.

Scott Sander is an associate clinical professor in the Department of Teacher Education at Miami University. His research interests include science-teacher education as it intersects with social justice, diversity, and inclusion. His work in large lecture courses looks to challenge traditional notions of science teaching and learning as he positions students as novice scientists/scholars who critically analyze both physical and social phenomena.

Brian D. Schultz is professor, chair, and Virginia Todd Memorial Scholar of curriculum studies in the Department of Teacher Education at Miami University. Prior to joining the faculty at Miami, Brian was Bernard J. Brommel Distinguished Research Professor and chair of the Department of Educational Inquiry and Curriculum Studies at Northeastern Illinois University in Chicago. Brian's research focuses on developing democratic, anti-oppressive, progressive education-based classrooms. Among his publications are the books *Teaching in the Cracks: Openings and Opportunities for Student-Centered, Action-Focused Curriculum* and the second edition of *Spectacular Things Happen Along the Way: Lessons from an Urban Classroom*.

Ling Shao is an assistant teaching professor in the Department of Economics at Miami University. She earned her PhD in economics from the University of Alabama, where she also taught introductory economics courses. She joined Miami University in 2012 as a visitor before being offered a permanent position in 2016. At Miami, Ling teaches Principles of Macroeconomics and International Economic Relations courses. She has published in journals such as *Applied Economics*. In addition to her research interests in empirical macroeconomics and international economics, she is also interested in pedagogical innovations such as writing to learn and team-based learning.

L. James (Jay) Smart is a professor in Miami University's Department of Psychology. He earned his PhD in experimental psychology (human factors) from the University of Cincinnati in 2000. His research broadly examines how to support people's ability to interact with technology. He teaches writing and research methods at the undergraduate and graduate level.

Pepper Stetler is an associate professor of art and architecture history and a Fellow of the Howe Faculty Writing Fellow at Miami University. She publishes on the history of photography and German architecture and culture in the early twentieth century. Her book, *Stop Reading! Look!: Modern Vision and the Weimar Photography Book,* was published by the University of Michigan Press in 2015.

Ann Updike was the associate director of the Howe Center for Writing Excellence at Miami University from 2013 until her retirement in 2021, where she supported faculty and graduate students as part of the Writing Across the Curriculum program. Her work appeared in *Diverse Approaches to Teaching, Learning, and Writing Across the Curriculum.*

Elizabeth Wardle is the Roger & Joyce Howe Distinguished Professor of Written Communication and director of the Howe Center for Writing Excellence at Miami University. She has served as the director of writing programs at the University of Central Florida and University of Dayton and the department chair at the University of Central Florida. She is the coauthor of *Writing about Writing*; *Naming What We Know*; *(Re)Considering What We Know*; *Composition, Rhetoric, and Disciplinarity*; and many articles and book chapters about writing pedagogy, transfer, and threshold concepts.

